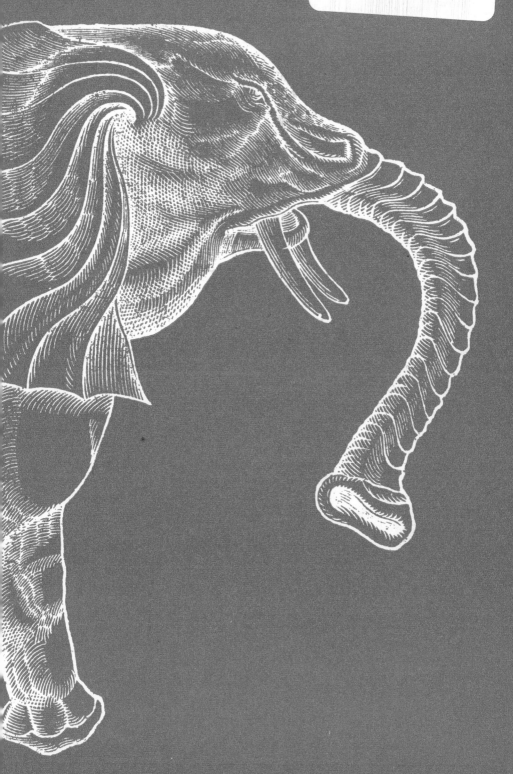

John Dunstall fecit.

The great Elephant brought into England and landed August y<sup>e</sup> third 1675

Printed & sould by John Overton at y<sup>e</sup> white Horse without Newgate

# elephants
## ancient and modern

## FCSillar and RM Meyler

A Studio Book
The Viking Press · New York

Duet for D and Christine

© F. C. Sillar and Ruth Meyler 1968

Published in 1968 by The Viking Press Inc.
625 Madison Avenue, New York, NY 10022
Library of Congress catalog card number: 69: 10348
Set and printed in 11 pt Plantin
Made and printed in Great Britain by
Richard Clay (The Chaucer Press) Ltd, Bungay, Suffolk

# Contents

# Contents

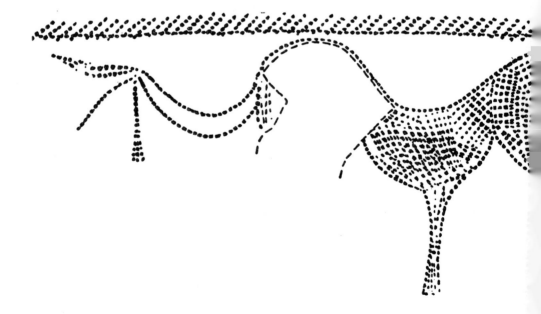

# First elephant

So hand in hand they passed, the loveliest pair
That ever since in love's embraces met—
Adam the goodliest man of men since born
His sons; the fairest of her daughters Eve.

.    .    .    .    .

                              About them frisking played
All beasts of the earth, since wild, and of all chase
In wood or wilderness, forest or den.
Sporting the lion ramped, and in his paw
Dandled the kid; bears, tigers, ounces, pards,
Gambolled before them; the unwieldy elephant,
To make them mirth, used all his might, and wreathed
His lithe proboscis; . . .

from the description of the Garden of Eden in *Paradise Lost*, Book IV, by John Milton

Schematic elephant; from a Meroitic Beerfoot excavated at Khartoum

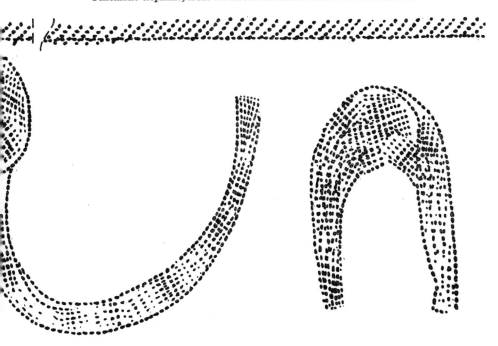

# Salute to elephants

In contemplating the elephant one is reminded of the Chinese civil servant who, on retirement, withdrew to a cavern in the remote hinterland of China and spent the last seventeen years of his life inscribing again and again all round the rocky walls of his refuge the words 'Oh, oh, strange business!' It is difficult to fault the old gentleman on his so simply expressed sentiment on the meaning of life. Life is indeed a strange business and the elephant is without doubt one of the strangest of life's manifestations.

Most people would agree that of all creatures the elephant has some of the most fascinatingly curious characteristics, the trunk alone being enough to attract the most uninterested of observers. The word 'trunk', it may be said in passing, is related to 'trump', which may well account for the elephant's trumpeting being so called.

The fascination of the animal has led large numbers of people to study it closely and to write about it. The majority of books on the elephant are devoted to its natural history, to the chase of the creature and to its use to and by humanity. We are more concerned with its presentation by writers and artists, and while stories connected with the chase or with the working of elephants will be found in this anthology—if that is the right word for this very miscellaneous work—the object of this book is to show the elephant as it has appeared to all sorts and conditions of men.

One of the most expressive references to elephants and their lumbering majesty is to be found in Saki's lines in *Reginald*, his first collection of stories to be published:

> Down to their homes from Himalayan heights
> The stale, pale elephants of Cooch Behar
> Roll like great galleons on a tideless sea!

The word 'elephant', at one time spelt 'olifaunt' or 'olifont', derives, of course, from the Greek ἐλέφας, which means either the beast itself or the ivory of its tusks. The origin of the word ἐλέφας is obscure. Some etymologists trace it to ELAPH, the Hebrew word for ox, and this in turn some derive from EBUR, Latin, originally Coptic, for ivory. This word itself can be traced back to Abu which, in Sir Wallace Budge's *Dictionary of Ancient Egyptian Hieroglyphics*, is used to denote both African and Indian elephants.

To all but professional zoologists the African and Indian species are both familiarly known as elephants. The African elephant, however, differs in so many particulars from his Indian counterpart that he has been placed by modern zoologists with a number of extinct forms in the genus Loxodonta—i.e. animals with oblique or crooked teeth. (This name has nothing to do with the tusks but refers to the teeth. In the African variety the grinding surfaces of the teeth become lozenge-shaped with wear—hence the classification.)

To the layman the most marked difference between the Indian and the African elephant is that the former has a convex back while the latter has a concave back. It would need a Darwin or a Huxley to explain why—and one would have imagined that this would have been the prominent characteristic from which the genus would have derived its name. But no; the zoologists must, positively must, get hold of something which no ordinary person would ever notice. (But such is the way of all zoological name-coiners. Look at puffins. Brehm insists that they be *Fratercula arctica grabae*. Well, well, you may say, why not? Why not, indeed. But then why insist upon the Manx Shearwater being *Puffinus puffinus puffinus*!)

While Aristotle and Pliny the elder were probably the first persons to write carefully and extensively about the elephant, the former in the fourth century BC and the latter in his *Historia Naturalis* somewhere about AD 60, there are, of course, other ancient references to the beast. Here, for instance, is how Kuo P'u, who wrote at the time of the Chiu Dynasty (third century BC), describes him:

> The elephant is a vast creature. His body is very heavy and has the strength of ten bulls. His appearance is very queer. When we look at him from the front, we think we are looking at his posterior because he has a trunk which looks like his tail. When he walks it is, as it were, as if a mountain moved, but ah, how hard to know whether he is coming or going!

It would be unfair to suggest that Hilaire Belloc was guilty of plagiarism when he wrote many centuries later:

> When people call this beast to mind,
> They marvel more and more
> At such a LITTLE tail behind,
> So LARGE a trunk before.

It is curious, too, to note the different scales by which the Chiu Dynasty and the twentieth century measured strength. 'The strength of ten bulls' says Kuo P'u—whereas a leader-writer in *The Times* in 1949 writes:

> Whatever the task at which they are called upon to lend a trunk, they lay on, unfortified by petrol coupons, enough willing horse-power to drive a tractor.

Cagey, though, do you not think? How many horses? Perhaps the need for stating exact horsepower when claiming petrol coupons during the war had made the writer unduly cautious.

Bulk, strength and trunk are the features which appear to have made the deepest impression on observers, as can be seen from the three instances quoted. Edward Lear, however, was profoundly impressed by the size of an elephant's eye, for he has no less than two poems describing it—'such little eyes' he says 'such little eyes'. And this is indeed true. The eye is minute for the size of the beast and gives an impression of roguish cunning.

Many people, of course, probe more deeply than merely to marvel at the outer shape and remark on the intelligence and character of the creature. In his *Essay on Man*, for instance, Pope writes:—

> How instinct varies in the grovelling swine
> Compared, half-reas'ning elephant, with thine!

Twixt that and reason what a nice barrier!
For ever separate, yet for ever near!

This sentiment is perhaps less than just to the elephant. We dare swear Elephant Bill would have snorted if he had read it. 'Half-reas'ning? Half? What's the man mean!' he would have ejaculated angrily. And he would have proceeded to tell innumerable stories in which elephants showed a reasoning power quite equal to that of humans. And an elephant if he were literate—and who knows how many are?—might well point to the poor powers of observation of many humans—the gardener, for instance, in Lewis Carroll's *Sylvie & Bruno*:

He thought he saw an elephant
That practised on a fife;
He looked again, and found it was
A letter from his wife.
'At length I realise' he said,
'The bitterness of life!'

There are many proofs of elephantine intelligence. Sometimes it is a somewhat 'back-handed' quality as in the case of the remarkable elephant in the zoo at Dresden who disposed of the unfortunate Mr Cornelius Appin. It will be remembered that Mr Appin had discovered how to teach animals to speak and wrought havoc among the guests in Lady Blemley's house-party by teaching the art to the cat Tobermory in Saki's story. The elephant destroyed Mr Appin because he had, according to the zoo authorities, been teasing the beast. Those who had experience with Tobermory, however, were convinced that he had been trying to teach the elephant German irregular verbs and that he got what he deserved.

We all know, of course, that elephants never forget. There are countless stories in which elephants after long years of separation meet again long lost friends and perform prodigies of remembrance. A slightly cynical connotation is given to this aspect of an elephant's character in Dorothy Parker's *Ballade of Unfortunate Mammals*. She writes:

Prince, a precept I leave for you,
Coined in Eden, existing yet:
Skirt the parlor, and shun the zoo—
Women and elephants never forget.

Perhaps the expression of the fact is slightly unkind to other creatures (though men would be the last to dispute it so far as women are concerned). Look at the memory displayed by many dogs. Consider the innumerable learned pigs, such as that one who used to perform at No. 55, opposite the Admiralty, Charing Cross, and who would tell any Lady's thoughts in company. Think of the faithful cat Mina who would not desert his young mistress Clementina's grave and lay upon it until he died. Think above all of Androcles' lion. That the quality is pinned to the elephant must be, one imagines, because the things remembered are so small while the remembrancer is so vast.

And there is no doubt about it. Regard, for instance, the Elephant's

Child. When he got home after his painful experience in acquiring his trunk—an experience so painful and frightening that one would have thought all other experiences would have been wiped from his mind—he remembered the chastisement he had received from all his uncles and aunts and repaid them in full measure.

It is indisputable that the elephant is not only a mysterious but an important member of creation. Both East and West place him upon a pinnacle and their artists and writers have used him as a model. He has often been in the thoughts of great men who have made pronouncements about him.

Disraeli, that great solvent of the mixture of East and West, moved a vote of thanks in the House of Commons in 1868 to Sir Robert Napier and his army after the Abyssinian campaign—'They brought the elephant of Asia,' he said, 'to convey the artillery of Europe to dethrone one of the kings of Africa, and to hoist the standard of St George upon the mountains of Rasselas.'

Splendid stuff! And, come to think of it, Dizzy had an eye not unlike an elephant's.

Another great man also thought of elephants. On 14 April 1865, a few hours before his assassination, Abraham Lincoln said to Charles A. Dala who was urging him to arrest one Jacob Thomson, a confederate commissioner who was trying to escape to Europe: 'When you have got an elephant by the hind-leg and he is trying to run away, it is best to let him run!' This is said to have been the President's last aphorism.

Few people have written in derogatory terms of the elephant. Indeed we have discovered none such. He is, in fact, benevolent and lovable. Samuel Butler writes of him:

> The docile and ingenuous elephant
> T' his own and only female is gallant:
> And she as true and constant to *his* bed
> That first enjoyed her single maidenhead.

Of course elephants are sometimes savage; who is not? The elephant as Kublai Khan's executioner is not a pleasant sight. Nor is Hyder Ali's elephant as described by Sir Walter Scott in that rather indifferent novel *The Surgeon's Daughter*. But is it, perhaps, significant that history is full of stories of elephants having to be artificially stimulated by wine, mulberries or frankincense in order to persuade them to behave in a brutal or even warlike manner? This hardly sounds as if elephants were by nature savage. So far as can be ascertained man is the only other animal that ever requires artificial stimulants to fight and kill his fellow men—which suggests, perhaps, the accuracy of the statement by Pliny that the elephant is of all creatures most akin to man. The wild elephant in the African bush has of course to defend himself in the midst of nature red in tooth and claw. This aspect of the elephant, as, indeed, of humanity and the animal kingdom in general, was uppermost in the mind of that cynical and splenetic divine, Dean Swift, when he wrote:

> So geographers in Afric maps
> With savage pictures fill their gaps,

And o'er unhabitable downs
Place elephants for want of towns.

Swift also gave us a glimpse of the obvious when he wrote in *Thoughts on various subjects*: 'Elephants are always drawn smaller than life, but a flea always larger.'

The opposite proposition would be in the category of the news said to be the test of what is acceptable by a good newspaper—'man bites dog'.

Naturally everyone has heard of 'rogue elephants'. They are the fellows who go off the rails and enjoy themselves as hooligans, beatniks or hippies. But one does not normally associate elephants with wickedness. Oddly enough, that gifted writer of first-class thrillers, Dorothy Sayers, did. In *The Nine Tailors* Hilary Thorpe discovers a piece of paper in the belfry at Fenchurch St Paul on which these cryptic words occur:

'I thought to see the fairies in the fields, but I saw only the evil elephants with their black backs. Woe: How that sight awed me . . .'

Who, one wonders, were these elephants and why were they evil?

The strangely mystical character of the elephant coupled with his strength has been the source of many Eastern legends, some of which are mentioned elsewhere in this book, but apart from his legendary life the elephant had—and has—a great influence on the thought and behaviour of Eastern peoples. One Major Snodgrass, reporting on the Burmese, remarked that so sensitive were they to the moods of the white elephant that an unusual grunt would have the effect of interrupting the most important business and of altering the whole course of the ship of state. And there is a tale of the most Western of Eastern people, the inhabitants of Constantinople, who were convinced that a great fire in the city was entirely due to the presence of an elephant, which had to be banished immediately.

There are three main spheres in which the elephant and man are in partnership—war, work and the provision of ivory. This last has led to much slaughter of elephants, showing up man's callous greed for gain. It would, of course, be foolish not to recognize the intrepidity of the hunter and his contribution to human knowledge, particularly of the vastnesses of Africa, as well as his gathering of ivory. Somehow, the *zeitgeist* of today is against the killing of creatures except for food. The story of Sinbad's seventh and last voyage is much more to our taste. Made by his master to shoot elephants for their tusks, Sinbad managed for two months to kill an elephant every day. At the end of this time when one day he was sitting in a tree waiting for a victim, his tree was suddenly surrounded by elephants. They tore the tree up by the roots and one of them seized Sinbad and placed him on his back. They set off on a long march and eventually put Sinbad, who had given himself up for lost, down in an open desert area. The elephants then departed and Sinbad recovering his senses looked around and saw that he had been brought to the elephants' graveyard where there were thousands of tusks merely for the trouble of picking them up. One likes to believe that this story is true and that the elephants had the intelligence to recognize that man would not give up his ivory but that cooperation would benefit both sides.

This dislike of killing is most penetratingly described by George Orwell in 'Shooting an Elephant', a story which is referred to later in this book.

Grace and prettiness are not attributes of the elephant. He who paints cats, horses and dogs (some dogs) is charmed, and charms, by the beauty of line and movement. Not so with the painter of the elephant. With the elephant there is magnificence and perhaps humour. The power of the creature is portrayed in the rock paintings such as those at Tassili in the Sahara. Hieronymus Bosch has symbolized his rock-like strength; Mantegna has painted his splendour and Rembrandt himself has drawn him in charcoal. But the most striking of all representations of the elephant are surely in the Indian and Persian miniatures such as those in the Akbarnama.

Sometimes even in the ancient orient, humour appears in pictures of elephants as in the Hindu paintings of the elephants suffering from colic and headache. In the first the animal's vitals are being severely constricted by a snake, while in the other the headache is being caused by demons.

The general appearance of the elephant is of course irresistible. Like that of the pig, the elephant's shape immediately brings a smile to one's lips. He does not perhaps rollick like the pig; his sense of dignity withholds him from playing the fool. Nor will he be made fun of. There was an elephant in the zoo in London who had once a sore tooth which he rinsed from time to time with a jet of water from his trunk, holding his face on one side to do so. It was comic to see and provoked considerable mirth among the spectators, which the elephant did not appreciate. One day there was a small crowd standing watching, smiling and laughing good-naturedly. Among them was an elderly gentleman who liked his joke—alas, he was a relative of one of the authors of this book. He planted himself in front of the elephant and each time that the elephant put his head on one side, rinsed and made his comic face, he put *his* head on one side and made a face at the elephant. The elephant bore this impertinence placidly for some time while the crowd shouted with laughter, egging on the two of them to make grimaces at each other. At last the old gentleman made such an excruciating face that the elephant upped with his trunk and hosed his opponent down well and truly—whereat the fickle crowd roared their ribs out. The old gentleman being a sportsman took it in good part but never reported whether there was a smile on the face of the elephant.

This incident occurred long before the days of the universal demand for publicity, which is doubtless why it never found its way into the columns of the daily press. Today, as everyone knows, not even an elephant can exist without a P.R.O.—or at least a press that keeps its image before the public. When the new elephant-house in the London Zoo was opened—designed by Sir Hugh Casson and his partners with top lighting, presumably to make the elephants think they were in the jungle—many newspaper men and women were invited to meet the elephants in their new home. The elephants were not much inclined to show off. One, Toto, gave a reluctant display in a warm bath. Another, Dicksie, more experienced, listened for a time with considerable patience to a series of idiotic questions. She treated with contempt a young woman who asked whether, when elephants were wrinkled, it meant they were getting old. She was equally scornful when a reporter asked whether she 'could get at us'. And when someone asked if she was eating 'dolly mixtures', she felt she'd had enough and lifted her trunk to spout over the assembled pressmen and into their whisky or champagne. Preposterous? Not a bit of it. What did Ogden Nash say?

> If you think an elephant's preposterous
> You've never seen a rhinoceros.

No doubt elephants have often soused people who have been plaguing them. There is, for instance, a well-authenticated case of an elephant who was brought to Rome in 1514. This elephant, having been made by his mahout to bow to the Pope, filled his trunk with water from a trough and sprayed the spectators, including his Holiness himself. In another authenticated case an elephant was expecting an apple from a visitor, who happened to be a tailor. Unhappily the tailor pricked the elephant's trunk with one of his needles. The incensed animal proceeded to drench the unfortunate man with a deluge of water. The story does not relate whether the tailor survived or was drowned.

Pigs and elephants share another characteristic—both regard themselves as equals of mankind, with whom they are prepared to make friends and cooperate (although as far as the pig is concerned, when one thinks of bacon, it is hard to understand); but both animals are ready to show affection to man and to be faithful in friendship. That supreme writer on elephants, Rudyard Kipling, has given us several stories on this theme—stories which one cannot but believe are firmly founded on truth. 'My Lord the Elephant', who held up the whole army in the Tangi pass, refusing to budge until they brought him his friend Mulvaney to talk to him, is a case in point. How Malachi, the elephant, knew that Mulvaney was in hospital close to the line of march none could guess. Yet that elephant knew it and would not budge until Mulvaney was brought out to say 'how do!'. And nothing is truer than John Wilmot's remark in the play *Valentinian* I. i.: 'The elephant is never won with anger'—but perhaps this is true of all animals except the wild cat which is never won at all.

Oddly enough, although pigs and elephants have an affinity, they dislike one another. Aelian tells a horrible story of how the citizens of Megara, attacked by Antipater, who had a multitude of elephants, collected a large number of pigs, covered them with pitch, set alight to them and drove them towards the elephants who were so terrified by the screams of the pigs that they fled in disorder. It was after this, some authorities say, that elephants were brought up with pigs to become accustomed to each other.

Shakespeare, who knew most things, well knew the elephant's equality with man. He does not talk a lot about them but, as always, when he does, it is to the point and pithy. When, in *Troilus and Cressida*, Agamemnon is come to persuade Achilles to the fight and Patroclus comes alone from Achilles' tent to say he will not, Ulysses remarks sardonically: 'The Elephant hath joints, but none for courtesy: his legs are legs for necessity not for flexure.'

This does suggest that Shakespeare thought that elephants could not kneel, which, in fact, they can do. But the structure of their legs is such that they cannot jump. And oddly enough, a few lines before, Thersites says spitefully, 'Shall the elephant Ajax carry it thus?'

However, the great poets have not had a great deal to say about elephants. John Donne, Milton and Southey, Joshua Sylvester and, above all, Rudyard Kipling are among the best known. We shall quote them by and by.

It is, of course, well known that the elephant plays a very prominent part in the religions of the orient. It is not so well known that he has also an important place in Christian mythology and that he appears in poetry and prose in mediaeval manuscripts. He is also to be seen in carvings on the capitals of pillars, on misericords and bench ends in many cathedrals and churches, both in England and on the continent. In fact, after pigs, of which there are no less than between 250 and 300, and cats, of which there are not quite so many, elephants come high in the census of numbers of carved animals in English cathedrals and churches and very high in order of importance. (It should, perhaps, be said for the comfort of dog lovers, that there are also many dogs, but while pigs, cats and elephants stand on their own feet, so to speak, dogs are nearly always lying as faithful hounds at the feet of their masters and mistresses—although there is one strange case where five pigs are devouring a dog!) However, the case of the ecclesiastical elephant will be found fully discussed later on.

From the church to the stage—or in this case, to the circus—is a not unusual step. Circus elephants, elephants of the entertainment world, are legion, and it would be very wrong not to give at least the more famous ones their proper place among their more august ecclesiastical and their more important warlike and workaday fellows; they will therefore appear in due time—as will the elephants of the inn sign and of the nursery.

Unlike cats and pigs, there are few proverbs about elephants and few other meanings of the word—other, that is, than the animal itself. There are two plants, *Elephant's Ear*, which is begonia and *Elephant's Foot*, which is a kind of yam. Elephant Penelope canvas is extremely coarse canvas, suitable for rug-making. An elephanter is an old Portuguese expression for violent storms which attend the termination of the monsoon. 'To see the elephant' is an American slang expression for 'to see life' or 'to see the world'. And 'double elephant' is a size of paper.

But this is small beer and the reader might justifiably beg us to desist by quoting the Latin proverb *'elephantem ex musca facis'*, 'you are making an elephant out of a fly'.

# The elephant

The torn boughs trailing o'er the tusks aslant,
The saplings reeling in the path he trod,
Declare his might—our lord the Elephant,
Chief of the ways of God.

The black bulk heaving where the oxen pant,
The bowed head toiling where the guns careen,
Declare our might—our slave the Elephant
And servant of the Queen.

by Rudyard Kipling from *Beast and Man in India* by J. Lockwood Kipling
The Tayu

1  Babur's victory over Rana Sangor

2 Chinese bronze ritual vase; Tcheou epoch, 11th–9th cent. BC

3 Cave painting at Tassili n'Ajjer, Sahara

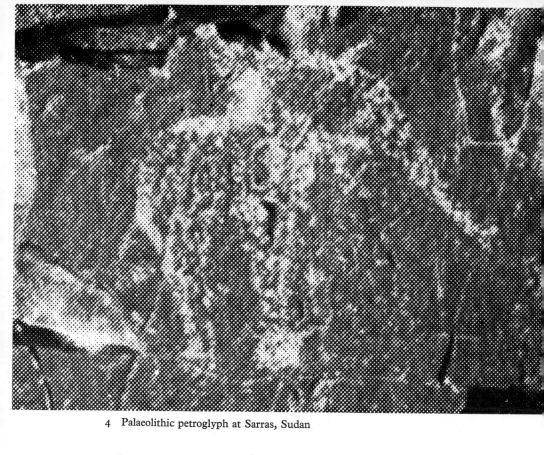

4 Palaeolithic petroglyph at Sarras, Sudan

5 Petroglyph in the Wadi Zirmei, Sahara

6  The Icthus Stone in Kintore Kirkyard, Aberdeenshire; 7th cent.

# Of the origin of elephants

The Matanga-Lila, which means 'Elephant-Sport', is the best Sanskrit work on elephantology. The translation of it from which a short extract follows was intended by the translator, Professor Franklin Edgerton, as an introduction to the elephant lore of the Hindus. The treatise was written by one Nilakantha, of whom, in fact, nothing is known. The work is written in verse and describes the origin of elephants, their care, character and points. The extract here included describes the mythological origin of elephants and their place in Brahmanism.

There was an overlord of Anga, like unto the king of the gods, famed under the name of Romapada. Once he was seated on a jeweled throne on the bank of the Ganges, in the city of Campa, surrounded by his retinue, when some people reported to him that all the crops of grain, etc., were being destroyed by wild elephants. The king reflected: 'Now what can I do?'

At this time the distinguished sages, Gautama, Narada, Bhrgu, Mrgacarman, Agnivesya, Arimeda, Kapya, Matangacarya and others, on divine instigation arrived in Campa. The king received them courteously with seats, flowers, and water, etc., and out of regard for him they granted the king of Anga a boon, to catch the wild elephants.

On the way the king's men, whom he despatched to catch the elephants, beheld as they roamed in the jungle a sage Samagayana who was staying in a hermitage. Near by a herd of elephants was grazing; and they saw the glorious hermit Palakapya, who was with the elephant herd, but was separated from it at morning, noon and night.

All this was reported to the lord of Anga by his servants. So he went and, while the hermit was gone into the hermitage, caught the elephants, and came straightway to Campa, and gave them over to the excellent sages Gautama, Narada, and the rest. But they fastened them securely to posts, and then dwelt there in peace, as did the other folk likewise.

Having performed his service to his father, the hermit Palakapya came out from the hermitage to the place where the elephant herd had been. Not finding it there, he searched everywhere, and so came to Campa, disturbed at heart with affection, and tended the elephants in their distress by applying medicaments to soothe their wounds, and in other ways.

Now Gautama and the other sages who were there saw this illustrious hermit who was spending his time in silence in the midst of the elephant herd; and so they asked him: 'Why do you anoint their wounds? What made you take compassion on the elephant herd?' Though the sages questioned him thus he made no reply.

Then the noble sages reported these facts; hearing which the king of Anga went thither, and paid respects to the hermit with foot-water and other courtesies, and asked him all about his family and name and the rest, being curious to hear. But when that blameless hermit made no reply to him, the king pressed him yet again with questions, bowing low in homage.

Then, propitiated, the sage Palakapya said to the lord of Anga: 'Formerly elephants could go anywhere they pleased, and assume any shape; they roamed as they liked in the sky and on the earth. In the

# Of the origin of elephants

northern quarter of the Himalaya Mountain there is a banyan tree which has a length and breadth of two hundred leagues. On it the excellent elephants alighted.[1]

'They broke off a branch [which fell] upon a hermitage place, where dwelt a hermit named Dirghatapas. He was angered by this and straightway cursed the elephants. Hence, you see, the elephants were deprived of the power of moving at will, and came to be vehicles for even mortal men. The elephants of the quarters, however, were not cursed.

'The elephants of the quarters, attended by all the elephant tribes, went and said to the Lotus-born:[2] "O god, when our kinsfolk have gone to earth by the power of fate, they may be a prey to diseases, because of unsuitable and undigested food due to eating coarse things and over-eating, and other causes!" Thus addressed by them in their great distress, the Lotus-born replied to them: "Not long after now there shall appear a certain sage, fond of elephants, well versed in medicine, and he shall right skilfully cure their diseases." Thus addressed by Fate[3] the elephants of the quarters went each to its own quarters while the others, their kinsfolk, went to earth in consequence of the curse.

'Rucira[4] was fashioned by the Creator as he fashioned Speech, by collecting the beauties belonging to sprites, men, demons, and gods. But once she was cursed by Fate because of her evil pride. Hence she was born as a daughter of the Vasus, from Bhargava, and was named Gunavati. Her great curiosity led her once to the hermitage of Matanga.

'Thinking "Nay, she has been sent by Indra to disturb my penance!" he cursed her, and she became an elephant cow. Then the sage, realizing that she was innocent, straightway said to her: "Fair elephant cow, when from drinking the seed of the hermit Samagayana a son shall be born to you, then your curse shall come to an end."

'A certain *yaksi*[5] once appeared to the hermit Samagayana in a dream. Then the noble hermit straightway went out from the hermitage and passed water. With the urine, seed came forth. That she drank when the hermit had re-entered the house, and speedily the elephant cow conceived and brought forth a son, from her mouth.

'Giving her son with joy to the sage, she left the form of an elephant cow and quickly went to heaven, freed from her curse, in peace. Pleased, that hermit Samagayana then performed the birth rite and other rites for him, and in accordance with a heavenly voice gave him the name of Palakapya.

'And he played with the elephants, their cows, and the young elephants, roaming with them through rivers and torrents, on mountain tops and in pools of water, and on pleasant spots of ground, living as a hermit on leaves and water, through years numbering twice six thousand, learning all about the elephants, what they should and should not

---

1. The elephants alighted after flying through the air
2. Lotus-born = Brahma
3. Fate = Brahma
4. Rucira was a nymph, the name meaning 'lovely'
5. Yaksi—a female sprite

eat, their joys and griefs, their gestures and what is good and bad for them and so forth.

'Know, King of Anga, that I am that hermit Palakapya son of Sama-gayana!' Thus addressed by that excellent sage, the King of Anga was greatly amazed. Then the sage, questioned further by that king with regard to elephants, told the prince about the origin of elephants, their favourable and other marks, their medical treatment, and other things, one after another.

The creation of elephants was holy, and for the profit of sacrifice to the gods, and especially for the welfare of kings. Therefore it is clear that elephants must be zealously tended.

The egg from which the creation of the sun took place—the Unborn[1] took solemnly in his two hands the two gleaming half shells of that egg, exhibited by the Brahmanical sages, and chanted seven samans at once. Thereupon the elephant Airavata[2] was born and seven other noble elephants[3] were severally born, through the chanting.

Thus eight elephants were born from the eggshell held in his right hand. And from that in his left hand in turn eight cows were born, their consorts. And in the course of time those elephants, their many sons and grandsons, etc., endowed with spirit and might, ranged at will over the forests, rivers and mountains of the whole world.

And the [eight] noble elephants [of the quarters] went to the battle of the gods and demons, as vehicles of the lords of the quarters, Indra, Agni and the rest. Then in fright they ran away to Virinca.[4] Knowing this, the spirit of *Must* was then created by Fate; when it had been implanted in them, infuriated they annihilated the host of the demons, and went with Indra and the rest each to his separate quarter.

from the *Matanga-Lila, or 'Elephant-Sport' of Nilakantha,* translated by Professor Franklin Edgerton

1. The Unborn = The Creator
2. Airavata was supposed to be a pure white elephant
3. These were the eight elephants of 'the quarters', or regions
4. Virinca = Brahma

# My name is Jumbo

'. . . An' the 'uttee's be'ind end was stickin' in the Pass, so we cheered *that*. Then they said that the bridge had been strengthened, an' we give three cheers for the bridge; but the 'uttee wouldn't move a bloomin' hinch.' So said Ortheris in 'My Lord the Elephant'. ''uttee' is the cockney soldier's attempt to pronounce 'Hathi', the Hindu name for the elephant. Considering the long years of the British Raj in India, it is strange that 'Hathi' did not invade the English language with words like 'Tiffin', 'Pukka', 'Sahib' and the rest. But we have stuck to the word 'elephant' which has only a remote, if any, connection with the Eastern names.

The animal played such an important, such an immense role in the East, that one would have thought one of the names given it in India or Burma at least would have found its way into Western languages.

As mentioned earlier, the origin of the word 'elephant' is obscure. This, in turn, some derive from A-bu, which according to Sir Wallace Budge in his *Dictionary of Ancient Egyptian Hieroglyphics* means both the Indian and the African Elephant. The possible derivation Abu is used by Ivan T. Sanderson in the title of his remarkable book on elephants *The Dynasty of Abu*.

Mr Sanderson does not use the word 'elephant' for the African variety but applies to it the zoological term 'Loxodont'. Nor does he examine the various eastern names as does the Chevalier P. Armandi in his history of elephants in war. In this history Armandi has an interesting note on the various names given to the animal in India: 'The devotion of the Indians to the Elephant', he writes, 'led to their choice of names for the animal; they were not just content to give the creature any old name; it had to be something that expressed one of its distinctive characteristics or habits. Here are some of the names I have come across:—

'*Gadja*, or *Gaja* This is the name of the elephant in Sanskrit. This name survives in modern Indian language and is the one most commonly used. The word is derived from the verb meaning to "move along" (cf. the word "go" in English and "Gehen" in German) and means in effect "the walker" or "the good-goer", in fact the Supreme Quadruped. The Sultan Djihan Guyr named his favourite elephant Indra-Gadga, that is "the elephant of Indras", one of the Hindu Gods.

'*Duipa* This means the creature which drinks twice; and *Anekapa* which means the creature which drinks repeatedly. These two names refer to the fact that the elephant draws water into his trunk and then squirts it into his throat, thus appearing to drink twice.

'*Karin* and *Hastin* are derived from *Kara* and *Hasta*, meaning "hand". (The Greek χειρ probably comes from *Kara*.) The similarity of function between the trunk of the elephant and the hand of a man must have struck people very early on. And, of course, the Greeks and Romans refer to the trunk as "the hand". Buffon uses the same term.

'It is from *Hastin* that the modern Hindustani name for an elephant, *Hati* or *Hathi* comes.

'The name *Dantin* comes from *danta* which means tooth—that is, the animal renowned for the strength and beauty of its teeth.

'*Duirada* is another name connected with teeth, from the root *rada* (cf. Latin, *rodere* and French *ronger* meaning to gnaw). It means the animal with "two defensive teeth".

'*Naga* is also one of the ancient names for elephant. It means "large snake" and is of course, a reference to the trunk.'

(Armandi refers to two subsidiary meanings of *Naga*, one being 'immense', and the other 'mountain' or 'woodland' thus 'immense beast' or 'mountain' or 'woodland' beast.

(It will be remembered that Rudyard Kipling gave the name Kala Nag to the elephant which took Toomai to witness the elephants' dance.)

'*Ibha*, sometimes written *Ipha*, is the most ancient Sanscrit name for the elephant.

'*Pil*, is the name for elephant in ancient Persian. The Arabs made *Fil* or *Al-Fil* out of this and it is most likely that it is from this that the Greeks made the form ἐλέφας. Other scholars, however, believe that ἐλέφας comes from *Ipha*, with the article "al" added by the Arabs, making *Al-ipha*.'

The elephant was one of the pieces used in India in the game of chess. The piece became *Al Fil* when the game reached Arabia. *Al Fil* passed from Africa via Spain to France, where it became *auphin*, which in Old French meant the Joker in chess, which was the same as '*läufer*' in German, or 'bishop' in the English version of the game. The word *Fil* is also the origin of *Morfil* (presumably 'mort-Fil') which is a term for ivory. In old maps the shores of Guinea are sometimes shown as the "Côte de Morfil"—the Ivory Coast.

Turning to Europe, Armandi remarks that it is strange that neither Hesiod nor Homer, 'who has given us such a vivid and truthful account of the customs and knowledge of his times', mention the elephant at all. 'Holy Writ,' he writes, 'is absolutely silent on the subject until the time of the Maccabees, which was much later than the period of Alexander— and this in spite of the fact that there are many descriptions of the armies of the ancient Asiatic kings.'

Job, of course, describes Behemoth which is interpreted by scholars as the water-ox. Samuel Bochart, who was an eminent French scholar and orientalist in the first half of the seventeenth century and wrote a work called *Hierozoicon . . . de animalibus sacrae scripturae*, used his learning to prove that Behemoth was in fact the hippopotamus. Antoine Augustin Calmet, however, another French scholar, who lived at the end of the seventeenth century and who taught philosophy and theology as a Benedictine at the Abbey of Moyen-Moutier, maintained fiercely in his *Dictionnaire Historique Géographique, Critique, Chronologique et Littéral de la Bible*, published in 1720, that Behemoth was indeed the elephant.

What does Job himself say that the Lord said to him? Here it is:

> Behold now behemoth which I made with thee: he eateth grass as an ox.
> Lo now, his strength is in his loins, and his force is in the navel of his belly.
> He moveth his tail like a cedar: the sinews of his stones are wrapped together.

His bones are as strong pieces of brass; his bones are like bars of iron.

He is the chief of the ways of God: he that made him can make his sword to approach unto him.

Surely the mountains bring him forth food, where all the beasts of the field play.

He lieth under the shady trees, in the covert of the reed, and fens.

The shady trees cover him with their shadow; the willows of the brook compass him about.

Behold, he drinketh up a river, and hasteth not: he trusteth that he can draw up Jordan into his mouth.

He taketh it with his eyes: his nose pierceth through snares.

It is difficult to think of the ox or, indeed, the hippopotamus as being 'chief of the ways of God' or that in either case 'his nose pierceth through snares'. Both these observations sound more applicable to the elephant.

Both Milton and Shelley appear to support the idea of behemoth being an elephant. In *Paradise Lost*, Book VII, describing the creation, Milton writes.

'. . . scarce from his mould
Behemoth, biggest born of earth
Upheaves his vastness . . .'

Shelley is, perhaps, not so convincing, but in *Prometheus Unbound* he refers to

'The jagged allegator and the might
Of earth-convulsing behemoth, which once
were monarch beasts . . .'

Rudyard Kipling, in the poem quoted in *Beast and Man in India*, refers to—'our Lord the Elephant, Chief of the Ways of God.'

And then, of course, there's Jumbo. Jumbo, the first of the name, the famous African elephant, came to London Zoo in 1865 and made a deep impression on the people—as had, indeed, the Indian elephant sent by St Louis to Henry III in 1255. But where did he get his name? He was a very large bull elephant or Loxodont and one can only surmise that as he came from Africa he was named after Mumbo-Jumbo, said to be a grotesque deity worshipped by certain Negro tribes.

As everyone knows, the name fitted the beast so well that it has been the generic name for elephants among English children ever since.

Somehow Mr Sanderson's 'Abu' does not appeal and is unlikely to be widely used. 'Loxodont', too, one cannot believe will catch on. Now that the British Raj has left India and Rudyard Kipling is no longer there to make India as familiar to us as our own Britain, Indian names for the beast are more likely to drop into oblivion in western countries.

The grace, the mystery, the magnificence of the word 'elephant' will remain. No name could better match the majesty of the creature.

Most elephants in man's service, whether as workers, in war or in entertainment, have been given names. It is said that the great emperor Akbar knew the names of his many thousands of elephants. The name of the elephant ridden personally by Hannibal was Surus—the Syrian—from which it is inferred that this one of Hannibal's elephants was of the Indian variety. Porus's elephant on which he was mounted at the Battle of Hydaspes, in which he was defeated by Alexander, was called Nicon. Antiochus's favourite elephant was Ajax.

The name of the elephant sent by Emanuel of Portugal to Pope Leo X was Hanno, while that sent to Charlemagne by the Caliph Haroun al Raschid was Aboul-Abbas. The elephant who refused to obey Abraha and march on Mecca was Mahmud.

Topsell, whose fascinating seventeenth-century disquisition on elephants will be found later in this volume, believed that '*elephantus*' in the 'Punicke tongue' signified '*Caesar*'; so that when Julius Caesar's grandfather slew an elephant 'he had the name of Caesar put upon him'.

Jumbo we have mentioned—but he shall have a story all to himself later on. A famous elephant in Exeter 'Change Menagerie, who had eventually to be shot—and who is said to have knelt down in order to make it easier for his executioners—was called Chuni, while an elephant in Mr Cross's menageries was Lutchmé.

The name of the first elephant to visit the United States is not known, but his successor—the second—was Old Bet.

Elsewhere in this book will be found a list of names of sixty-six of Akbar's elephants. Some are singularly dull—'Short', 'Tall', 'Handsome'; others have a flavour of rollicking affection—'Heart-Opener', 'Father's Gift', 'Always Drunk'; yet others are splendid—'Over-Comer in War', 'Enemy-treader', 'Earth-shaker'—the latter reminding one of the earth-shaking beast of Macaulay's *Lays of Ancient Rome*. But perhaps the oddest of the lot is 'Good Ball'—why, one would like to know, call your elephant 'Good Ball'? Did he respond to kicking?

One of the most charming of elephant names was the name of the elephant which Richard Halliburton rode over the Great St Bernard. When beast and rider reached the Hospice at the top of the pass they were required to put their names on registration forms. Richard Halliburton said that the elephant could only get a bit of one foot through the door, so he had to get down and sign for both himself and his mount, taking, as he says, the elephant's dictation through the window.

'Name—Elysabethe Dalrymple. But please add,' said the elephant, 'that everybody calls me "Dally"—my real name is too silly.'

Elysabethe Dalrymple was really a very remarkable elephant: her passage of the Alps is described by Halliburton (an equally remarkable traveller and writer), in his book of travellers' tales called *Seven League Boots*. The passage of the Alps was only achieved at the second attempt. On the first occasion Halliburton left it too late and the passes were closed. He had wasted too much time trying to buy a suitable animal. The first he found was in a French circus, the 'Cirque d'Hiver'. There he fell in love with an elephant called Lulu and saw her in his mind's eye marching down to Rome. She appeared to return his affection but, alas, she was by nature a too affectionate beast and was on the point of a confinement. So she had to be abandoned.

Halliburton inspected three other elephants in the circus—Marie, Josephine Baker and Yvonne. He chose Yvonne and all was fixed, but at the last minute the owner of the circus remembered that his posters advertised sixteen elephants and if he let Yvonne go he would lose face, so Yvonne too had to stay behind.

It was then that he met Elysabethe Dalrymple, the perfect elephant, in the Paris Zoo. Once more everything was arranged and Elysabethe Dalrymple started from the Bois in good order. Unhappily in the Porte Maillot she became terrified by the traffic. A taxi driver sounded a blast on his horn at the elephant's stern and the animal bolted down the Avenue de la Grande Armée at top speed, scattering cabs and pedestrians in all directions, until stopped by a solid block of traffic in front of the Arc de Triomphe. Poor Dally, squealing and shaking, was led back to the zoo where she gradually recovered, though too late for the proposed journey.

Halliburton, however, was a determined fellow; although he had only six days left before the St Bernard was expected to close until the spring he managed to buy a splendid elephant named Bertha from Hanover. Even so, it proved too late and winter closed the route and the project had to be abandoned.

Halliburton got his second opportunity in the following July. Dally was put into training for traffic and was ready to start after only two weeks' experience. The journey was triumphantly accomplished in spite of rarefied air and an encounter near the top of the pass with an Italian Army on manoeuvres whose gunfire terrified the animal out of her senses. Nevertheless, after several adventures the expedition reached Turin in safety and eventually Dally returned to the peace of her old home in the Bois de Boulogne. As a parting gift Halliburton gave her an outsize harmonica which he left her blowing vociferously.

One could fill pages with the names of elephants, attractive, comic, sometimes sinister. Some have meaning, some not. Mulvaney's elephant, the 'uttee' that sat down in the Tangi pass, was called Malachi—at least that's what Mulvaney called him. 'Elephant Bill's' most famous elephant was Bandoola, named after the Burman patriot, Maha Bandoola who fought the British in 1824. But we had better bring this list to a close—perhaps with another of 'Elephant Bill's' elephants, whose name was Ma Pin Wa—which, being translated, means 'Miss Fat Bottom'.

# Of the elephant

The Elephant came first by his name of the Greeke verbe *Elephio*, which signifieth huge or like a hill. He is of exceeding great body, his tushes are of Iuerie: his becke is holpen with that snowt, that helpeth him euen as our hand doth. The Medes and Persians use to carie in their warfare their Casteles and other preparaunce on the Elephants backe: he is of good memorie and long mindfull of a good tourne. Plinie saith, that amongest all the beastes of the wild forrest, he is most mens frind. Insomuch that if a mans iourney lieth so, that he must nedes through the Forrest (least he himself so monstrous and huge should first feare him), he goeth a little a side out of his way: furder if the Dragon should assault the man, he goeth forwith and warreth with the Dragon and keepeth him off from the man: so that whilst these two be at strife, the man passeth away. Aristotle saith, that this kind is without his Gall, and therefore it may be that he is so quiet and peasible. Solinus saith, that they seeme to haue some skill in the art of Astronomie, and play the Phisicion, his part euerie moneth in purgation taking and purging themselues: for after euery new Moone they hauke after the cleare riuers, and so wash off all filthinesse, such as may cumber the body. After that they bathe them, and this being so done, they go again al frolike to their woonted pastures. And to the intent that their youth should keepe good rule and not go at royat, they haue them with them.

Such care haue they ouer them. They haue a meruelous and most honest shamefastnesse in the acte of generation. Therefore when the time commeth that this must nedes be done, the Female witting the Male his pleasure, goeth straying before towardes the deserts of the East, seketh the most secret place where that their intent may be done and ended closely. The Male he anone hasteneth after and before their meeting of coniunction had togither, they are busied awhile in seking out the herb Mandrage, which the Female taketh and reciueth to make hir of more fertill nature and pregnant: and the Male also eateth of it to procure a more earnest desire. Of al things that it standeth in feare of it is most afraide of the sily Mouse, which fretteth him then most when as hee is tied to the Maunger and cannot away.

from *A Greene Forest or a naturall Historie*. Compiled by John Maplet, M. of Arte and student in Cambridge: entending hereby that God might especially be glorified; and the people furdered, 1567

# Noah's elephant

The Elephant there comming to imbarque,
And as he softly getteth up the Ark,
Feeling by his great waight, his body sunck,
Holds by his huge Tooth, and his nervy Trunck: ...

from *Every Living Creature* by Michael Drayton, 1563–1631

So they came in two by two,
The elephant, the kangaroo,
And the gnu,
And the little tiny shrew

from *The History of the Flood* by John Heath-Stubbs, 1918–

## An Israeli legend

There is an ancient Israeli legend that, during the sojourn of Noah
and the animals in the Ark, the vessel was on the point of capsizing because of the huge deposits of dung on one side. Desperately Noah asked
the Deity what could be done. He was told to move the elephant to the
other side. This he did, with the surprising result that large numbers of
rats and mice were released from below the disturbed heap of dung.
These rodents began to gnaw holes in the timbers of the Ark. Again
Noah asked for instructions. He was told to smite the lion on the nose.
He did so and promptly the lion sneezed out two cats—the first in creation—who proceeded to dispose of the rats and mice and thus save the
Ark. It is interesting that in this story the elephant and the lion, tradi-
tional enemies, were employed on the same side.

# The elephant according to Pliny

Pliny, or to give him his full name, Gaius Plinius Secundus, lived in the first century AD from AD 23 to AD 79. He was born at Como. He lived through the reigns of several Emperors, including Nero and Vespasian, with the latter of whom he was on intimate terms. His nephew, Pliny the Younger, gives a fascinating description of his uncle. He tells us how he would call upon Vespasian before dawn and then when he had completed his official duties he went home where he would study and write. The whole of his time during holidays was given up to study and he even had a secretary sent to him while he was in his bath and he often dictated while he was being dried and rubbed down after his bath. When he travelled he kept a shorthand writer hard at work, and he saw that he had gloves in cold weather, so that nothing should hold up the work. He never walked but was carried in a litter so as not to lose a moment from his studies and he actually reproved his nephew for wasting valuable time walking. He died in the eruption of Vesuvius which destroyed Herculaneum and Pompeii. At the time he was prefect of the Roman fleet and was stationed at Misenium. When the eruption occurred he went over to the southern shore of the Bay of Naples to help those in danger but died of suffocation from the dust.

His great work on Natural History appeared in AD 77. While much is sound sense, chiefly gathered from Aristotle, so far as biology is concerned, he was not unlike Herodotus in believing tall stories, such as of men whose feet were the wrong way round; men without mouths who lived on the scent of things; men with 'umbrella feet' which they used as parasols; animals which buried their heads, because, if a man met their gaze, he fell dead.

His writings on the elephant are surprisingly accurate and extraordinarily interesting—so much so as to be worth quoting extensively. The elephant is the first of the beasts he describes and it occupies chapters 1 to 12 of Book VIII. He does not confine himself to purely zoological matters, but writes of the animal's place in society in peace and war. He describes, for instance, their breastplates and talks of their skin as 'a lattice-work of wrinkles' (*cancellata cutis*). In a coin illustrated by Cuperus the lattice-work makes the animal look as if it were dressed in tartan. (See illustration on page 93.)

Pliny writes of the elephant:

'These animals are well aware that the only spoil that we are anxious to procure of them is the part which forms their weapon of defence, by Juba called their horns, but by Herodotus, a much older writer, as well as by general usage and more appropriately, their teeth. Hence it is that, when their tusks have fallen off, either by accident or from old age, they bury them in the earth. These tusks form the only real ivory, and, even in these, the part which is covered by the flesh is merely common bone, and of no value whatever; though, indeed, of late, in consequence of the insufficient supply of ivory, they have begun to cut the bones as well into thin plates. Large teeth, in fact, are now rarely found, except in India, the demands of luxury having exhausted all those in our part of the world. The youthfulness of the animal is ascertained by the whiteness of the teeth. These animals take the greatest care of their teeth; they pay especial attention to the point of one of them, that it may not

33

be found blunt when wanted for combat; the other they employ for various purposes, such as digging up roots and pushing forward heavy weights. When they are surrounded by the hunters, they place those in front which have the smallest teeth, that the enemy may think that the spoil is not worth the combat; and afterwards, when they are weary of resistance, they break off their teeth, by dashing them against a tree, and in this manner pay their ransom.

'It is a wonderful thing, that most animals are aware why it is that they are sought after, and what it is, that, under all circumstances, they have to guard against. When an elephant happens to meet a man in the desert, who is merely wandering about, the animal, it is said, shows himself both merciful and kind, and even points out the way. But the very same animal, if he meets with the traces of man before he meets the man himself, trembles in every limb, for fear of an ambush, stops short and scents the wind, looks around him, and snorts aloud with rage; and then, without trampling upon the object, digs it up and passes it to the next one, who again passes it to the other, till it comes to the very last. The herd then faces about, returns, and ranges itself in order of battle; so strongly does the odour, in all cases, attach itself to the human footstep, even though, as is most frequently the case, the foot itself is not naked. In the same way, too, the tigress, which is the dread of the other wild beasts, and which sees, without alarm, the traces even of the elephant itself, is said at once, upon seeing the footsteps of man, to carry off her whelps. How has the animal acquired this knowledge? And where has it seen him before, of which it stands in such dread? Doubt there can be none, that forests such as it haunts are but little frequented by man! It is not to be wondered at, if they are astonished at the print of a footstep before unknown; but how should they know that there is anything that they ought to dread? And, what is still more, why should they dread even the very sight of man, seeing that they are so far superior to him in strength, size, and swiftness? No doubt, such is the law of Nature, such is the influence of her power—the most savage, and the very largest of beasts have never seen that which they have reason to fear, and yet instantly have an instinctive feeling of dread, when the moment has come for them to fear.

'Verrius informs us, that they fought in the Circus, and that they were slain with javelins, for want of some better method of disposing of them; as the people neither liked to keep them nor yet to give them to the kings. L. Piso tells us only that they were brought into the Circus; and for the purpose of increasing the feeling of contempt towards them, they were driven all round the area of that place by workmen, who had nothing but spears blunted at the point. The authors who are of the opinion that they were not killed, do not, however, inform us how they were afterwards disposed of.

'There is a famous combat mentioned of a Roman with an elephant, when Hannibal compelled our prisoners to fight against each other. The one who had survived all the others he placed before an elephant, and promised him his life if he should slay it; upon which the man advanced alone into the arena, and, to the great regret of the Carthaginians, succeeded in doing so. Hannibal, however, thinking that the news of this victory might cause a feeling of contempt for these animals, sent some horsemen to kill the man on his way home. In our battles with Pyrrhus it was found, on making trial, that it was extremely easy to cut off the trunks of these animals. Fenestella informs us, that they fought at Rome in the Circus for the first time during the curule aedileship of Claudius Pulcher, in the consulship of M. Antonius and A. Postumius, in the year of the City 655; and that twenty years afterwards, during the curule aedileship of the Luculli, they were set to fight against bulls.

'In India they were caught by the keeper guiding one of the tame elephants towards a wild one which he has found alone or has separated from the herd; upon which he beats it, and when it is fatigued mounts and manages it just the same way as the other. In Africa they take them in pit-falls; but as soon as an elephant gets into one, the others immediately collect boughs of trees and pile up heaps of earth, so as to form a mound, and then endeavour with all their might to drag it out. It was formerly the practice to tame them by driving the herds with horsemen into a narrow defile, artificially made in such a way as to deceive them by its length; and when thus enclosed by means of steep banks and trenches, they were rendered tame by the effects of hunger; as a proof of which, they would quietly take a branch that was extended to them by one of the men. At the present day, when we take them for the sake of their tusks, we throw darts at their feet, which are in general the most tender part of their body. The Troglodytae, who inhabit the confines of Aethiopia, and who live entirely on the flesh of elephants procured by the chase, climb the trees which lie near the paths through which these animals usually pass. Here they keep a watch, and look out for the one which comes last in the train; leaping down upon its haunches, they seize its tail with the left hand, and fix their feet firmly upon the left thigh. Hanging down in this manner, the man, with his right hand, hamstrings the animal on one side, with a very sharp hatchet. The elephant's pace being retarded by the wound, he cuts the tendons of the other ham, and then makes his escape; all of which is done with the very greatest celerity. Others, again, employ a much safer, though less certain method; they fix in the ground, at considerable intervals, very large bows upon the stretch; these are kept steady by young men remarkable for their strength, while others, exerting themselves with equal efforts, bend them, and so wound the animals as they pass by, and afterwards trace them by their blood. The female elephant is much more timid by nature than the male.

'Elephants of furious temper are tamed by hunger and blows, while other elephants are placed near to keep them quiet, when the violent fit is upon them, by means of chains. Besides this, they are more particularly violent when in heat, at which time they will level to the ground the huts of the Indians with their tusks. It is on this account that they are prevented from coupling, and the females are kept in herds separate from the males, just the same way as with other cattle.

'The vulgar notion is, that the elephant goes with young ten years; but, according to Aristotle, it is two years only. He says also that the female only bears once, and then a single young one; that they live two hundred years, and some of them as much as three hundred. The adult age of the elephant begins at the sixtieth year. They are especially fond of water, and wander much about streams, and this although they are unable to swim, in consequence of their bulk. They are particularly sensitive to cold, and that, indeed, is their greatest enemy. They are subject also to flatulency, and to looseness of the bowels, but to no other kind of disease.

'Their teeth are very highly prized, and from them we obtain the most costly materials for forming the statues of the gods. Luxury has discovered even another recommendation in this animal, having found a particularly delicate flavour in the cartilaginous part of the trunk, for no other reason, in my belief, than because it fancies itself to be eating ivory. Tusks of enormous size are constantly to be seen in the temples; but, in the extreme parts of Africa, on the confines of Aethiopia, they are employed as door-posts for houses; and Polybius informs us, on the authority of the petty king Gulussa, that they are also employed as stakes in making fences for the folds of cattle.'

# Harmlesse great thing

Nature's great master-peece, an Elephant,
The onely harmlesse great thing; the giant
Of beasts; who thought, no more had gone, to make one wise
But to be just, and thankfull, loth to offend,
(Yet Nature hath given him no knees to bend)[1]

Himselfe he up-props, on himselfe relies,
And foe to none, suspects no enemies,
Still sleeping stood; vex't not his fantasie
Blacke dreames; like an unbent bow, carelessly
His sinewy Proboscis did remisly lie.

from *The Progress of the Soul* by John Donne

1. It was an ancient belief that elephants' legs were so constructed that they could not bend. This same belief was expressed in Ulysses' remark in *Troilus and Cressida*. (See page 17)

# The elephant in art and legend

The proper study of mankind is man, said Alexander Pope, but when one regards the elephant, one wonders. Every creature has, of course, its devotees. Chesterton and, one suspects, Orwell puts the pig on a pinnacle. Humanity in general contemplating the animal 'Kingdom' has pronounced the lion to be the King of Beasts. The English worship the dog and the horse while the ancient Egyptians gave the cat the supreme place and looked upon it, with considerable justification, as Divine. But there has been nothing quite like the relationship between man and the elephant. The cat may be divine; the lion may be royalty; the dog and the horse may be faithful yeomen; but the elephant is surely Plato's philosopher-statesman, ready, indeed eager to cooperate with mankind for the good of creation as a whole.

The elephant is not only the source of quantities of legends but has formed the subject as well as furnished the material for many works of art. No other creature has provided the artist with the substance for a whole branch of art, a substance which, whether in its natural state or in the form of artifacts, is a delight to eye and hand alike, and there are probably more representations of elephants fashioned in ivory than in any other material.

The elephant appears among the very earliest works of man as artist, taking his place in prehistoric cave paintings with the mammoth and the moufflon, the boar and the bison and other creatures. Some of the most interesting of these paintings and carvings are to be found in the central regions of the Sahara, on the plateau of Tassili n 'Ajjer in the South of Algeria described in the *Rock Paintings of Tassili* by Lajoux and Elgar; in the Wadi Zirmei in Eghei on the northern edge of Tibesti, about 600 miles south east of Tassili, described by Dr A. J. Arkell (one time Director of Archaeology in the Sudan) in his book *Wanyanga*; and at Sarras, just south of the second cataract on the Nile, illustrated in Dr Arkell's *History of the Sudan* (see also schematic elephant pages 8 and 9).

According to Elgar, the Tassili paintings are believed to have a magical or religious character, the artists having had no conception of aesthetics. The painted passages and shelters were holy places and the painters of the mesolithic and neolithic age drew the men and animals as a propitiatory rite. Yet in writing of the Altamira paintings the Abbé Breuil says 'Si l'art pour l'art n'était pas né, l'art magique ou religieux n'aurait jamais existé'.

The photographs of an elephant at Sarras and in the Wadi Zirmei (plates 4 and 5) are paleolithic or possibly neolithic and are significant as evidence of the dessication of the area, no elephant being found today in the Nile Valley until well south of Khartoum.

Historical Egypt provides various early representations of the elephant. There is, for instance, a wall-painting in the tomb of Rekhmere (c. 1500 BC) at Thebes showing an Indian bringing a tusk on his shoulder and leading an elephant no bigger than a large dog to Tuthmosis III; and from the tomb of Rameses III (c. 1200 BC) a small ink drawing on a limestone chip was discovered, doubtless an artist's sketch or trial piece for a wall-painting showing an elephant of the distinctively Indian variety.

Asia is, of course, the main source of elephant paintings, ivories and

7 Carving from Elephant Terrace, Angkor Thom, Cambodia

8 Elephants among the lotuses, Anuradhapura, Ceylon; 7th cent.

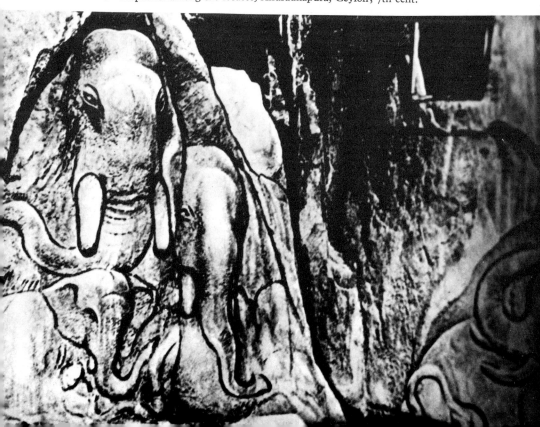

9  Elephant and castle

10  Raising fallen elephant

11 Elephant and draco

12 Elephant and castle

13 Birth of elephant in water

14 Elephant and castle on tight-rope

Man leading elephant; wall-painting in tomb of Rekhmere, Thebes

sculptures. Among the earliest are prehistoric seals of the so-called Indus valley culture, about the middle of the third millennium BC. The 4th and 5th centuries BC provide terracotta figures from the city of Muttra (ancient Mathura), among them figures of elephants and from the same source come punch-marked coin symbols. There are many hundreds of the latter; again the elephant is among them. From this time on the elephant is constantly appearing in sculpture, relief and painting. At Barhut there is a great stupa, the remains of which are now in Calcutta, which had an elaborately decorated railing, many of the carvings depicting scenes from the life of Buddha, including, of course, elephants. Another remarkable relief comes from the vihasa (or monastery) of Bhaja and shows the god Indra seated on his cloud-elephant Airavata. Airavata was the first divine elephant to be created. After the sunbird Garuda came into existence Brahma sang seven holy melodies over the two halves of the eggshell which he held in his hands. The result was sixteen elephants: eight male led by Airavata and eight female. These sixteen became the ancestors of all elephants and the caryatids of the universe, supporting the world at the four cardinal points and the four intermediate points.

C

The original elephants and their offspring had wings and roamed the sky. Unhappily they settled on a banyan tree and broke off a branch on to a sage who was teaching beneath. The sage cursed them and they then became earthbound.

The myth that the world is supported on the backs of elephants has had a very wide currency. Originating in India, it spread to Africa and thence, doubtless though the slave trade, to America. The theory is that the earth rests on the backs of four elephants who stand upon a tortoise. When asked what the tortoise stood on, one Negro sage declared that it stood upon an elephant. 'And what does that elephant stand upon?' 'Oh,' said the sage 'it's elephants and tortoises all the way down!'

So many Eastern myths and legends are associated with elephants, it would require volumes to record them. Many are mirrored in the arts throughout Asia and give rise to some of the most splendid carvings, reliefs and paintings. One finds, for instance, in the great Elephant Terrace at Angkor, where so much of the Khmer people's sculpture was created, a splendid relief of an elephant struggling with a lion. It is said that there is a natural antagonism between the two animals, the lion being wise and strong, and the elephant being loving and merciful. There is a story in the *Yuan Hsieh* of an emperor who, presumably inadvertently, caused a panic among the Imperial elephants by having dancers who were to perform the Lions' Dance (the Shih-tsu Wu) dressed up as lions. Another tale tells of the Tsung Chueh who was sent to deal with barbarians in the South Country of Lin Yi. The cavalry of Tsung Chueh were unable to stand up against the Lin Yi elephant troops. So Tsung Chueh covered his horses with skins to look like lions, which deceived the elephants, who scattered in terror—a story reminiscent of the iron horses designed by Iskandar in his fight with Fúr.

The Japanese also have elephant legends, a number of them centering on the famous courtesan known as the 'Tayu' who is sometimes depicted sitting on an elephant. In a painting by Goshun she is shown on a six-tusked white elephant emerging from the clouds.

There is a splendid story of an elephant in the *Wakan Jumbutsu Shu*, a Japanese book on ancient Chinese myths. One night in the time of the T'ang dynasty a renowned warrior named Wu was wakened by a loud knocking on his door. It was a 'shojo', a gnome popular in Japanese folklore. The gnome explained that he had come at the behest of an elephant to say that some hundreds of miles away there was a terrible and gigantic dragon or serpent which was in the habit of seizing elephants in the forest and devouring them. The elephants besought Wu to come and deal with the serpent. Wu, thinking this would be a worthwhile adventure, set out and found the monster lying in the mouth of a cave. It had a terrible horned head with glittering eyes and teeth like the blades of swords. Quite unperturbed, Wu, hiding behind a rock, shot a poisoned arrow into each eye and the serpent perished in a series of convulsions, roars and flashings of light. Wu then entering the cave found mountains of elephants' bones. The elephants were delighted and presented Wu with a lot of ivory tusks—whence comes an Eastern saying 'The serpent swallows the elephant and after three years the bones of the elephant come out of the serpent'.

This story of the elephant and serpent is of special interest in view of the legend of the enmity of the elephant and the serpent depicted in the mediaeval manuscripts and carvings in English and other cathedrals.

There are large numbers of elephants in sculpture, paintings, ivory, bronze, silver and gold, shown as mounts for various gods, priests and sages in the arts of India, Tibet, Japan and other oriental countries. Among the most famous are Indra on his cloud elephant, Airavata, already referred to, dated about 200 BC; Samantabhadra Bodhisatva on his elephant mount, from Tibet, in bronze coated with silver nearly a thousand years later; and the 'image of Fugen' (Samantabhadra) of the Fujiwara period (twelfth century) in the national museum, Tokyo.

The most famous elephant god is, of course, Ganesha. Properly speaking Ganesha is an elephant-headed man, the eldest son of Shiva and Parvati. He is shown with an elephant's head to symbolize his sagacity and is invoked on the title page of books, especially account books, as he is believed to bring prosperity in trade.

There are various versions of the story of his acquiring an elephant-head. In one of these, Parvati was proudly exhibiting her offspring, inviting all the gods to come and see him. With the rest came Sani (the planet Saturn). He looked upon the infant and his glance burnt off the child's head. Vishnu the Preserver, seeing what had happened, rushed off on his 'vahan' or vehicle, the bird Garuda. Finding an elephant asleep he cut off its head and rushed back to clamp it on Ganesha's neck. Ganesha is generally shown with four arms but only one tusk. The other he is supposed to have lost, preventing an intruder from entering his father Shiva's chamber. One of the most striking Indian sculptures is to be found at Sanchi where, on the great stupa, the legend known as the Chaddanta Jataka is illustrated. This tells of one of the early incarnations of the Buddha, when he ruled as king of a herd of elephants who enjoyed the possession of six tusks. One of his two wives suffered from acute jealousy and after various stratagems disposed of her husband with the help of an assassin. The elephant, as he died, presented his tusks to his murderer, who took them to the Queen. When she saw them, her heart broke. The story appears on the lower architrave of the Western gate; its date is the second half of the first century BC. •

There is also a representation of the Chaddanta Jataka on a Tondo on the stone 'hedge' in the stupa of Barhut. Another tondo (plate 61) from the same stupa illustrates the Dream of Maya, mother of Gautama. She dreams that the Buddha is descending in the form of a white elephant and she conceives. These tondi date from the second century BC.

Among the most celebrated sculptures of elephants in the Far East are those dating from the twelfth century on the great terrace of the elephants at Angkor, the ancient royal capital of the Khmer people, in the forests of Cambodia. Examples of Khmer art and reproductions of many of its manifestations can be studied in the remarkable book on the subject by Madeleine Giteau, of the National Museum at Phnomh Penh.

Equally celebrated are massive carvings of elephants among the lotuses of the seventh century, to be seen near Anuradhapura in Ceylon; the elephants on the great sculpture at Mahamallapuram, known as 'The Descent of the Ganges', of the Pallava period of Indian Art (about the seventh century); and the cave paintings in the Buddhist caves at Ajanta, in the jungle of the western Ghats, not far from Bombay. These are the oldest surviving Indian paintings, dating from the fifth century, among them the remarkable ceiling painting known as 'The Pink Elephant' in cave XVII.

Undoubtedly the most exquisite eastern elephant paintings—or perhaps one should say paintings with elephants as prominent features—are those to be found in the Akbarnama and among the Persian miniatures. For wealth of invention, brilliance of colour and exquisite execution they are unsurpassed. In a recent exhibition in the Victoria and Albert Museum, the Persian miniatures were described by one critic as an aristocratic art. Among the finest of these are to be found in the Shahnama of the Persian poet Firdausi; and the Khamsa of Nizami. One manuscript of Nizami's 'Romance of Alexander' seems to have been made for the namesake of the hero whose feats are described, the Timurid Iskander Sultan. Of this the catalogue of the Exhibition remarked, 'The dilapidated state of this little manuscript, which was formerly in the Mughal Imperial Library in Delhi, may be partly due to its having been carried about by Iskander Sultan in his pocket (or equivalent) on his campaigns'.

The same critic who referred to the miniatures as an aristocratic art writes that this quality is not alone due to their social and cultural background, but that the description is apt because of their extraordinary concentration; the extreme force of the design within the very small space available to it. 'It is an *élite* art in the sense that gestures are never wasted.'

The earliest appearance of the elephant in European art occurs in coins of Carthaginian and Roman origin. Authoritative studies on these in connection with Hannibal appear in the Numismatic Chronicle by H. H. Scullard and in *African Affairs* by Sir Ernest Gowers: some of them are illustrated on plate 44. Hannibal's elephants were mostly African, as can be seen from the coins. In Polybius, the elephants' directors or mahouts are termed Ἰνδοι, but the rider shown on one of the Carthaginian African elephants is considered to be an African. Italian coins of the period do show unmistakable Indian elephants which suggest that Hannibal had at least some in his army.

There is a long treatise in Latin on the elephant on coins and medals by one Gisbertus Cuperus in which he includes numerous illustrations. Some of the most interesting of these depict the supposed religious observance of elephants, particularly in connection with their worship of the sun, moon and stars. A Neapolitan coin has on one face the diademed head of Apollo, the sun god, and on the reverse the tripod of the Delphic oracle with an elephant worshipping it (see page 47).

This notion of the elephant worshipping the sun is referred to by Pliny who wrote: 'The elephant has a religious respect also for the stars, and a veneration for the sun and moon. It is said by some authors, that at the first appearance of the new moon herds of these animals come down from the forests of Mauretania to a river the name of which is Amilo; and that they there purify themselves in solemn form by sprinkling their bodies with water; after which, having saluted the heavenly body, they return to the woods, carrying before them the young ones which are fatigued.'

Cuperus also quotes Aelian who writes that elephants adore the rising sun, stretching up their trunks as if they were hands to the sun's rays. The same author goes on to say that at the new moon elephants break off branches in the woods and raise them aloft to the moon in the hope that by waving them gently about they will persuade the moon to be propitious.

Pliny's story of the elephants coming down to the River Amilo from the mountains of Mauretania and purifying themselves in the water and then paying homage to the moon is illustrated on a coin struck by Cardinal Zabarella. Here can be seen the elephant in the river with the trees near by and the moon across the sun's face and with the stars in the heavens. There is also a striking picture in Athanasius Kircher's *China Illustrata* of 1667 showing an elephant raising its trunk and its left foot, worshipping the sun and moon together (see page 202).

Some coins have on the one face representations of religious articles such as a sacrificial knife, a chalice and an aspergill, and on the other the figure of an elephant, sometimes with the name Caesar. Some authors, according to Cuperus, have argued that elephants were named Caesar in parts of Africa, pointing out that Mauretania was divided by Caligula into two provinces of which one was called Mauretania Caesariensis. (See ref. to 'Elephantus' as Punic for Caesar on page 29.)

Some of these coins show an elephant crushing a serpent under his feet and Cuperus argues that this commemorates Julius Caesar's victory over the African king Juba, the elephant and serpent being shown because Africa is full of elephants and serpents—'*Horrendos angues, habitataque membra venenis et vastos elephantes habet*'. The illustrations on page 92 are supposed to symbolize Caesar's victory over the Sons of Pompey.

Elephant worshipping tripod (see also p. 92).

SOLI DEO

Cuperus also quotes an anonymous Italian numismatist who infers from a coin on which the elephant standing upon a serpent and on the reverse certain sacrificial instruments such as a sacrificial knife, a chalice and an aspergill are engraved, that the serpent is connected with some aspect of divinity.

He thinks that these coins were struck by Augustus in honour of Julius Caesar and conjectures that the elephant on them signifies Caesar's deification.

Many of the Roman or other ancient coins and medals with elephants stamped upon them are drawing chariots or triumphal cars. One such commemorates Alexander's victory over Porus at the battle of the Hydaspes.

From the Roman Empire onwards elephants seem to have been forgotten in Europe for several centuries. They occur again towards the end of the first millennium AD—from AD 700 on—in Scotland. At the side of the road at the foot of Bennachie, about a mile north west of Chapel of Garioch in Aberdeenshire, there is a Pictish sculptured stone of the first period—that is about AD 700—known as the 'Maiden' stone. It is a beautiful pillar of red granite ten feet high with a big chip out of one side and shows on the front a man between two fish monsters—sometimes called 'Jonah and the two whales', the enriched cross and shaft and a panel with an enriched disc and other decorative details. The back is divided into four compartments showing (1) Beasts and a centaur-like figure, (2) a rectangle and Z rod, (3) an elephant, (4) a mirror and comb symbol.

The so-called elephant symbol is very common in Pictish sculptured stones of which there are literally hundreds in north-east Scotland. Two of the best known besides the Maiden stone are Sueno's stone in Forres and the 'ichthus' stone in Kintore kirkyard a few miles north of Aberdeen (plate 6).

Sueno's stone is fully described in the *Annals of the Royal Borough of Forres* by Robert Douglas, one-time medical officer of health for the Borough. He describes it as a four-sided Runic obelisk covered with carvings of men and horses on the top, while on the east side there is an elephant. Douglas quotes a number of theories about the origin of the stone, among them the views of another archaeologist, T. L. Mason, who suggests that figures similar to the elephant emblem are to be found among the stucco figures in ruins in Mexico and other countries. A more probable suggestion is made in the Wardlaw manuscript that the stone was erected by the Danes (Sueno being the Latin for Sweyn) and that when King Malcolm visited Forres in 1060 he observed the monument and ordered its preservation. Others argue that it was erected to celebrate the expulsion of the Danes from Scotland. The attribution of some connection with Denmark is interesting. There is no particular link between the elephant and Denmark with the exception of the remarkable silver cauldron found at Gundestrup in Jutland. This, known as the Gundestrup Bowl, has a number of figures inside and outside in relief. Included among them is the figure of an elephant. One cannot connect this in any way directly with the elephant on Sueno's stone because there is something like a thousand years between them, as the bowl is believed to date from the first century BC. T. G. E. Powell writes that the mythological scenes and figures in high relief can be compared to Celtic iconography in Gaul and mythological allusions in Irish Literature. The stylistic aspects of the various creatures, including the elephant, point to a middle Danubian origin for the bowl, Celts having settled along the middle Danube. Although there is no known link, the Gundestrup elephant may be the ancestor of those on the Pictish stones.

Modern authorities tend to believe that the so-called elephant emblem on the Pictish stones is in fact a crude and distorted representation of a tusked boar, an animal perfectly familiar to the local inhabitants, but against this is the self-evident fact that the carvings do look more like elephants than pigs.

A local Aberdeenshire historian writes of the Kintore stone as a monument of Christian significance because of the fish symbol and remarks that the elephant represents Christ 'mighty to save' (*vide infra*); the late Rev. J. G. Dawson Scott wrote of this stone:

> The elephant is there as weel,
> That beast sae gran' an' fu' o' micht,
> Rome's sodgers wid the story tell,
> They cam' tae teach as weel as fecht.

There is a long description of the Kintore stone in Bishop G. F. Browne's *Antiquities in the Neighbourhood of Dunecht*. According to Bishop Browne the fish on the stone is a salmon. Of the elephant he writes: 'The elephant here as in other of the cases in this district shows that the tusks were treated as the jaw. The trunk comes very clearly out of the forehead.'

Pictish stones in Scotland are classed as I (seventh century), II (eighth century), and III (ninth century). Class I have entirely pagan symbols, class II pagan symbols and the cross, class III the cross alone. Strangely, the Maiden stone, regarded as belonging to class I, has a cross. There is a tradition that in the fifth century St Ninian came from Candida Casa on the Isle of Whithorn (so called because according to the Venerable Bede, the building on the Isle of Whithorn was of stone) and founded a chapel at Oyne, quite close to the Maiden Stone. There would thus be a remote Christian tradition in the area on which sculptors of the Pictish stones may have drawn.

For the true elephants of mediaeval Christendom—for these Pictish elephants despite their appearance may not, as has been explained, be elephants at all but may in fact be pigs—one has to search the manuscripts of the Middle Ages, chiefly the bestiaries, and examine the carvings in both wood and stone in the cathedrals and churches of the Romanesque period. Such elephants, particularly those in the manuscripts, are often strange-looking beasts with only a remote resemblance to the natural animal. Many, if not most of them, were executed by monks or craftsmen who had never seen an elephant. According to E. H. Gombrich, writing in *The History of Art* (Phaidon Press, London, 1950) thirteenth-century artists were not in the habit of copying from nature, but used pattern books. Thus the illuminators of manuscripts copied from earlier manuscripts so that the earlier errors of representation were frequently repeated. The ecclesiastical carvers copying from the manuscripts produced the same grotesque features.

Oddly enough, however, one of the earliest manuscript illustrations of an elephant shows a very natural creature. This is the splendid illustration in Parker Manuscript 16 in the possession of Corpus Christi College, Cambridge. It is a picture drawn from life by the monk Matthew Paris in AD 1255 of the elephant presented by Louis IX of France—St Louis—to Henry III of England. Louis is said to have acquired this elephant during his expedition to Palestine. The animal which, from the illustration, is clearly an African elephant, is believed to have arrived in England in AD 1254. It is said to have landed at Whitsand and an entry in the Close Rolls of January 1255 quotes a mandate from the King ordering the Sheriff of Kent to arrange with one John Gouch to provide for bringing 'the king's elephant from Whitsand to Dover and, if possible, to London by water'.

The illustration shows the elephant standing fastened to a stake by the ankle, with his keeper, whose name is given in an inscription on the MS. as Henricus of Florence, standing between the tethered leg and the trunk. Henry of Florence is shown feeding his charge and is an indication of the size of the beast.

The King in a precept to the Sheriff of London orders 'we command you, that, of the farm of our city, ye cause without delay, to be built at our Tower of London one house of forty feet long and twenty feet deep, for our elephant'.

This elephant is remarkably well drawn and it is of great interest that many of the elephants in manuscripts and carvings of later date are grotesquely inaccurate.

It is reported that Bishop Bruere, or Briwere, was responsible for the elephant carving on a misericord in St Peter's Cathedral, Exeter and that this represents Henry III's elephant; but this seems to be impossible as the Bishop's dates were 1224-44, at least ten years before Henry III's elephant arrived in England. The Bishop is said to have spent five years in the east and doubtless knew well what elephants looked like. One authority suggests that Bishop Bruere helped to hurry Henry's elephant to England and that it had been delayed on the way. This may be so, but it does not prove that the misericord in Exeter represents Henry's elephant—and if indeed its date is, as believed 1244, it cannot be Henry's. In any case it is very remarkable that the Exeter elephant is much more naturalistic than many later cathedral carvings.

The bestiaries are manuscripts which in general derive from the *Liber Physiologus*, the first of them; according to Druce, this was probably compiled by a Greek monk of Alexandria. The first actual reference to *Physiologus* is in 496 when it was declared by Pope Gelasius to be a heretical book. No original manuscript of *Physiologus* is in existence. The earliest dates from the second half of the tenth century and is in MS. 10074 at the Bibliothèque Royale in Brussels. G. C. Druce considers that the original *Physiologus* probably did not contain many of the details to be found in the later bestiaries, which drew much of their information from Isidore's *Etymology* and the *De Universo* of

Rabanus. A great deal of the information in the bestiaries is drawn from the natural history writings of Pliny, Aristotle, Aelian and others. Physiologus was attracted by the symbolic method of teaching, popular with the early Christian divines. The manuscripts are not, of course, merely concerned with natural history, but use the legend of the elephant to preach on ethics and the meaning of Christianity. The legend is given a religious interpretation and this—the Sermo as it is called—is illustrated in many of the miniatures. The legend is closely connected with the stories of the serpent, or Draco, and the strange man-plant, the Mandrake.

G. C. Druce, whose essay on the elephant in mediaeval legend and art in the *Archaeological Journal* is one of the most authoritative studies on the subject, observes that the legend is repeated in most of the bestiaries but bases his main account on the bestiary in the Harleian Manuscript No. 3244 in the British Museum.

The manuscript begins by explaining that the elephant is so called because it is mountainous in size: 'For in Greek a mountain is called ἐλεφιο.' (Druce here quotes another MS. which uses the word elephon which is said to be a corruption of the Greek word λοφος from Isidore's *Etymology*, which is interpreted as the Latin *jugum*, the ridge or brow of a hill.) The manuscript repeats much of Pliny and Aristotle which can be read elsewhere in this book. It records the belief that elephants are very unwilling to mate and the female leads the male to the Mandragora (or Mandrake) tree and gives him the fruit of the tree. When the male has eaten the fruit, the female conceives and in due time she goes into a deep pool to give birth while the male keeps guard against the elephant's enemy, the serpent.

When an elephant falls down it was supposed to be unable to get up again because according to the theory (false, of course) it had no leg joints—so it cried out loudly until another great elephant appeared. This elephant was unable to raise his friend, so they both trumpeted until twelve more elephants arrived. Even they were unable to raise the fallen elephant and all made a great trumpeting. Then there appeared a little elephant which placed its mouth with its trunk under the big elephant and lifted it up. 'Now the little elephant has this nature that, when a fire is made of its hair and bones, no evil will come, nor dragon.'

'The great elephant and his wife,' the Bestiary continues, 'represent Adam and Eve. For when they were in the Flesh and pleased God before their Fall, they knew not sexual intercourse, nor did they know anything of sin; but when Eve ate of the fruit of the tree, that is to say, the mandragora, which is the tree of knowledge, and gave to Adam, then she became pregnant and because of this they went out from Paradise. For while they were in Paradise Adam knew not Eve. For it is written; Adam knew his wife, and she, conceiving, gave birth to Cain above the waters of shame, about which the prophet says: "Save me, O God, for the waters are come into my soul" (*Psalm* 69 v. 1) and immediately the Dragon (that is, the Serpent) deceived them and caused them to become strangers from their home in the mountains. This is not the way to please God. Then came the great elephant, that is, the law, and did not raise him up, in the same way that the priest did not raise that man up who fell among thieves. Nor did the twelve elephants, that is the multitude of prophets, raise him up, as neither did the Levite him that was wounded whom we have mentioned; but it was the wise elephant, that is our Lord Jesus Christ. Since he is greater than all, he is made the smallest of all, because he humbled himself, being made obedient unto Death, that he might raise mankind. He is the wise Samaritan who placed him on his beast. For himself (that is to say, Christ) being wounded bore our infirmities and carried our sins. Now we understand by the Samaritan a preserver, about which David says: "The Lord preserveth the simple" (*Psalm* 116 v. 6). And where the Lord is present, the devil will not be able to come near.'

This last sentence, according to Druce, refers to the burning of hair and bones of the little elephant which drives away serpents. In some of the manuscripts there are very odd additions to this legend, itself sufficiently strange to modern minds. For instance, in the Westminster bestiary it states: 'Alexander frightened these beasts (that is elephants) away from his camp by the grunting of swine' (plate 34) (*cf* the story told elsewhere in this book of the elephants and swine at Megara). The Westminster MS. also mentions that the dragon or serpent 'drinks the blood of the elephant for the purpose of cooling his burning intestines'.

The allegorical method of teaching the people the meaning of Christianity runs through the various manuscripts. It is not easy for the mind of today to grasp the symbolism. The strange business of the burning of the skin and hair of the little elephant as a charm against the serpent, or evil, is hard to understand. One version of the elephant legend, by Hugo de Folieto towards the end of the twelfth century, appears in the *De bestiis et aliis rebus* of Hugo de Sancto Victore and other thirteenth-century manuscripts. Druce observes that while the events described are the same, the symbolism varies—although the variations are not major ones. The Hugo de Folieto version declares 'For in whatever place or house the bones and skin of the elephant may be burnt, immediately the smell of them drives out and puts to flight serpents, or if there have been any harmful and poisonous reptiles there, they do not approach. So too the works and commands of God purify the heart of anyone who has the will within himself, and no thought of a contrary nature is able to enter there, but whatever is harmful and foul, immediately every such thought leaves him and vanishes away, so that no evil spirit or contrary thought nor any mischief thence arising is any longer in evidence.'

The whole legend as woven into the symbolism, used to stimulate the minds of the readers of the bestiaries, is fascinating. Summarized shortly, we find ourselves taken to the east of the Garden of Eden—Paradise. The unwillingness of elephants to breed—described by the classical writers—is supposed to be due to the coldness of their blood and is used to symbolize the chastity of Adam and Eve. The elephants overcome their inhibition by eating Mandrake, the Tree of Knowledge, chosen because of its property of promoting conception. It is interesting to find in *Genesis* 30, 14:

> And Reuben went in the days of wheat harvest and found man-drakes in the field and brought them unto his mother Leah. Then Rachel said to Leah give me, I pray thee of thy son's mandrakes and she said unto her is it a small matter that thou hast taken my husband? And wouldest thou take away my son's mandrakes also. And Rachel said therefore he shall lie with thee to-night for thy son's mandrakes. And Jacob came out of the field in the evening and Leah went out to meet him and said thou must come in unto me for surely I have hired thee with my son's mandrakes. And he lay with her that night. And God hearkened unto Leah and she conceived and bare Jacob the fifth son.

The Dragon is in the bestiary symbolism in place of the serpent. The birth of the young elephant in water represents the birth of Cain, 'above the waters of shame'. The pool in which the elephant is born is the world full of troubles into which Adam and Eve are cast. This is the first part of the legend referring to the fall.

Then comes the story of the redemption. The preacher, using the ancient belief that the elephant had no leg-joints, tells how the big elephant, Adam, has fallen through a tree. (The theory was that elephants slept leaning against a tree, which was then half-cut by hunters so that the elephant broke off the trunk and fell through.) Neither the first great elephant, Moses, that came in response to the fallen elephant's cries for help, nor the next twelve elephants, symbolizing the lesser prophets, could raise him up. But, the little elephant, which is Christ who came to redeem mankind, succeeded in raising him.

The perpetual strife between the elephant and the serpent or Draco is symbolic of the struggle between good and evil and is an integral part of the legend. As the story goes, the serpent lies in wait for the elephant and catches it in its coils as it passes, suffocating it so that it falls down. The elephant falls upon the serpent and they thus perish together. One of the most striking descriptions of the serpent is given in Sloane MS. 278, the version of Hugo de Folieto:

> The scripture teacheth us that the mightiest of the serpents is the dragon, which causes death by its poisonous breath and with blows of its tail. . . . It lies in wait for the elephant, the most chaste of animals and coiling itself round the elephant's legs endeavours to suffocate it with its breath. As the elephant falls dead upon it, it is crushed to death . . . the reason for the enmity between them is this: The Dragon's poison boils with very great heat while the elephants' blood is exceedingly cold. The dragon therefore wants to cool its own heat in the blood of the elephant. . . . The dragon, the greatest of all serpents, is the devil, the king of evil. As it causes death by means of its poisonous breath and blows of its tail, so the devil destroys the souls of men by thought, word and deed. He kills their thoughts by the breath which is pride; he poisons their words with malice; he strangles them by the performance of evil deeds, as it were with his tail. By the dragon the air is disturbed, and so is the peace of men of spiritual thought disturbed thus. It (the serpent) lies in wait for a chaste animal (the elephant); so he

persecuted to death Christ, the guardian of chastity, being born of a chaste virgin; but he was overcome, having been crushed by him (the elephant, that is, Christ) in his Death. The precious colour which it got from the ground (the earth soaked by the blood of the serpent and the elephant in their death was supposed to produce a very valuable pigment, called 'cinnabar', used for producing blood colour in painting) that is the Church of Christ adorned by his precious blood. The dragon is the enemy of a pure animal, likewise is the devil the enemy of the Virgin's Son.

Pliny has a long account of the enmity of the vast serpents and elephants in India and it is clear from his description of the serpent waiting in a tree for the elephant and then hurling itself on the animal as it passes that he is referring to a python or boa constrictor. The notion that the elephant's blood is cool while the serpent's is hot is unexplained. Nor is there an explanation of the dragon's hot breath; but Aelian has an extraordinary tale of a serpent seventy feet long in a cave which Alexander's army passed. The serpent was annoyed by the noise of passing troops and hissed loudly, terrifying the soldiers with blasts of hot breath.

Pliny and Aelian also describe the hostility between the elephant and the rhinoceros, and how the latter attacks by ripping up the elephant's belly. For illustrations of this, however, one has to wait nearly 2,000 years to look at the pictures in Thomas Williamson's *Oriental Field Sports*. Aelian observes that the elephant and rhinoceros generally fight about pasture. The rhinoceros sharpens its horn upon rocks and when fighting gets under the legs of the elephant and tears its belly open. If it isn't quick enough to get in the first blow the elephant seizes it in its trunk and rips it in pieces with its tusks.

The elephant and castle, of which there are a great many illustrations in the bestiaries and other manuscripts, is not, so far as the castle is concerned, part of the legend of the elephant. But the illustrations are remarkable in their variety, originality and oddity. Often the elephants resemble pigs and have bell-mouthed trunks; their colours are of every hue from grey to green, red to blue. They frequently have claw-like feet, horses' tails and are covered with hairs. The castles are generally much too large in proportion to the animal and they are often packed with knights in full armour. The elephant is frequently controlled by a keeper who guides it by means of a rope attached to its trunk, which is sometimes pierced to take the rope. In one St John's College, Oxford, manuscript the elephant has a keeper twice as tall as the beast—which reminds one of the Egyptian wall painting at Thebes of 1500 BC where an Indian is leading an elephant to Tuthmosis III, the animal being about the size of a Labrador dog (page 43).

The strangest manuscript representation of the elephant and castle is perhaps the one to be seen in an Icelandic bestiary (MS. 673A Copenhagen University Library) of which there are only two fragments transcribed in 1889 by Verner Dahlerup in *Physiologus i to Islandske bearbejdelser*. The bestiary is thirteenth century. The elephant is much more like a wolf than an elephant with feet that are a cross between cloven hoofs and a wolf's pads. The creature has a shield on its trunk

Elephant and castle; from Icelandic Bestiary

which hides most of its head. The castle is like a wooden stockade, as large as the elephant, and contains seven armed men of whom only the heads, helmets and shields are visible. The elephant, the shield and the warrior's shields are pink, the armour green and the castle self-colour.

One of the favourite subjects illustrated in the manuscripts is the Romance of Alexander. There are a number of manuscripts of this, one of the most magnificent being that produced for Charles the Bold (Charles le Téméraire), Duke of Burgundy, in the fifteenth century. This is now in the Bibliothèque Nationale in Paris. The life and adventures of Alexander the Great were the basis for many romances of the Arthurian type in mediaeval Europe as well as being used by the Persian poets, Firdausi in his Shahnama and Nizami in his writings on Iskander Sultan.

From the mediaeval manuscripts it is a short step to the stone and wood carvings in the great cathedrals and in many of the early churches. Our principal authority, G. C. Druce, felt that the miniatures actually illustrating the legend were few compared with its importance in mediaeval religious teaching. The same is true of the ecclesiastical elephants. Probably the oldest in England is the badly damaged carving on the twelfth-century font at Dunkeswell in Devon. This illustrates the struggle between the dragon and the elephant. The only example of this on a misericord in England is in Carlisle Cathedral, where the elephant is hardly recognizable as such, having an extraordinary trunk, quite short,

55

rather like a beak. (It is so short it reminds one of the 'Elephant's Child' in Kipling's story which had a nose like a boot before it was stretched by the crocodile.) The elephant is being furiously assaulted by a winged dragon with two legs. The dragon has got its tail over the elephant's back, which it is savagely biting. The elephant has its foot on the dragon's back. The date is the fifteenth century.

A much earlier carving of elephants is to be found in Canosa Cathedral in Apulia, where two elephants support the episcopal throne, the date being about 1080. Other elephant carvings in Italian cathedrals can be seen at Bari and Trani.

Twelfth-century examples are to be found at Aulnay, Surgères and Loulay, all in Charente Maritime, France. These are on pillar capitals; at Aulnay, below the abacus, have been inscribed the words, HI SUNT ELEPHANTES. The examples in Charente Maritime are in a sense outliers, the majority of elephant carvings in France being in Burgundy, within the orbit of the exceptionally learned clerics of Cluny. Elephants are to be found in cathedrals or churches at Andlau (in Alsace), at Chartres, Moutierneuf, Perrecy-les-Forges, Vézelay, Poitiers, Caen, Vorly (near Poitiers), Saint-Engrâce in the Hautes-Pyrénées, Notre-Dame-la-Grande, Saint-Benoît-sur-Loire and La Charité-sur-Loire. Those at Andlau are of particular interest, being accompanied on a frieze by a dromedary. All these elephants belong to Romanesque, or, as we should say, to Norman art and such carvings more or less ceased with the growth of the Gothic tradition.

In English cathedrals and churches there are many representations of elephants, a number of which are illustrated in this book. More often than not these have castles on their backs. Among the more interesting are those at Apethorpe, Northants., and at Haslemere in Surrey, on painted or stained glass, depicting biblical scenes; at Wickham Church, Berkshire, where, on the roof of the North aisle, there are eight papier-mâché elephants brought from the Paris Exhibition of 1862. In *Double Lives*, William Plomer describes how, when he enquired why they were there, the incumbent replied that, the elephant being a symbol of wisdom, a quality notably lacking in his parishioners, it was a comfort to him to address his sermons to the sagacious-looking elephants' heads suspended above their own. The author adds that this might well be described as 'preaching over the heads of the congregation'. At Kilpeck Church, Herefordshire, an elephant's head appears on the string course holding a man in its trunk. In Ripon Cathedral, flanking the bishop's throne, a splendid elephant, also holding a man in its trunk, has a castle with nine men in it on its back; it stands upon a turtle, which is reminiscent of the Eastern myth that the elephants supporting the world stand upon tortoises. Elephants appear on misericords [1] in the cathedrals at Carlisle, Exeter, Gloucester and Manchester. On one of the two elephant misericords in Beverley Minster, the

---

1. Misericords are the ledges on the underside of seats in cathedral and other choir stalls. The seats are hinged so that the occupant could raise them to a vertical position and stand in the stall. To stand throughout a service was exhausting for elderly monks and the ledges were provided for them to rest on without actually sitting down. Most misericords are richly carved. Poppy-heads are the decorated knobs or pinnacles on bench ends, so called from the French *poupée*, a doll (see following page).

elephant is being pursued by an ape with a cudgel. There are also elephants on misericords in St Mary's, Beverley; St Helen's, Garstang;
Cartmel Priory; and St George's Chapel, Windsor. There are elephant
carvings on poppy-heads, bench ends and other wood ornaments at
Burwell, Cambridgeshire; in Chester Cathedral; Christchurch, Hamp-
shire; Denston, Suffolk; Detling, Kent; Earl Soham, Suffolk; Exeter
Cathedral; Holbeton, Devon; Holme Hale, Norfolk; Lakenheath,
Suffolk; South Burlingham, Norfolk; South Lopham, Norfolk; Thur-
garton and Tuttington, Norfolk; Westhall, Suffolk; Willian, Hertford-
shire; and Yaxham, Norfolk. Most of these carvings belong to the
thirteenth, fourteenth or fifteenth centuries. Some are reasonably realistic,
while others, often following the bestiaries, are essentially pig-like, or
have extraordinary trunks, such as those at Denston, South Lopham
and South Burlingham.

There are also processions of animals including elephants giving
praise to their Creator at High Bickington, Devon; on a cornice at
Kersey, Suffolk; and at Twywell, Northants. There is an elephant
carved in stone on a corbel at Norton Malreward, Somerset, and an
elephant's head on a capital at Ottery St Mary, Devon. There are elephant roof-bosses, sometimes heraldic, in Canterbury; Lacock Abbey,
Wilts; Queen Camel, Somerset; and Selby Abbey, Yorkshire. There is
a modern font supported on a elephant at Lea, Herefordshire; and
ancient fonts with elephants carved upon them at Berrington, Salop
and Dunkeswell, St Nicholas, Devon. In Dunkeswell, Holy Trinity,
and at Muchelney, Somerset, there are several floor-tiles with elephants
and castles. Besides these purely ecclesiastical elephants there are a
number of heraldic elephants on tablets and brasses. One of the most
interesting accounts of the elephant in heraldry is in a treatise in 1494 by
Sir William Cummings, Marchemont Herald of Scotland and Lyon
King of Arms. This gives the symbolic interpretation which applied to
the knight who first bore the device; he writes:

> The eliphant yet is callit barro be yaim of ynd for his cry is callit
> barritus of wham ye teith ar ywoir[1] & for gueulle[2] has growing[3]
> ande amang al ye othir bestes he is ye maistir of body and of vertu.
> Ande yais for yai of medee and of perse puttis upon yaim toures de
> bost[4] in ye whilkis thai fecht ande ar of gud understanding ande
> of gude memour and ganges togidder in gret cumpany when yai
> gang in forestes ande in wateres. And ganges faner[5] in secret
> places and lewis yair fans[6] in ye place whar thai fane at yai be nader
> tane[7] nader dragonys and bores thair fans two yeres or yai fane
> thaim. And liffes 111° yheres as sais ysodre.[8] And signifies he yat
> first ber thame in armes has voce & name terrible & wes of strang
> figour in his face gret of body & of vertu berand gret birdings[9]

1. ywoir = ivory
2. gueulle = gules
3. there is something missing here
4. bost = wood
5. faner = faoner—Old French for 'give birth'
6. fans = infants
7. tane = toad
8. Ysodre = Isidore, author of Isidore's *Etymology*
9. berand gret birdings = bearing great burdens

and man of gret mynd and understanding. And in his dedes in wattir and in land sterklie cumpaingnit with follres of his estate. And his generacioun wes born ii yheres & vas of lang lif and his generacioun eas langlestande ande worthy of memour and yis may suffice of bestis to say. And gif it was demandit of yaim yat ar nocht heir men may get ye significatioun in ye buk yat spekes of propirteis ye whilk may be gottin in many places.'

The illustration which goes with this text shows a thin scraggy creature much more like Don Quixote's Rosinante than an elephant, although there is a trunk and tusks. The elephant has a castle of stone with corner towers and a postern gate.

Heraldic elephant

Drawing of brass to Visct Beaumont in Wivenhoe Church

Also in Scotland, there are some splendidly odd elephants, possibly heraldic, on the painted ceiling at the top of a tower in Delgatie Castle, an ancient stronghold of the Clan Hay, in Aberdeenshire. The date of the painting is believed to be 1597. The best-known heraldic elephant is on a brass in the cloisters of Canterbury Cathedral, but the most striking are on brasses such as that to Sir Henry Vernon and his widow Margaret in Tong Church in Shropshire. Her feet rest on an elephant (plate 31) which, though unmistakably an elephant, is in the attitude of a crouching dog. Among other splendid brasses are those to Viscount Beaumont in Wivenhoe Church near Colchester in Essex (pp. 58 and 59). And there is a fine elephant on a brass shield to one John Onley in Withington Church.

15 Elephant and draco; Norman font Dunkeswell St Nicholas, Devon

16 Saddled elephants on capital from Poitiers; 11th cent.

17 Elephant; 13th-cent. misericord, Exeter Cathedral

18 Elephant and draco; 15th-cent. misericord, Carlisle Cathedral

Drawing of brass badge in canopy in Wivenhoe Church

An important sphere of art in which the elephant plays a part is in ivory. Here the elephant not only provides the subject but the material as well. In the east, particularly in India, one finds exquisite representations of Ganesha, the elephant-headed god, and other deities. It is not proposed to go into the history of the use of ivory but only to refer to one or two examples of ivory elephants. One of the most important of these is the game of chess, where the king and his chief minister are often shown mounted on elephants.

The game has been called 'the king of games and the game of kings'. In India, where it is believed to have started, the Queen, known to modern times as the most powerful piece on the board, did not exist. The early piece with her powers was the king's chief minister, or the Grand Vizier. Some of the finest of the early pieces came with a set which was sent by the Khalif Haroun al Raschid to Charlemagne as a gift. They are in the Cabinet des Médailles, once in the Trésor de Saint-Denis. The pieces are signed with an Arab name, Yousouf el Nahili.

In Europe in the Middle Ages, the elephant itself disappeared from the chess-board and there appeared various pieces which seemed to have no connection with him, such as the bishop in England, *Le Fou* in France, the Runner or *Läufer* in Germany. In fact, the elephant in Arabia was *al fil*. A corruption of this appears in old French *auphin*, which signified *le fou* or *l'évèque* or bishop. The piece had horns or, as in the case of the bishop, a mitre, which some have said derived from the elephant's tusks. In the time of Louis XVI the elephant came back to the chess-board, but this time represented with the castle; this later became like a dungeon rather than the edifice on the elephant's back for war in oriental countries.

One of the most remarkable as well as one of the earliest sculptured elephants is the so-called Camondo bronze elephant in the Musée Guimet in the Place d' Iéna in Paris. This magnificent specimen from China is almost a metre long. It is in the form of a vessel in which food was contained to be offered in the performance of sacrifices to the spirits of Heaven, of ancestors, of streams and hills and to the God of earth. Such vessels were regarded as of great importance as aids to the acts of worship. The decoration on the vessel was to protect the contents from evil spirits. It was evidently thought in this case that a vessel in the form of an elephant provided more efficient protection than a small elephant engraved on the surface of a vessel. According to Bachofer the elephant belongs to an early period in the Shang Dynasty, between c. 1500 to 1200 BC. It is probable that the elephant was known to the Shang as the most powerful animal in existence. It is interesting that while in the churches and in manuscripts many of the elephants depicted are grotesque, there were artists such as Mantegna in Italy and the weavers of Flanders who were producing pictures or tapestries in which zoologically correct elephants appeared. Some of these can be seen in Hampton Court.

Mantegna was born at Vicenza in 1431. When he was eleven years old he went to Padua and was in the academy of Francesco Squarcione where he learned his job and was lucky enough to witness the craft of Donatello who lived in Padua from 1444 to 1450. Mantegna became wedded to the idea of a rebirth of the spirit and art of the ancient classical world and perhaps his most famous work is the series of paintings of the 'Triumphs of Caesar'. These were bought by Charles I and are now at Hampton Court, much damaged and much repainted. It is in No. 5, known as 'the elephants', that Mantegna's own hand can be most clearly distinguished.

The tapestries in Hampton Court in which elephants appear are those known as the 'Triumphs of Petrarch' and follow the theme of his allegorical poem *I Trionfi*. This describes the triumph of Love, of Chastity over Love, of Death over Chastity, of Fame over Death, of Time over Fame, and of Eternity. Splendid elephants appear in the scenes showing the triumph of Fame over Chastity, where four magnificent animals draw Fame's chariot, and in the triumph of Death over Fame, where Fame's elephants are raising their trunks in horror and rage.

These tapestries were bought by Wolsey in 1523. There are, of course, other textiles in which elephants appear, one of the most famous being of a much earlier date. This is a fragment of silk woven about AD 960, a thousand years ago; it came from Khorassan in Persia. On it are two formalized elephants facing one another. There are camels on one border. This very fine piece was found, strangely, in the church of St Josse-sur-mer, near Boulogne, in 1920, and is now in the Louvre.

Among the many eastern paintings of elephants are two eccentric pictures which remind one of Hieronymus Bosch. In the one an elephant is suffering from a bad headache and this is indicated by the artist showing an imp boring into the animal's skull. In the other the elephant has stomach ache, which is caused by a boa-constrictor squeezing the beast in its coils. It is not impossible that the latter is connected with the legend of the enmity between elephants and serpents referred to above.

Elephant suffering from colic

Elephant suffering from headache

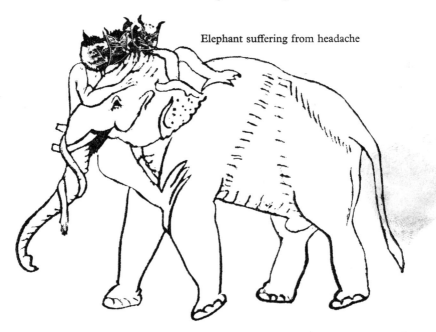

# The elephant in art and legend

Hieronymus Bosch has in fact produced a picture of a fantastical elephant playing the part of a fortress, round, over and in which all sorts of struggles and strange actions are taking place (plate 63).

Luini has a picture of an elephant in his *Adoration of the Magi* which in the cathedral at Como. In this, the elephant with a vast castle on his back is following other animals towards the Holy Family in the train of the Magi.

There is a highly dramatic Italian picture of the destruction of the Egyptians in the Red Sea, in which an elephant and castle are being overwhelmed by the waters. So far as is known there is no historical evidence of elephants having been in Pharaoh's army pursuing the Israelites on that occasion.

One of the most striking drawings by a European artist of an elephant is by Rembrandt himself. It is in chalk and charcoal and it is curious to note that the feet are not complete (plate 74).

It would be tedious to try to catalogue all the elephants in art and in this book we have tried to give some of the more interesting. One may perhaps conclude with a reference to one of the strangest of all. This is an elephant standing eight or ten feet high in a private garden in Peckforton in Cheshire. It was constructed about 1740 by a local mason with a fantastic turreted castle on its back—as in so many of the manuscripts, the castle is as big if not bigger than the elephant; the castle has glass windows and the whole was constructed for use as—a beehive.

Drawing of beehive at Peckforton, Cheshire

# Elephant and dragon

Of all the beasts which thou *This-Day* didst build,
To haunt the Hils, the Forrest, and the Field,
I see (as Vice-Roy of their Brutish Band)
The *Elephant*, the Vant-guard doth command:
Worthy that Office; whether we regard
His Towred back, where many Souldiers ward;
Or else his Prudence, wherewithall he seems
T'obscure the wits of human-kinde somtimes:
As studious scholar, he self-rumineth
His lesson giv'n, his King he honoureth,
Adores the Moon: moved with strange desire
He feels the sweet flames of the *Idalian* fire,
And (pierc't with glance of a kinde-cruell eye)
For humane beauty, seems to sigh and dye.
Yea (if the *Graecians* doe not mis-recite)
With's crooked trumpet he doth somtimes write.
But, his huge strength, or subtile Wit, cannot
Defend him from the sly *Rhinocerot*:
Who (never with blinde fury led) doth venter
Upon his Foe, but (yer the lists he enter)
Against a Rock he whetteth round about
The dangerous pike upon his armèd snout:
Then buckling close, doth not (at random) hack
On the hard Cuirass on his Enemie's back;
But under's belly (cunning) findes a skin,
Where (and but there) his sharpned blade will in.
   The scaly *Dragon*, being else too lowe
For th' *Elephant*, up a thick Tree doth goe,
So, closely ambusht almost every Day,
To watch the Carry-Castle in his way:
Who, once approaching straight his stand he leaves,
And round him he so closely cleaves
With's wrything body; that his Enemy
(His stinging knots unable to untie)
Hastes to some tree, or to some Rock, whereon
To rush and rub-off his detested zone;
The fell embraces of whose dismal clasp
Have almost brought him to his latest gasp.
Then suddenly, the *Dragon* slips his hold
From th' *Elephant*, and sliding down, doth fold
About his fore-legs, fetter'd in such order,
That stock'd there he now can stir no further;
While th' *Elephant* (but to no purpose) strives
With's winding Trunk t'undoe his wounding gyves,
His furious foe thrusts in his nose, his nose,
Then head and all; and there-withall doth close
His breathing passage: but, his victory
He joyes not long; for his huge Enemy
Falling down dead, doth with his weighty Fall
Crush him to death, that caus'd his death withall:

from *The Divine Weeks* by Joshua Sylvester, 1563–1618

# Prester John's elephant

But as for Wild Beasts, *Abissinia* breeds more, and more bulkie than any other Region: of which, we shall give a short account, beginning from those which appear most Monstrous in their Creation. In the first place *Elephants*, conspicuous for bulk of Body and Docility, heard together in the Plain and woody places in great Numbers. *H. Ludowic Azevedez* saw in *Tigria* a hundred of them together differing in Bigness; and he attests, that as great a Number went but a little before them. But it is almost incredible to be told what a havock they make in the Fields and Woods: they will shake Trees bigger than themselves in Bulk, so long, till either their Trunks break, or the whole Tree be torn up by the Roots, as with an Earthquake. Smaller Trees they snap off about a hands breadth from the Ground. As for shrubs and underwoods, and all sorts of fruit Trees, they either eat 'em up, or trample 'em under their feet. *Gregory* was wont to say, that they open'd *High-Ways*, and where they had gone before, Travellers would rather choose to follow, as being less cumbersome. But least Food should be wanting to such Massie Creatures, Providence has provided: For in those Places grow certain Trees about the bigness of cherry-trees, full of Pith, like Elder; upon which they banquet, as upon Grass. Of all the dumb Beasts, this Creature certainly shares the most of Human Understanding: kind usage exercises Their Ambition, contumely fires their Revenge. Of which many examples are extant among the writers of Natural Historie. *Gregory* told us, that where they like their Entertainment, they are very punctual in observing the Laws of Hospitality though one of the Females would have serv'd her Host but an ugly trick after her departure from her Lodging. This Elephant had brought forth a Young one, in a certain Field which her Landlord had sow'd with Corn; who willing to dislodge such an unwelcome guest, had resolv'd to kill the said elephant; his Neighbours dissuaded him, assuring him, that the slaughter would not be unreveng'd; but on the other side, that she would defend his ripe Harvest against all others, and therefore advis'd him to let her alone till she had brought up her Cubb; but withal, so soon as she had done that, forthwith to reap his Harvest. The Husbandman following this Counsel, preserv'd his Harvest untouch'd, suffering no other injury than what the Beast spoiled in her passage to and fro. After the Female had carryed away her young one from that Place, the Husbandman by the help of his Neighbours got in his Harvest with all speed. The next night the Elephants came in Troops, with an intention to have supp'd with their Landlord before their departure, but found the Table taken away, and the Buttery Empty. The People of the Country aver, that they are not their Teeth, but their Horns of which the Ivory is made; and indeed their substance and situation demonstrate the same thing: for they grow out of the Head and not out of the Jaws; and besides that, they only adorn the brows of the Males; the Females like our Does have none at all. The Elephant never offers to attempt upon any person, unless provok'd; if he be threaten'd with sticks or cudgels, he hides his *Probosces* under his Belly, and goes away braying; for he is sensible it may easily be chop'd off: the extream parts of it being very nervous and tender, which causes him to be afraid of hard blows. At the end of it three little sharp pointed Langets come forth, by the help of which, he can take up the smallest thing that is, as men do with their fingers. They never take care to tame them here, when there is no use of them, either in Peace or War, among so many high Mountains.

*from A New History of Ethiopia being a Full and Accurate Description of the Kingdom of Abessinia vulgarly, Though erroneously called the Empire of Prester John* by The Learned Job Ludolphus, 1682

# Of the elephant

There is no creature among al the Beasts of the world which hath so great and ample demonstration of the power and wisdome of almighty God as the elephant: both for proportion of body and disposition of spirit; and it is admirable to behold, the industry of our ancient forefathers, and noble desire to benefit us their posterity, by searching into the qualities of every Beast, to discover what benefits or harmes may come by them to mankind: having never beene afraid either of the Wildest, but they tamed them; the fiercest, but they ruled them; and the greatest, but they also set upon them. Witnesse for this part the Elephant, being like a living Mountain in quantity & outward appearance, yet by them so handled, as no little dog became more serviceable and tractable. The great use of the consideration of an elephant

Among all the Europeans the first possessor of Elephants, was Alexander Magnus, and after him Antigonus, and before the Macedonians came into Asia, no people of the world except the Affricans and the Indians, had ever seen Elephants. When Fabritius was sent by the Romanes to King Pyrrhus in Ambassage, Pyrrhus offered to him a great summe of money, to prevent the Warre, but he refused private gain, and preferred the service of his Country: the next day he brought him into his presence, and thinking to terrifie him placed behind him a great Elephant, shadowed with cloth of Arras; the cloth was drawne and the huge beast instantly layed his trunke uppon the head of Fabritius, sending forth a terrible and direfull voice: whereat Fabritius laughing, perceiving the pollicy of the king gently made this speech; The first man in Europe possessor of elephants

> *Neque heri aurum neque hodie bestia me promovit.*
> I was neither tempted with thy Gold yesterday, nor terrified with the sight of this beast today:

and so afterward Pyrrhus was overcome in War by the Romans, and Manlius Curius Dentatus, did first of all bring Elephants in Tryumphe to Rome, calling them Lucanae Boves, Oxen of the wood, about the 472 year of the city: and afterwards in the year of Romes building 502, when Metellus was high priest, and overthrew the Carthagenians in Sicily, there were 142.

Of all earthly creatures an Elephant is the greatest: for in India they are nine cubits high, and five cubits broad; in *Affrica* foureteen or fifteene ful spans, which is about eleven foot high and proportionable in bredth, which caused *Aelianus* to Write, that one Elephant is as big as three Bugils; and among these the males are ever greater then the females. In the kingdome of *Melinda* in *Affricke*, there were two young ones, not above six monthes old, whereof the least was as great as the greatest Oxe, but his flesh was as much as you shall find in two Oxen; the other was much greater. The height & stature of elephants

Their colour is for the most part mouse-colour, or blacke; and there was one all white in *Ethiopia*. The skinne looketh pieled and scabby; it is most hard on the backe, but softer underneath the belly, having no covering of hair or gristes nor yet helpe by his taile to drive away the flies, for that evill doth this beast feele in his great body but alway hath crevices in his skin, which by their savour doe invite the little flies The colour and severall parts to a continual feast, but when by stretching forth they have received the swarmes, by shrinking together again, they inclose the flies and so to kill them: so that these crevices in his skin, are unto him insteede of a mane, taile, and haire: yet there are some few haires which grow scattering uppon his hide, whereof some have beene brought out of *America* into *Germany*, which were two palmes long, but not so stiffe as Swines.

Their skinne is so hard and stiffe, that a sharpe sworde or iron cannot pierce it. Their head is very great, and the head of a man may as easily enter into their mouth, as a finger into the mouth of a Dog; but yet their eares and eyes are not aequivalent to the residew of their proportion: for they are small, like the wings of a Bat or a Dragon, those of the *Ethiopian Sambri* want eares altogither. Their eies are like the eies of Swine, but of their teeth very red, they have teeth of either side foure, wherewith they grinde their meate like meale, and they have also two other which hang forthe beyond the residue, in the males downeward, and these are the greater and crooked: but in the females upwarde, and they are the smaller and straight: the one of them they keepe alway sharpe, to revenge injuries, and with the other they root up plants and trees for their meate: so that nature hath armed both sexes with these, for their chiefest defence; and with these the females are calved at the first, and indued from the mothers belly, and appeare so soone as they come foorth: The males not so quickly, but rather after the maner of bores and Sea-horsses, they hang out of their mouthes, and grow to be ten foot long, whereof they make posts of houses in some countries, and cal them *Ebora*, that is, young ivory: which caused *Martiall* to write thus:

> Grandia taurorum portant qui corpora quaeris
> An lybicas possint sustinuisse trabes.

It hath been affirmed by *Aelianus* & some writers following *Pliny*, that these teeth are Horns, and that Elephants are horned Beasts, which errour rose upon the occasion of these words of Pliny; Elephantos et arietes candore tantum cornibus assinulatis, in Santonum littore reciprocaos destituit Oceanus: where Aelianus finding a resemblance betwixt Rams and Elephants in their white horns, was contented to apply that name to them both, which appertaineth onely to one: for Pliny himselfe Lib 18. sheweth his meaning by another like speech, of the whetting their hornes upon trees, and Rhinocerotes upon stones: for except he had named hornes in the first place it might have been questioned whether Rhinocerotes had any hornes, but rather teeth in the second place.

The toung is very small though broad, his truncke called *Proboscis* and *Promuscis*, is a large hollow thing hanging from his nose like skinne to the groundward: and when he feedeth it it lyeth open, like the skin upon the bill of a Turkey-cock, to draw in both his meate and drinke, using it for a hand, and therefore improperly it is called a hand. For by it he receiveth of his keeper whatsoever he giveth him, with it he overthroweth trees, and wheresoever he swimmeth, through it he draweth breath. It is crooked, gristly, and inflexible at the roote, nexte to the nose: within, it hath two passages, one into the head and bodie by which he breatheth, and the other into his mouth, whereby he receiveth his meate: and herein is the woorke of God most woonderfull, not onely in giving unto it such a diverse proportion and anatomie, but also giving him reason to knowe this benefite of it, that so long as he is in the water and holdeth up that trunck, he cannot perish.

With this hee fighteth in warre, and is able to take up a small piece of money from the earth: with it he hath beene seene to pull downe the toppe of a tree which twenty foure men with a rope could not make to bend. With it he driveth away his hunters when he is chased, for he can drawe up therein a great quantity of water, and shoote it forth againe, to the amazement and the overthrow of them that persecute him. The Moores say that he hath twoe heartes, one wherewithall he is incensed, and another whereby hee is pacified.

He bendeth his hinder legs like a mans when he sitteth, but by reason of his great waight hee is not able to bend on both sides together, but either leaneth to the right hand or to the left and so sleepeth: It is false that they have no joints or articles in their legs, for when they please they can use, bend, and move them, but after they grow old, they use not to lie downe or straine them by reason of their great weight, but take their rest leaning to a tree: and if they did not bend their legs, they could never go any ordinary and stayed pace. Their feet are round like a horsses, but so as they reach from the middle every way two spans length, and are as broad as a bushell, having five distinct toes upon each foot, the which toes are very little cloven, to the intent that the foot may be stronger; and yet parted, that when he treadeth upon soft grounde, the weyght of his body presse not downe the legge to deepe. Hee hath no nailes upon his toes, his taile is like an Oxes taile, having a little haire at the end, and the residue thereof peeled and without haire: He hath not any bristly hairs to cover his back: and thus much for their severall parts and their uses.

There is not any creature so capable of understanding as an Elephant, and therefore it is requisite to tarry somewhat the longer in expressing the severall properties, and naturall qualities thereof, which sundry and variable inclinations, cannot choose but bring great delight to the reader. They have a wonderful love to their owne Countrey, so as although they be never so well delighted with divers meats and joyes in other places, yet in memory thereof they send forth teares, and they love also the waters, rivers, and marishes, so as they are not unfitly called *Riparii* such as live by the rivers sides: although they cannot swim by reason of their great and heavy bodies, untill they be taught. Also they never live solitary but in great flocks, except they be sicke or watch their young ones, and for either of these they remaine adventurous unto death, the eldest leadeth the herd, and the second driveth them forward, if they meet any man they give him way, and goe out of his sight.

*Their inward natural parts*

*The Places of their abod*

Their voice is called by the word *Barrire*, that is to bray, and thereupon the Elephants themselves are called *Barri*; for his voice commeth out of his mouth and nostrils togither, like as when a man speaketh breathing; wherefore *Aristotle* calleth it rawcity, or hoarsnes, like the low sound of a Trumpet, this sound is verie terrible in battailes as shall be afterward declared.

They live upon the fruits of plants and rootes: and with their truncks and heads, overthrow the tops of trees, and eat the boughes and bodies of them, and many times upon the leaves of trees he devoureth Chamaelons, whereby he is poisoned and dieth if hee eat not immediately a wilde Olive. They eat earth often without harme, but if they eat it sildome, it is hurtfull and procureth paine in their bellies; so also they eat stones. They are so loving to their fellowes, that they will not eat their meat alone, but having found a prey, they go and invite the residue to their feastes and cheere, more like to reasonable civill men, then unreasonable brute beasts. There are certaine noble melons in *Aethiopia*, which the Elephants being sharpe-smelling-beastes do winde a great way off, and by the conduct of their noses come to those Gardens of Melons, and there eat and devour them: When they are tamed they will eat Barlie either whole or grounde: of whole at one time is given them nine Macedonian Bushels, but of meale six, and of drinke eyther wine or water thirty Macedonian pintes at a time, that is fourteen gallons, but this is observed, that they drinke not wine except in warre, when they are to fight, but water at all times, whereof they will not tast, except it be muddy and not cleare, for they avoid cleare water loathing to see their own shaddow therein; and therefore when the Indians are to passe the water with their Elephants, they choose darke and cloudy nights wherein the moone affordeth no light. If they perceive but a mouse run over their meate, they will not eat thereof, for there is in them a great hatred of this creature. Also they wil eat dryed Figges, Grapes, Onions, Bulrushes, Palmes, and Ivy leaves. There is a Region in India called Phalacrus, which signifieth Balde, because of an herbe growing therein, which causeth every living thing that eateth thereof, to loose both horne and haire, and therefore no man can be more industrious or warie to avoide those places, then is an Elephant, and to beare every greene thing growing in that place when he passeth thorough it.

It will forebeare drinke eight daies together, and drinke wine to drunkenesse like an Ape. It is delighted above measure with sweet savours, oyntments, and smelling flowers, for which cause their keepers will in the Summer time lead them into the medowes of flowers, where they of themselves will by the quickness of their smelling, chuse out and gather the sweetest flowers, and put them into a basket if their keeper have any; which being filled, like daintie and neat men, they also desire to wash, and so will go and seeke out water to wash themselves, and of their owne accord returne backe again to the basket of flowers, which if they find not, they will bray and call for them. Afterward being led into their stable, they will not eat meat untill they take of their flowers and dresse the brimmes of their maungers therewith, and likewise strew their roome or standing place, pleasing themselves with their meat, because of the savour of the Flowers stucke about the cratch, like dainty fed persons, which set their dishes with greene herbs, and put them into their cups of wine.

They are never so fierce, violent, or wilde, but the sight of a Ramme tameth and dismayeth them, for they feare his hornes; for which cause the *Egiptians* picture an Elephant and a Ramme, to signifie a foolish king that runneth away for a fearefull sight in the field. And not onely a Ramme, but also the gruntling clamour or cry of Hogs: by which meanes the Romanes overthrew the Carthaginians, and *Pirrhus* which trusted overmuch to their Elephants. When *Antipater* besieged the *Megarians* very straitly with many Elephants, the Citizens tooke certaine Swine and annointed them with pitch, then set them on fire and turned them out among the Elephants; who crying horribly by reason of the fire on their bodies, so distempered the Elephants, that all the wit of the Macedonians could not restraine them from madnesse, fury, and flying upon their owne company, onely because of the cry of the Swine. And to take away that feare from the Elephants, they bring up with them when they are tamed, young Pigges and Swine ever since that time. When Elephants are chased in hunting, if the Lions see them, they runne from them like Hinde-calfes from the Dogges of Hunters, and yet *Iphicrates* sayeth, that among the *Hesperian* or westerne Aethiopians, Lions set upon the young Calves of Elephants and wound them: but at the sight of the mothers, which come with speede to them, when they heare them cry, the Lions runne away, and when the mothers find their young ones imbrued in their owne bloud, they themselves are so inraged that they kill them, and so retire from them, after which time the Lions returne and eat their flesh. They will not indure the savour of a Mouse, but refuse the meat which they have run over: in the river *Ganges* of *India*, there are blew Wormes of sixty cubits long having two armes; these when the Elephants come to drink in that river, take their trunks in their handes and pull them off. There are Dragons among the Aethiopians, which are thirty yards or paces long, these have no name among the inhabitants, but Elephant-killers. And among the *Indians* also there is an inbred and native hatefull hostility betwixte Dragons and Elephants: for which cause the Dragons being not ignorant that the Elephants feed upon the fruites and leaves of green trees, doe secretly convey themselves into them or to the toppes of rocks; covering their hinder parts with leaves, and letting his head and foreparts hang down like a rope on a suddaine when the Elephant commeth to crop the top of the tree, she leapeth into his face, and diggeth out his eies, and because that revenge of malice is to little to satisfie a Serpent, she twineth her gable-like-body about the throat of the amazed Elephant, and so strangleth him to death.

Again they marke the footsteps of the Elephant when he goeth to feed, and so with their tailes, net in and intangle his legs and feet: when the Elephant perceiveth and seeth them, he putteth downe his truncke to remove and unty their knots and ginnes; then one of them thrusteth his poisoned stinging-head into his Nostrils, and so stop up his breath, the other prick and gore his tender-belly-parts. Some againe meet him and flye upon his eies, and pull them foorth, so that at the last he must yeeld to their rage, and fall downe upon them, killing them in his death by his fall, whom he could not resist or overcome being alive: and this must be understood, that forsomuch as Elephants goe togither by flocks and heards, the subtill Dragons let the foremost passe, and set upon the hindmost, that so they may not be oppressed with multitude.

Also it is reported that the blood of an Elephant is the coldest blood in the world, and the Dragons in the scorching heate of Summer cannot get any thing to coole them, except this blood; for which cause they hide

A secret of a cruelty in India

The fear of rammes swine and other beasts

The cruelty of the female to their wounded Calves

themselvs in rivers and brooks whither the Elephants come to drinke, and when he putteth downe his trunke they take hold thereof, and instantly in great numbers leape up unto his eare, which is naked, bare, and without defence: where out they sucke the blood of the Elephant untill he fall downe dead, and so they perish both together.

Of this blood commeth that ancient Cinnabaris, made by commixture of the blood of Elephants and Draggons both together, which alone is able and nothing but it, to make the best representation of blood in painting. Some have corrupted it with Goats-blood, and call it *Milton*, and *Mimum*, and *Monochroma*; it hath a most rare and singular vertue against all poisons, beside the unmatcheable property aforesaid.

These Serpents or Dragons are bred in *Taprobona*, in whose heads are many precious stones, with such naturall seales or figurative impressions, as if they were framed by the hande of man, for *Podisippus* and *Tzetzes* affirme, that they have seen one of them taken out of a Dragons head, having upon it the lively and artificiall stampe of a Chariot.

Elephants are enemies to wilde Bulles, and the Rhinocerots, for in the games of *Pompey*, when an Elephant and a Rhinoceros were brought together, the Rhinoceros ranne instantly and whet his horne upon a stone, and so prepared himselfe to fight, striking most of all at the belly of the Elephant, because he knewe that it was the tenderest and most penetrable part of the body.

There were certaine officers and guiders of these Elephants, which were called *Elephantarchae*, who were the governors of sixteen Elephants, and they which did institute and teach them *Martiall* discipline, were called *Elephantagogi*. The millitary Elephant did cary 4-persons on his bare backe, one fighting on the right hand, another fighting on the left hand, a third which stood fighting backward from the Elephants head, and a fourth in the middle of these holding the raines and guiding the beast to the descretion of the Souldiers, even as the pilot in a ship guideth the sterne, wherein was required an equall knowledge and dexterity, for they understand any language quickly, for when the *Indian* which ruled them said, strike heere on the right hand, or els on the left, or refraine and stand stil, no reasonable man could yeald readier obedience. They did fasten by iron chaines, first of all upon the elephant that was to beare ten, fifteene, twenty, or thirty men, on eitherside, two panniers of iron bound underneath their belly, and upon them the like panniers of wood hollow, wherein they place their men at armes, and covered them over with small boards, for the trunke of the elephant was covered with a maile for defence, and upon that a broad sword, and two cubits long: this (as also the wodden Castle or paniers aforesaid) were fastened first to the necke, and then to the rumpe of the elephant. Being thus armed, they entered the battell, and they shewed unto the beast to make them more fierce, wine, red liquor made of rice, and white cloth, for at the sight of any of these, his courage and rage increaseth above all measure; then at the sound of the Trumpet he beginneth with teeth to strike, teare, beat, spoyle, take up into the aire, cast downe again, stamp upon men under feet, overthrow with his trunke, and make way for his riders to pierce with Speare, shield, and swords; so that his horrible voice, his wonderfull body, his terrible force,

Of Cinnabaris or the best red colour

The fight of the Elephants

The instruction of Elephants for war

his admirable skill, his ready and inclinable obedience, and his strange and sildome seene shape, produced in a maine battell no meane accidents and overturnes. For this cause we read how that *Pirrhus* first of all, produced elephants against the Romans in *Lucania*: afterward *Asdruball* in *Affrica*, *Antiochus* in the East, and *Jugurtha* in Numidia.

To conclude, elephants are afraid of fire, and *Martiall* made this *Epigram* of a Bul slaine by an elephant, which was wont to domineer in all their triumphant games, wherewithall I will conclude this discourse.

> Qui modo per totam flammis stimulatus arenam
> Sustulerat raptas Taurus in astra pilas
> Occubuit tandem cornuto ardore petitus
> Dum facilem tolli sic elephanto putat.

*Mutiannus* which was thrice Consull affirmed to *Pliny*, that he saw an Elephant which learned the Greeke letters, and was able with his tongue to Write these words: Autos egoo Tadegrapsa laphura tekelt anetheca: that is, I Wrote these things and dedicated the Celtican spoyls: but in these actions of Writing, the hand of the teacher must be also present to teach him how to frame the Letters, and then as *Aelianus* sayeth they will Wryte uppon Tables, and followe the true proportion of the Characters expressed before their face, whereupon they look as attentively as any *Grammarian*. In *India* they are taught many sportes, as to Daunce and Leape, which caused *Martiall* to Wryte thus; <sup>Their learning in letters</sup>

> Turpes esseda quod trahunt bisontes
> Et molles dare iussa quod choreas
> Nigro bellua nil legat magistro
> Quis spectacula non putes decorum.

When the Prizes of Germanicus Caesar were played; there were many Elephants which acted strange feates or partes, foure of them went uppon Ropes and over the Tables of meate, whereon they set their feete so warily that they never touched any of the ghests, the boardes or standing Cuppes being fully furnished. And also they learned to daunce after Pipes, by measure, sometime Dauncing softly, and sometime apace, and then againe leaping upright, according to the number of the thing sung or played upon the instrument: and they are apt to learne, remember, meditate, and conceive such things, as a man can hardly perform.

Their industrious care to performe the thinges they are taught, appeareth heerein, bycause when they are secret and alone by themselves, they will practice leaping, dauncing, and other strange feats, which they could not learn suddenly in the presence of their maisters (as Pliny affirmeth) for certaine truth of an Elephant which was dull and hard of understanding, his keeper found him in the night practicing those thinges which hee had taught him with many stripes the day before, and could not prevail by reason of the beasts slow conceit.

There was an Elephant playing upon a Cymball, and others of his fellowes, dauncing about him, for there was fastened to either of both his forelegs one Cymball, and another hanged to his truncke, the beast would observe just time, and strike uppon one, and then the other, to the admiration of all the beholders. There was a certaine banquet pre-pared for the Elephants upon a low bed in a parlour set with divers dishes and pots of Wine, whereinto were admitted twelve, sixe males, apparelled like men, and sixe females apparelled like women: when they saw it, they sat downe with great modesty, taking heere and there like discreet, temperate ghests, neither ravening upon one dish or other, and when they should drinke, they tooke the cup receiving in the Liquor very manerly, and for sport and festivity would through their trunckes squirt or cast a litle of their drink upon their attendants; so that this beast is not only of an admirable greatness but of a more wonderful meakenesse and docibility.

the reverence of Elephants to Kings

They are said to discerne betwixt kings and common persons, for they adore and bend unto them, poynting to their Crownes, which caused Martiall to Wryte this Tetrastichon:

Quid pius et supplex elephas te Caesar adorat
Non facit hoc jussus, nulloque docente magistro
Hic modo qui tauro tam metuendus erat
Crede mihi numen sentit et ille tuum.

3 kindes of elephants

The King of Indians was watched with foure and twenty Elephants, who were taught to forbeare sleepe, and to come in their turnes at certaine houres, and so were they most faithfull, carefull, and invincible. And as there be of them three kindes, the *Palustrians* or Marishye Elephantes are hare brained and inconstant, the Elephantes of the Mountaines are subtill and evill natured, lying in wait to destroy and devoure, but the Campestriall Elephants are meeke, Gentle, Docible, and apt to imitate men; In these is the understanding of their country language of obedi-ence to Princes, gouvernment, and offices; the love and pleasure of glory and praise: and also that which is not alway in men; namely, equity, wisedome, and probity.

the religion of elephants

They have also a kind of Religion, for they worshippe, reverence, and observe the course of the Sunne, Moone, and Starres; for when the Moone shineth, they goe to the Waters wherein she is apparent, and when the Sunne ariseth, they salute and reverence her face: and it is observed in Aethiopia, that when the Moone is chaunged untill her prime and appearance, these Beastes by a secret motion of nature, take boughes from of the trees they feede upon, and first of all lift them up to heaven, and then looke uppon the Moone, which they doe many times together; as it were in supplication to her. In like manner they reverence the Sunne rysing, holding up their trunke or hand to heaven in con-gratulation of her rising.

Juba was woont to say, that this beast was acceptable to those Gods which ruled Sea and Land, bycause of their reverence to Sunne and Moone, and therefore *Ptolomeus* Philopator, offered foure Elephants in a sacrifice (to recover the quietnesse of his mind) thinking that the Gods would have beene well pleased therewith, but finding that his fearefull dreames and visions departed not from him, but rather his disquietnesse increased, fearing that the Gods were angry with him for that action, he made foure Elephants of brasse, and dedicated them to the sun, that so by this deede he might purchase pardon for the former offence.

Elephants sacrificed and what followed thereupon

# Of the elephant

This religion of theirs, also appeareth before their death, for when they feele any mortall woundes, or other naturall signes of their later end, either they take up the dust, or else some greene herbe, and lift it up to heaven in token of their innocence and imploration of their owne weakenes: and in like manner do they when they eate any herbe by natural instinct to cure their diseases: first they lift it up to the heavens (as it were to pray for a devine blessing upon it) and then devoure it.

I cannot omit their care, to bury and cover the dead carkases of their companions, or any others of their kind; for finding them dead they passe not by them till they have lamented their common misery, by casting dust and earth on them, and also greene boughes, in token of sacrifice, holding it execrable to doe otherwise: and they know by a naturall instinct some assured fore-tokens of their owne death. Besides when they waxe old and unfit to gather their owne meate, or fight for themselfes the younger of them feed, nourish, and defend them, yea they raise them out of Ditches and trenches into which they are fallen, exempting them from all labour and perill, and interposing their owne bodies for their protection: neither do they forsake them in sicknesse, or in their woundes, but stand to them, pulling Darts out of their bodies, and helping both like skilfull Chirurgians, to cure their woundes, and also like faithful friendes to supply their wants.

Again how much they love their young which is a naturall part of religion we have shewed before. *Antipater* supposeth that they have a kinde of divination or divine understanding of law and equity, for when King Bochus, had condemned thirty men to be torne and trod in pieces by Elephants, and tying them hand and foote to blocks or pieces of Wood, cast them among thirty Elephants, his servants and officers could not by all their wit, skil, or provocation, make the beasts touch one of them: so that it was apparent, they scorned and disdained to serve any mans cruell disposition, or to be the ministers of tyranny and murther. They moreover have not onely an observation of chastity among themselves, but also are, revengers of whoredome and adulterers in other, as may appear by these examples in History. *[margin: Their understanding of justice and in equity]* *[margin: The revenge of adulterys by Elephants]*

A certaine Elephant seeing his Maister absent, and another man in bedde with his Mistresse, he went unto the bed and slew them both. The like was done at Rome where the Elephant having slaine both the adulterer and adulteresse, he covered them with the bed clothes untill his keeper returned home, and then by signes drew him into his lodging place, where he uncovered the adulterers, and shewed him his bloody tooth that tooke revenge uppon them both for such a villainy: whereat the maister wondering, was the more pacified because of the manifest-committed iniquity. And not onely thus deale they against the Woman, but they also spare not to revenge the adultery of men, yea of their owne keeper: for there was a rich man which had married a Wife not very amiable or lovely, but like himselfe for wealth, riches and possessions, which he having gained, first of all set his heart to love another, more fitting his lustfull fancye, and being desirous to marry her, strangled his rich il-favored Wife, and buried her not farre from the Elephants stable, and so married with the other, and brought her home to his house: the Elephant abhorring such detestable murther, brought the new married

19 Elephant and castle; 15th-cent. bench-end, S. Burlingham, Norfolk
20 Elephant and castle; 15th-cent. poppy-head, S. Lopham, Suffolk

21 Elephant and castle; 14th-cent. misericord, Gloucester Cathedral

22 Elephant and castle; 15th-cent. bench-end, Holme Hale, Norfolk
23 Elephant and castle; bench-end (1520), Beverley Minster

24 Elephant; 15th-cent. poppy-head, Denston, Suffolk
25 Elephant and castle; bench-end (1385), Chester Cathedral

Wife to the place where the other was buried; and with his teeth digged uppe the ground and shewed her the naked bodye of her predecessour, intymating thereby unto her secretly, how unworthely she had married with a man, murtherer of his former wife.

Their love
to their
keepers and
all men that
harme them
not

Their love and concord with all mankind is most notorious, especially to their keepers and Women: for if through wrath they be incensed against their keepers, they kill them, and afterwards by way of repentance, they consume themselves with mourning: And for the manifesting of this point *Arrianus* telleth a notable story of an *Indian*, who had brought up from a Foale a white Elephant, both loving it and being beloved of it againe, he was thereupon carried with great admiration. The king hearing of this White Elephant, sent unto the man for it, requiring it to be given him for a present, whereat the man was much grieved, that another man should possesse that which he had so tenderly educated and loved, fitting him to his bowe and purposes, and therefore like a ryvall in his Elephants love, resolved to deny the king, and to shift for himself in some other place: whereupon he fled into a desert region with his Elephant, and the king understanding thereof grew offended with him, sent messengers after him to take away the Elephant, and withall to bring the man backe againe, to receive punishment for his contempt.

When they came to the place where he remained and began to take order for their apprehension, the man ascended into a steepe place and there kept the kings messengers off from him by casting of stones, and so also did the beast like as one that had received some injury by them, at last, they got neare the Indian and cast him downe but the Elephant made upon them, killing some of them, and defending his maister and nourisher, put the residue to flight, and then taking up his maister with his trunke carried him safe into his lodging, which thing is worthy to be remembered as a noble understanding part both of a loving friend and faithfull servant.

The like may be said of the Elephant of *Porus*, carrying his wounded maister the king in the battel he fought with Alexander, for the beast drew the Darts gently out of his maisters body without all paine, and did not cast him untill he perceived him to be dead and without blood and breath, and then did first of all bend his owne body as neare the earth as he could, that if his maister had any life left in him, he might not receive any harme in his alighting or falling downe. Generally as is already said they love all men after they be tamed, for if they meet a man erring out of his way they gently bring him into the right againe, yet being wilde are they afraide of the foot-steps of men if they winde their treadings before they see their persons, and when they find an herbe that yeeldeth a suspition of a mans presence, they smell thereunto one by one, and if al agree in one savour, the last beast lifteth uppe his voice and crieth out for a token and watchword to make them all flie away.

*Cicero* affirmeth that they come so neare to a mans disposition, that their small company or Nation seemeth to overgoe or equall most men in sence and understanding.

Their love
of beautiful
women

At the sight of a beautifull woman they leave off all rage and grow meeke and gentle, and therefore Aeliannus saith, that there was an Elephant in Egypt which was in love with a woman that sold Corrals,

E

the selfe same woman was wooed by Aristophanes, and therefore it was not likely that she was chosen by the Elephant without singular admiration of hir beauty, wherein Aristophanes might say as never man could, that he had an Elephant for his rivall, and this also did the Elephant manifest unto the man, for on a day in the market he brought her certaine Apples and put them into her bosome, holding his Trunke a great while therein, handling and playing with her brests. Another likewise loved a Syrian woman, with whose aspect he was suddainely taken, and in admiration of her face stroked the same with his trunke, with testification of farther love: the woman likewise failed not to frame for the Elephant amorous devises with Beads and corals, silver and such things as are gratefull to these brute beastes, so shee enjoyed his labor and diligence to her great profit, and he hir love and kindness without al offence to his contentment, which caused *Horace* to write this verse:

quid tibi vis mulier nigris dignissima barris

At last the woman died, whom the Elephant missing, like a lover distracted betwixt love and sorrow fell beside himselfe and so perished. Neither ought any man to marvel at such a passion in this beast, who hath such a memory as is attributed unto him, and understanding of his charge and business as may appeare by manifold examples, for *Antipater* affirmeth that he saw an Elephant that knewe againe and tooke acquaintance of his maister which had nourished him in his youth, after many yeares absence.

When they are hurt by any man, they seldome forget a revenge, and so also they remember on the contrary to recompence al benefits as it hath bin manifested already. They observe things done both in waight and measure, especially in their owne meate. *Agnon* writeth that an Elephant was kept in a great mans house in Syria, having a man appointed to bee his overseer, who did daily defraude the Beast of his allowance: but on a day as his maister looked on, he brought the whole measure and gave it to him: The Beast seeing the same, and remembering howe he had served him in times past, in the presence of his maister exactly devided the corne into two partes, and so laied one of them aside: by this fact shewing the fraud of the servant to his maister. The like storie is related by *Plutarch* and Aeliannus, of another Elephant, discovering to his maister the falsehood and privy theft of an unjust servant.

About *Lycha* in *Affricke* there are certaine springes of water, which if at any time they dry up, by the teeth of Elephants they are opened and recovered againe. They are most gentle and meeke, never fighting or striking man or Beast, except they be provoked, and then being angered they will take up a man in their trunke and cast him into the ayre like an Arrow, so as many times he is dead before him come to ground. Plutarch affirmeth, that in Rome a Boy pricking the trunke of an Elephant with a goad, the beast caught him, and lift him up into the air to shoote him away and kill him: but the people and standers by seeing it, made so great a noise and crye thereat, that the beast set him downe againe faire and softly without any harm to him at all; as if he thought it sufficient to have put him in feare of such a death.

*Their revenge of harmes & observation of the measure of their meat*

In the night time they seeme to lament with sighes and teares their captivity and bondage, but if any come like unto modest persons they refrain suddenly, and are ashamed to be found either murmuring or sorrowing. They live a long age, even to 200 or 300 yeares, if sickness or woundes, prevent not their life and some but to 120 yeares; they are in their best strength of body at three score, for then beginneth their youth.

The medecinnal vertues in this beast are by Authours observed to be these: The blood of an Elephant and the ashes of a Weasill, cure the great Leprosie: and the same blood is profitable against all Rhewmaticke fluxes and the *Sciatica*. The flesh dryed and cold, or heavy fat and cold is abhominable for if it be sod and steeped in vineger with fennel-seede, and given to a Woman with child, it maketh her presently suffer abortement. But if a man tast thereof salted and steeped with the seede aforesaid, it cureth an old cough. The fatte is a good Antidote either by oyntment or perfume: it cureth also the payne in the head.

The Ivory or tooth is cold and dry in the first degree, and the whole substance thereof Corroborateth the hart and helpeth conception; it is often adulterated by fishes and Dogges bones burnt, and by White marble. There is a Spodium made of Ivory in this manner. Take a pound of Ivory cut into pieces, and put into a raw new earthen pot, covering & glewing the cover with lome round about, and so let it burne til the pot be thrughly hardened: afterward take off the pot and beate your Ivory into small powder, and being so beaten, sift it, then put it into a glasse and poure upon it two pounds of distilled rose Water, and let it dry. Thirdly beate it unto powder againe, and sift it the second time, and put into it againe so much rose water as at the first, then let it dry, and put thereunto as much Camphire as will lye upon three or foure single Groats, and worke it altogether upon a marble stone into little Cakes, and so lay them up where the ayre may nott corrupt and alter them. The vertue heereof is very precious against spittyng of bloode, and the bloody-flixe, and also it is given for refrigeration without daunger of byndinge or astriction.

After a man is delivered from the lethargye, pestilence, or sudden forgetfulnesse, let him be purged and take the powder of Ivory and Hiera Ruffi, drunke out of sweete water: This powder with Hony atticke, taketh away the spottes in the face: the same with wilde mints drunk with water, resisteth and avoydeth the Leprosie at the beginning. The powder of Ivory burnt and drunke with Goates blood doeth wonderfully cure all the paynes and expell the little stones in the raynes and bladder: Combes made of Ivory are most wholesome, the touching of the trunke cureth the headache: the liver is profitable against the falling evill, the same vertue hath the gall (if he have any against the falling evill).

The same, by annointing, cureth a lowsie skin, and taketh away that power which breedeth these vermine: the same perfumed easeth Agues, helpeth a woman in travaile, and driveth gnats or marsh-flyes out of a house.

from *The Historie of Foure-Footed Beasts* by Edward Topsell

# The moral elephant

'Why,' asks a shepherd, 'is this bank unfit
For celebration of our vernal loves?'
'Oh swain', returns the wiser shepherdess,
'Bees swarm here, and would quick resent our warmth!'
Only cold-blooded fish lack instinct here,
Nor gain nor guard connubiality:
But beasts, quadrupedal, mammiferous,
Do credit to their beasthood: witness him,
That Aelian cites, the noble elephant,
(Or if not Aelian, somebody as sage)
Who seeing much offence beneath his nose,
His master's friend exceed in courtesy
The due allowance to that master's wife,
Taught them good manners and killed both at once,
Making his master and all men admire
Indubitably, then, that master's self
Favoured by circumstance, had done the same
Or else stood clear rebuked by his own beast.

from *Dominus Hyacinthus de Archangelis* by Robert Browning

# Apocryphal elephants

## Antiochus marches against Judas Maccabaeus

Now when the King heard this, he was angry: and he called together all his friends, and the captains of his army, and them that were over the horsemen. . . .

And the number of his army was an hundred thousand footmen, and twenty thousand horsemen, and thirty two elephants, trained to battle.

And they went through Idumea, and approached to Bethsura, and fought many days, and they made engines: but they sallied forth, and burnt them with fire, and fought manfully.

And Judas departed from the castle and removed the camp to Bethzacharam, over against the king's camp.

And the king rose before it was light and made his troops march on fiercely towards the way of Bethzacharam: and the armies made themselves ready for the battle, and they sounded the trumpets:

And they showed the elephants the blood of grapes, and mulberries to provoke them to fight.

And they distributed the beasts by the legions: and there stood by every elephant a thousand men in coats of mail, and with helmets of brass on their heads: and five hundred horsemen set in order were chosen for every beast.

These before the time wheresoever the beast was, they were there; and whithersoever it went, they went, and they departed not from it.

And upon the beast, there were strong wooden towers, which covered everyone of them: and engines upon them: and upon everyone thirty two valiant men, who fought from above, and an Indian to rule the beast.

And the rest of the horsemen he placed upon this side and upon that side at the two wings, with trumpets to stir up the army, and to hasten them forward that stood thick together in the legions thereof.

Now when the sun shone upon the shields of gold, and of brass, the mountains glittered therewith and they shone like lamps of fire.

And part of the King's Army was distinguished by the high mountains, and the other part by the low places: and they marched on warily and orderly.

And all the inhabitants of the land were moved at the noise of their multitude, and the marching of the company, and the rattling of the armour, for the army was exceeding great and strong.

And Judas and his army drew near for battle: and there fell of the King's Army six hundred men.

And Eleazar the son of Saura saw one of the beasts harnessed with the King's harness: and it was higher than the other beasts: and it seemed to him that the king was on it.

And he exposed himself to deliver his people and to get himself an everlasting name.

And he ran up to it boldly in the midst of the legion, killing on the right hand, and on the left, and they fell by him this side and that side.

And he went between the feet of the elephant, and put himself under it: and slew it, and it fell to the ground upon him, and he died there.

from the *First Book of the Maccabees*, chapter six

## Apocryphal elephants

It is interesting that in the original Greek, the word ἔδειξαν is used to describe how the elephants were stimulated. This word, the aorist of δείκνυμι, normally means 'showed' and Dr More in his *Enthusiasmus Triumphatus* in 1656 construes the word literally in this sense. Others have, however, argued that to show elephants 'the blood of grapes and of mulberries' could have had no possible effect and that ἔδειξαν should be interpreted as 'forced them to drink'.

This argument is supported by the story of the persecution of the Jews by Ptolemy Philopator in Alexandria in 210 BC. The author of the Third Book of the Maccabees in the Greek Septuagint relates that the king, as preparation for causing his elephants to trample the Jews to death in the Hippodrome ordered one Hermon, their keeper, to dose them—ποτίσαι—the day before with frankincense and undiluted wine.

Here is the story:

### Ptolemy Philopator sets his elephants on the Jews

Then he called Hermon who was in charge of the elephants, and filled with bitter anger and wrath, and altogether inflexible, ordered him for the next day to drug all the elephants—in number five hundred—with copious handfuls of frankincense, and abundance of unmixed wine, and then when they were maddened by the plentiful supply of drink to bring them in to compass the fate of the Jews. And giving this order he turned to his feasting, having gathered together those of his friends and army who were most hostile to the Jews, while [Hermon] the ruler of the elephants attended to the injunction with all care. And the servants who were in charge of the Jews went out in the evening and bound the hands of the hapless wretches, taking all other precautions to keep them safe through the night, imagining that the nation would at one blow meet its final destruction. But the Jews who seemed to the heathen to be destitute of all protection, on account of the constraint and bonds which encompassed them on every side, with crying that would not be silenced, all called with tears on the almighty Lord and ruler of all power, their merciful God and father, beseeching him to frustrate the wicked design against them and to deliver them by a glorious manifestation from the fate yawning ready before them. So their prayer ascended fervently to heaven; but Hermon, having given the pitiless elephants drink till they were filled with the plenteous supply of wine and sated with frankincense, came early in the morning to the palace to report to the king about this. But the good creature, bestowed night and day from the beginning of time by him who gives the portion of sleep to all, *even* to whomsoever he will, *this* he sent upon the king; and he was overborne by a sweet and heavy *slumber* by the operation of the Lord, thus being greatly foiled in his lawless purpose, and utterly disappointed in his unchangeable design. But the Jews having escaped the appointed hour praised their holy God, and again besought him who is ready to forgive to manifest the might of his all-powerful hand before the proud eyes of the heathen. But when the middle of the tenth hour had nearly come he who was in charge of the invitation, seeing the guests assembled, went to the king and shook him. And having woken him up with difficulty, he pointed out that the hour for the banquet was already passing, reminding him of the circumstances. And the king considering these, betook himself to his cups and ordered those who had come for the banquet to take their places over against him. And when this had been done he called on them to give themselves up to revelry, and counting themselves highly honoured to reckon as a joy the feast, late as it was. And when the entertainment had gone on for some time, the king called Hermon and asked with fierce threats why the Jews had been allowed to survive that day. But when he pointed out that he had completely carried out the order overnight, and his friends confirmed him, the king with a rage more fierce than Phalaris, said that *the Jews* might thank his sleep for the *respite* of the day; but, he added, make ready the elephants in the same manner without further delay for the following day to destroy utterly the accursed Jews. When the king had spoken, all who were present readily assented with joy with one accord, and each one departed to his own house. But they did not spend the night season in sleep, so much as in devising all manner of cruel insults for those whom they thought to be in such a wretched plight.

So as soon as the cock had crowed in the morning, Hermon harnessed the beasts and began to put them in motion in the great colonnade. And the multitudes in the city assembled for the piteous spectacle, eagerly looking for the break of day. But the Jews drawing their last breath for but a brief moment more, with tearful supplications and strains of woe, raising their hands to heaven, besought the most high God again to help them speedily. The rays of the sun were not yet scattered abroad, and the king was receiving his friends, when Hermon came to his side and invited him to go forth, explaining that the desire of the king was ready to be fulfilled. When the king understood him, he was astonished at the unusual *summons* to go forth, having been overwhelmed with complete ignorance, and asked what was the matter on account of which this had been so zealously completed. But this was the operation of God the ruler of all, who had put in his mind forgetfulness of his former devices. But Hermon and all his friends pointed to the beasts and the army; It is prepared, O king, according to thine eager purpose. But he was filled with fierce anger at the words, because by the providence of God he had entirely lost his wits on this matter, and looking on him said threateningly. If thy parents or offspring were here, I would have furnished them as this rich banquet for the fierce beasts in place of the Jews against whom I have no charge and who have shown in a preeminent degree a full and unshaken loyalty to my ancestors. And indeed, if it were not for the affection *kindled* by our life together and thy service, thou shouldst have died instead of these. So Hermon met with an unexpected and dangerous threat, and his eyes and countenance fell. And *the king's* friends, slinking away sullenly one by one, sent away the assembled crowds, each to his own business. And the Jews hearing the words of the king, praised the Lord God who had manifested *his glory*, the king of kings, having obtained this help also from him.

But the king, having arranged the banquet once more in the same way, ordered them to turn to their pleasures. And calling Hermon he said threateningly, How often, thou wretched creature, must I give thee orders about these very things? Even now make ready the elephants for the morrow to destroy the Jews. But his kinsmen who sat at table with him wondered at his shifting purpose, and remonstrated, How long, O King, dost thou make trial of us as though we were fools, now for the third time giving orders for their destruction, and once more when the matter is in hand changing and cancelling thy decree? Wherefore the city is in a tumult through its expectation, and being crowded with throngs of people has now been several times in danger of being put to plunder. On this the king, a Phalaris in all things, was filled with madness, and, reckoning nothing of the changes of mind which had been wrought in him for the protection of the Jews, swore strongly a fruitless oath that he would without delay send to the grave the Jews mangled by the knees and feet of the beasts, and would march against Judaea and quickly level it to the ground with fire and sword, and burning to the earth their temple which we might not enter would quickly make it empty for all time of those who sacrificed therein. Then his friends and kinsmen went away joyfully with good confidence, and ordered the army to the most convenient places of the city to keep guard. And the ruler of the elephants, having driven the beasts into a state almost, one might say, of madness by fragrant draughts of wine mingled with frankincese, and having fitted them in a fearful guise with implements, at dawn, the city being now filled with countless multitudes thronging towards the hippodrome, entered the palace and urged on the king to the business that lay before him. And he, his impious heart filled with fierce anger, started forth with all his force with the beasts, determined with an unfeeling heart and his own eyes to gaze on the grievous and piteous destruction of the afore-mentioned *Jews*. And when they saw the dust raised by the elephants going out at the gate, and the armed force accompanying them, and the movement of the crowd, and heard the far-sounding tumult, thinking that the last crisis of their life had come and the end of their miserable suspense, they betook themselves to lamentation and groans, and kissed one another, embracing their relatives and falling on their necks, parents and children, mothers and daughters; and others with new-born babes at their breast drawing their last milk. But none the less, reflecting on their former deliverances sent from heaven, with one accord they threw themselves on their faces, and took the babes from their breasts, and cried out with an exceeding loud voice, beseeching the ruler of all power by a manifestation to show pity upon them now that they were come to the gates of death.

But a certain Eleazar, a man of note among the priests of the country whose years had already reached old age, and who was adorned with every virtue of life, made the elders who were round him cease from calling on the holy God, and prayed thus: King of great power, most high, almighty God, who governest all creation with loving kindness, look upon the seed of Abraham, the children of Jacob thy sanctified one, the people of thy sanctified inheritance, who are unjustly perishing, strangers in a strange land. O Father, thou didst destroy Pharaoh, the former ruler of this Egypt, with his multitude of chariots, when he was lifted high in his lawless insolence and a tongue speaking great things, drowning him together with his proud host, and didst cause the light of thy mercy to shine upon the race of Israel. Thou, when Sennacherib, the cruel king of the Assyrians, was puffed up by his countless hosts, after he had taken the whole earth captive by his sword, and was lifted up against thy holy city speaking grievous words of boasting and insolence, thou, Lord, didst break him in pieces, making manifest thy power to many nations. Thou, when the three friends in Babylonia freely gave their life to the flames that they should not serve vain things, didst make as dew the fiery furnace, and deliver them unharmed even to the hair of their head, turning the flame upon all their adversaries. Thou, when Daniel was cast through the slanders of envy to the lions beneath the ground as food for wild beasts, didst bring him up to the light unhurt. And when Jonah was languishing unpitied in the belly of the sea-born monster, thou didst restore him, O Father, uninjured to all his household. And now thou hater of insolence, rich in mercy, protector of all, quickly manifest thyself to the saints of Israel's line, in their insolent oppression by the abominable and lawless heathen. And if our life has been ensnared in impious deeds during our sojourning, save us from the hand of the enemy, and destroy us, O Lord, by whatever fate thou choosest. Let not the men whose thoughts are vanity bless their vain *gods* for the destruction of thy beloved, saying, Neither has their God delivered them. Thou who hast all might and all power, the Eternal, look now upon us; pity us who by the mad insolence of lawless men are being sent to death as traitors; and let the heathen to-day fear thy invincible might, thou glorious one, who hast mighty works for the salvation of the race of Israel. The whole multitude of babes with their parents beseecheth thee with tears. Let it be shown to all heathen that thou art with us, O Lord, and hast not turned thy face away from us; But as thou hast said, Not even when they were in the land of their enemies have I forgotten them, even so bring it to pass, O Lord.

And when Eleazar was even now ending his prayer, the king with the beasts and the whole insolent array of his army came to the hippodrome. And the Jews beholding it raised a great cry to heaven, so that now the surrounding valleys re-echoed it, and caused in all the hosts, an incontrollable trembling. Then the greatly glorious, almighty, and true God, making manifest his holy face, opened the gates of heaven, from which two glorious angels of terrible aspect descended, visible to all but the Jews and withstood them and filled the army of the adversaries with confusion and terror, and bound them with immovable fetters. And a great horror seized on the body of the king as well, and his fierce insolence was forgotten. And the beasts turned round against the armed hosts that followed them and began to tread them under foot and destroy them.

from the *Third Book of the Maccabees*, chapter five

# Alexander defeats Porus
## at the battle of the Hydaspes, 326 BC

The battle of the Hydaspes was one of the great battles of history in which elephants played a major part. The river Hydaspes is the modern Jhelum, a tributary of the Indus. It flows down through the West Punjab in Pakistan, halfway between Lahore and Rawalpindi.

The Indian Army, commanded by the Rajah Paurava or, in Greek, Porus, awaited Alexander on the East bank of the river.

The accounts of Alexander's invasion of India come chiefly from Diodorus, Quintus Curtius, Plutarch and Arrian. These historians were able to draw on the writings of historians contemporary with Alexander, some of whom were associated with Alexander himself and were eye-witnesses of the events they describe. Arrian (c. AD 150) whose account of the Battle of the Hydaspes follows[1] said himself that his principal authorities were Aristobulus of Cassandreia who was with Alexander in India and Ptolemy, one of Alexander's generals who later became King of Egypt and founded the great library of Alexandria. Unfortunately all but a few fragments of the contemporary writings have been destroyed. The work from which the account of the battle is taken is the *Anabasis*, which contains the history of Alexander from his accession in 336 BC until his death in Babylon in 323 BC.

In a preliminary cavalry engagement Alexander defeated a body of the Indian horse. Arrian proceeds:

Four Hundred of the *Indian* Horse were there slain, and among them *Porus*'s Son; and most of their Chariots, with their Horses, were taken, they being heavy and troublesome in Flight, and even in the Battle (by reason of the slippery Soil of the Place) altogether unserviceable. As soon as the Horse who had escaped from this Conflict, arriv'd at their main body, and gave *Porus* notice that *Alexander* was already pass'd over the River, with the greatest part of his Army, and that his Son was slain in Battle, he was so much moved, that he knew not what Course to take; especially because the Forces which were posted over against his grand Camp, and commanded by *Craterus*, were also endeavouring to pass the River: However, at last, he resolved to march against *Alexander*, and attack the *Macedonians*, as the strongest Body; and, at the same time, to leave a part of the Army, and some Elephants, behind in the Camp, to fright Craterus's Horse as they approach'd the Bank of the River. He therefore, with his whole Body of Horse, which were about four Thousand, and three Hundred Chariots, with two Hundred Elephants, and near thirty Thousand Foot, march'd forwards, and when he came to a Plain, where the Soil was not incommodious, by reason of the slippery Clay, but firm and sandy, and every way fit for wheeling his Chariots round upon, he resolv'd there to draw up his Army, which he did in the following manner: First he plac'd the Elephants in Front, at the distance of one Hundred Foot from each other, to cover the whole Body of Foot, and at the same time to strike a terror into *Alexander*'s Horse; for he imagined that none, either Horse, or Foot, would be so hardy as to endeavour to penetrate through the Spaces between the Elephants: The Horsemen, he thought, could not, because their

1. From Arrian's *History* translated by Mr Rooke in 1729

88

Horses would be terrify'd at the Sight, and the Foot would not dare, because the arm'd Soldiers would be ready to gall them on each Hand, and the Elephants to trample them under their Feet. The Foot possessed the next Rank, they were not indeed plac'd in the same Order with the Elephants, but so small a way behind, that they seem'd to fill up the interspaces. At the Extremities of each Wing, he plac'd Elephants, bearing huge Wooden Towers, wherein were arm'd Men: The Foot were defended on each Hand by the Horse, and the Horse by the Chariots, which were plac'd before them.

*Porus*'s Army stood ranged thus; but as soon as *Alexander* saw the *Indians* drawn up in order of Battle, he commanded his Horse to halt, 'till the Foot could come up; and even when the Body of Foot, had, by degrees, join'd with the rest of the Forces, he would not proceed immediately to marshalling them lest he should expose them, breathless and weary with a long March, to the fury of the fresh *Barbarians*; but surrounding them with his Horse, he gave them time to take Breath, and recover their Spirits: Then, viewing the Disposition of the Enemy's Troops, he came to a Resolution not to make his first Attack in Front (where the greatest part of the Elephants were posted, and the Ranks of Foot were much thicker in the intermediate Spaces) for the same Fears which induced *Porus* to range that part of the Army thus, hinder'd *Alexander* from attacking them there first. But knowing himself to be much superior to the *Indians* in Horse, he, with the best part of them, mov'd towards *Porus*'s left Wing, resolving to break in upon that Quarter; and dispatch'd *Caenus* with his own and *Demetrius*'s Troops to the Right, with Orders, that when he perceiv'd the *Barbarians* turn their Horse to resist the Fury of his Attack, he should fall upon their Rear. The Phalanx of Foot, he order'd to be led on by *Seleucus*, *Antigonus* and *Tauro*; and commanded them not to engage before they saw the Enemy's Horse and Foot in disorder, by his, and *Caenus*'s Attacks. But when they came within reach of their missive Weapons, they should immediately dispatch about a Thousand Archers against the Enemy's Left Wing, that by the Violence of those, and the Irruption of the Horse, that part of the Army might be put into disorder: He, with his auxiliary Horse, flew swiftly to the left Wing, with design to engage them warmly, before they could recover themselves from the Confusion which his Archers must necessarily bring them into.

The *Indians*, perceiving themselves environ'd on all Hands, first led on their Horse, to resist the Attacks of Alexander, when immediately Caenus, with his Forces, as he had been order'd, fell upon them in Flank, which caused them to divide their Forces into two Parts, and resolve to lead the best and most numerous of them against *Alexander*, and face about with the other, to meet Caenus; and this serv'd to break the Ranks, as well as the Courage of the *Indians*. *Alexander* taking this Opportunity of their dividing their Forces, immediately rushed forwards upon that Party designed against him, which were scarce able to sustain the first Shock of his Horse, before they fled to the Elephants, as to a friendly Wall for Refuge, whose Governours stir'd up the Beasts to trample down the Horse; but the *Macedonian* Phalanx gall'd not only the Beasts themselves, but their Riders also, with their Arrows; and this was a Manner of Fighting altogether new, and unheard-of among the *Macedonians*: For which-way-soever the Elephants turn'd, the Ranks of Foot, however firm, were forc'd to give Way. The *Indian* Horse, now perceiving their Foot in the heat of Action, rally'd again, and attack'd *Alexander*'s Horse a second time, but were again forc'd back with Loss (because they were far inferior to them, not only in Number, but in Military Discipline) and retreated among the Elephants. And now all Alexander's Horse being joyn'd together in one Body, (not by any command of his, but by Chance, and a casual Event in the Battle) wherever they fell upon the *Indians*, they made dreadful Havock among them. And the Beasts being now pent up in a narrow Space, and violently enrag'd, did no less Mischief to their own Men, than the Enemy; and as they toss'd and mov'd about, Multitudes were trampl'd to Death; besides, the Horse being confin'd among the Elephants, a huge Slaughter ensu'd, for many of the Governours of the Beasts being slain by the Archers, and the Elephants themselves, partly enrag'd with their Wounds, and partly for want of Riders, no longer kept any certain Station in the Battle, but running forwards, as if Madness had seiz'd them, they pushed down, slew, and trampl'd under Foot, Friends and Foes without distinction: Only the Macedonians having the Advantage of a more free and open Space, gave way, and made room for the furious Beasts to rush through their Ranks, but slew them whenever they attempted to return: But the Beasts at last, quite wearied out with Wounds and Toil, were no longer able to push with their usual Force, but only made a hideous Noise, and moving their fore Feet heavily, pass'd out of the Battle. Alexander having surrounded all the Enemies Horse with his, made a signal for the Foot to close their Shields fast together, and haste that way, in a firm Body, and by this means the *Indian* Horse being every way overpower'd, were almost all slain. Nor was the Fate of their Foot much better, for the Macedonians pressing them vehemently on all Sides, made a great Destruction among them, and, at last, all of them (except those whom Alexander's Horse had hemm'd in) perceiving their Case desperate, turn'd their backs and fled.

In the mean while, *Craterus*, and the Captains who were with him on the other side of the River, no sooner perceived the Victory to encline to the *Macedonians*, than they pass'd over, and made a dismal Slaughter of the *Indians* in the pursuit; and being fresh Soldiers, they succeeded those who had been wearied out in the heat of the Battle. Of the *Indian* Foot, little less than twenty Thousand fell that Day; of their Horse about three Thousand. All their Chariots were hack'd to pieces: Two of *Porus*'s Sons were slain; as was *Spitaces*, Governour of that Province, all the Managers of their Elephants, and their Charioteers; and almost all the Captains of Horse, as well as Foot, belonging to *Porus*. The Elephants also, which were not kill'd, were every one taken. Of *Alexander*'s Foot, which consisted at first of six Thousand, and gave the first onset, about Eighty were lost, of his Equestrian Archers, Ten; of the Auxiliary Horse, Twenty; and of all the rest of the Troops of Horse, about Two Hundred. *Porus*, who behav'd himself with the utmost Prudence, and acted the part, not only of an experienc'd General, but of a stout

Soldier, all that Day; seeing the Slaughter made among his Horse, and some of his Elephants lying dead, others without Managers, running about, mad with their Wounds; and the greatest part of his Foot cut off, behav'd not like *King Darius*, who left the Field among the very first of his Troops; but as long as ever he could see any Party of his *Indians* keep their Ground, he fought bravely; but receiving a Wound on the right Shoulder, which place alone was bare during the Action (for his Coat of Mail being excellent both for Strength and Workmanship, as it afterwards appear'd easily secured the rest of his Body) he turn'd his Elephant out of the Battle and fled. *Alexander* having observ'd his gallant and generous Behaviour in that Days Action, desir'd, above all things, to have his Life sav'd; and accordingly sent *Taxiles*, the Indian Prince to him, who, when he overtook him, and came as near as was safe, for fear of his Elephant, he requested him to stop his Beast (for that all his Endeavours to escape were vain) and receive *Alexander*'s Commands. *Porus* seeing it was *Taxiles*, his old Enemy, run against him with his Spear, and had perhaps slain him, if he had not immediately turn'd away his Horse and escap'd out of his sight. However, all this was not sufficient to incense *Alexander* against him; but he sent others, and after them more, among whom was *Meroe*, an *Indian*, because he understood that there had been an old Friendship between him and *Porus*. *Porus* overcome with *Meroe*'s exhortations, and almost dead with Thirst, caus'd his Elephant to kneel down, and then alighted from him; and as soon as he had refrsh'd himself with a little Water, he accompanied *Meroe* to *Alexander*.

Obverse and reverse of coin from Cuperus showing Alexander's triumph over Porus

# Alexander defeats Porus at the battle of the Hydaspes, 326 BC

*Alexander* being inform'd of the Approach of *Porus,* advanc'd a little forwards, before his Army; and accompanied by some of his Friends, went to meet him; and stopping his Horse, was seiz'd with Admiration at his Tallness, (for he was above five Cubits high) as well as at his Beauty, and the Justness of the Proportion of his Body; and he was no less amaz'd to find, that he seem'd still far from entertaining any humble or servile Ideas in his Mind, tho' he was conquer'd: He consider'd besides, that he was a generous Man, who had contended with another of equal Generosity, and that he was a King who had strove to preserve his Dominions from the Invasions of another King. Then *Alexander* first directing his discourse to him, commanded him to ask what he should do for him; to whom Porus made answer, *That he would use him Royally. Alexander* smiling, reply'd, *That I would do for my own sake;* but say what I shall do for thine. *Porus* told him, *All his Wishes were summ'd up in his first Petition.* Alexander over-joy'd at this Answer of his, not only restored him straight to Liberty, and the full Possession of his former Dominions, but also gave him another Empire beyond his own, and treated him in so royal and so generous a Manner, that he ever after had him his fast Friend. Thus concluded the Wars of *Alexander* against *Porus,* and the *Indians,* beyond the River *Hydaspes* in the Month of *Munychion,* when *Hegemon* was Archon of *Athens.*

Coin with Julius Caesar's head from Cuperus.

# Alexander defeats Porus at the battle of the Hydaspes, 326 BC

Elephant in armour, compared by Pliny to the skin, which he described as *cancellata cutis*: coin from Cuperus

# Sikandar

The earth was mountain-like with elephants.
The army stretched four miles with troops behind
And elephants in front.
   Now spies arrived
From Hind before the world-lord and informed him
At large of how the elephant contendeth
In warfare: 'It will rout two miles of horse.
No cavalier will dare to face that beast,
Or, if he did so, ever come again.
Because its trunk is higher than the air,
And Saturn is its helper in the sky.'
   They drew a picture of an elephant,
And showed it to Sikandar who commanded
That the philosophers of Rúm should model
One out of wax for him, and then inquired:—
'Who can propound a scheme to cope with such?'
The sages held a session and devised
A plan in all its details. Then the Sháh
Assembled all the master-smiths of Rúm,
Of Misr, and Párs, twelve hundred men in sum,
Who made a horse, with saddle and with rider
Complete, of iron, fastening the joints
With bolts and rivets. Horse and man were furbished.
They charged it with black naphtha, and then ran it
On wheels before the troops. At sight thereof
Sikandar was well pleased for, being wise,
He felt the gain thereof, and bade to make
A thousand such and more: who e'er beheld
On chargers dappled, chestnut, black and grey
An iron host? The matter took the month,
And then the workmen rested from their labours.
Thus led they forth on wheels an iron host
That of all things resembled horsemen most.
Now when Sikandar was approaching Fúr,
And from afar one host beheld the other,
On both sides rose the shout and dust of battle.
And eager for the fray the warriors
Advanced. They lit the naphtha in the steeds:
Fúr's troops were in dismay. The naphtha blazed:
Fúr's troops recoiled because those steeds were iron,
Whereat the elephants, when their own trunks
Were scorched, fled likewise, and their drivers marvelled.
Thus all the Indian host and all those huge,
High-crested elephants were put to flight.
Sikandar like a raging blast pursued
The foe until the air turned indigo,
And opportunity for fight was over.

from the *Shahnama of Firdausi*

26  Archbishop Urso's throne, *c.* 1080 Canosa Cathedral, Apulia

27 Font supported on elephant, 1907

# Some travellers' tales

Very many travellers have included stories of elephants in the accounts of their journeys. Many of the details recorded appear in one form or another in several of these writings and it would be tedious to include more than a few of them here. One, John Ranking, who describes himself as a 'Resident Upwards of Twenty Years in Hindoostan and Russia', has collected a great number of facts and fantasies on elephants and other matters in a large volume, published in London in 1826, entitled '*Historical Researches on the Wars and Sports of the Mongols and Romans in which Elephants and Wild Beasts were Employed or Slain*'. Among the writers upon whom John Ranking has drawn are Samuel Purchas, who compiled similar works at the beginning of the seventeenth century; Vincent le Blanc, who wrote of his travels in India and the East in 1660; John Bell of Antermony who travelled to Pekin and wrote an account of life and customs there in 1763; Baron d'Aubonne, J. B. Tavernier, who published *Les Six Voyages de Jean-Baptiste Tavernier* in 1769. Some extracts from Ranking's work are given below:

In the thirteenth and fourteenth centuries of the Christian Era, the Mongol Grand Khans who resided in Pekin, and the viceroys their relations in Shensi, Yunan, etc., possessed many thousands of elephants; those animals being part of the considerable war establishment. Since that period, elephants appear to have been kept for parade, hunting and beasts of burden. Ships on the Kiang-keou are drawn by elephants to Quinsay.

Emanuel Carvalius was at Cambalu (Pekin) in the year 1598, when the Emperor had four hundred elephants, which were brought from Malacca and Pegu.

When Mr Bell was at Pekin, he says: After dinner we saw the huge elephants richly caparisoned in gold and silver stuffs. Each had a driver. We stood about an hour admiring these sagacious animals who, passing before us at equal distances, returned again behind the stables, and so on, round and round, till there seemed to be no end to the procession. The plot, however, was discovered by the features and dress of the riders; the chief keeper told us there were only sixty of them. The Emperor keeps them only for show and makes no use of them, at least in these northern parts. Some of them knelt and made obeisance to us; others sucked up water from vessels, and spouted it through their trunks among the mob, or wherever the rider directed.

His Majesty sent to the Grand Seignior a throne of solid gold, ornamented with large pearls, and two chain elephants that had been taught at the sound of instruments to dance.

For the defence of Delhi against Timur, Mahmoud's force consisted of ten thousand horse, forty thousand foot, and elephants armed with cuirasses and poisoned daggers upon their tusks. They had wooden towers upon their backs, in the form of bastions, in which were cross-bowmen and archers, who could fight under cover. On the side of the elephants were flingers of fire and melted pitch, and rockets shod with iron, which give repeated blows where they fall. The soldiers feared the elephants might fling them into the air. The learned doctors wished

to be placed near where the ladies were, if his Majesty pleased! . . .
Timur placed his standard upon the walls of Delhi. . . . A hundred
and twenty elephants and twelve rhinoceroses were brought before
Timur; and having been trained for such purposes, they placed themselves in a humble posture and made a cry as if demanding quarter.

After the death of the Burman conqueror, his son, finding the King of
Ava, his tributary and uncle, was plotting a conspiracy, seized forty
Avan Noblemen, had them conducted into a wood, which was set
fire to, and those who escaped the flames were killed by the sword. The
two kings agreed to try their fate by single combat upon elephants;
and the king of Pegu obtained the conquest. . . .

The king [of Pegu] hath four white elephants; and if any other hath
any, he will seek them by favour or force. They are fed in vessels of
silver gilt. One of them, when he goes to the river, passes under a canopy
of cloth of gold, or silk, carried by six or eight men; as many going before, playing drums or other instruments. On his coming out of the
river a gentleman washes his feet in a silver bason. There were black
elephants nine cubits high. The king is said to have about five thousand
elephants of war . . . one wife . . . three hundred concubines and . . .
ninety children.

They load their elephants and horses with iron and steel hoops, three
fingers broad, keen as razors, and dart them dexterously, and swift as
arrows; they poison them and the large wounds they make are mortal.

An English mastiff [more probably it was a bull-dog] seized an elephant
by the trunk, and kept his hold so fast, that the elephant, having tossed
him in the air for some time, at last swung him off; but did not care to
come near him a second time. This being told to the Mogul, enhanced
the reputation of English dogs; they were carried about in palankines
along with his Majesty, and he fed them himself with a pair of silver
tongs made for that purpose.

# Elephants conquer the Alps

## Hannibal's invasion of Italy

One of the greatest exploits which history records is undoubtedly the invasion of Italy in 219 BC by Hannibal the Carthaginian. The Romans, prepared for attacks by sea, never imagined the crossing of the Alps by an army of sufficient size and strength to threaten Rome itself.

Many military commentators regard Hannibal as the greatest general of all time and there is no doubt that his victories were models of generalship. But it is in carrying out the duties as his own quartermaster general—in his mastery of what is today called logistics—that we may marvel at him most.

To have led his army with its elephants the whole way from Spain through much hostile country and over the high passes, when one remembers that the great beasts from tropical Africa were totally un- used to ice and snow, is a feat of astonishing competence and daring.

In all the various accounts of the use of elephants in war, the animals do not appear to have played the decisive part which their size and pro- minence would suggest. Their tremendous strength and carrying power seem to have dazzled the eastern races into thinking that they were in- vincible. Both Alexander and the Romans succeeded in defeating them and it is one of the most surprising things about Hannibal that he was so convinced of their value that he accepted the risks and difficulties of the passage of the Alps rather than face the Invasion of Italy without them.

In the course of his march from Spain to Italy, Hannibal had to transport his army of 38,000 infantry, 8000 cavalry and thirty-seven elephants, together with his baggage train, across the Rhone.

The point he chose for the crossing was from Fourques to Arles where the river is about 900 feet wide and reasonably shallow and slow.

The crossing was resisted by the Gauls, and Hannibal sent a force under Hanno about thirty miles upstream to cross where there was an island and to fall upon the Gauls in the rear.

Enough boats were then collected and the army crossed. But the elephants presented a problem. Here is Polybius's account of how it was solved:

> They then constructed several rafts of great strength and size and lashing two together side by side they fastened them firmly to the bank of the river. Together they formed a platform fifty feet wide. To these they fastened further rafts extending the structure about 200 feet out into the stream. They attached the upstream side by means of cables to trees further up the bank thus ensuring the immobility of the structure against the current.
> To the outer end they fastened further rafts of the same width with ropes which could easily be detached, at the same time con- necting these detachable rafts by tow-ropes to boats which would draw them over the river. The whole affair was then covered with earth to make it level with and of the same colour as the approach road on the river bank.
> The elephants would always obey their drivers, going as far as the edge of the water but on no account would they ever enter it. The drivers now led two elephant cows on to the raft bridge. The rest

followed obediently. As soon as sufficient number were on the detachable raft, the hawsers were cast off and the raft towed rapidly out and across the stream. At first the elephants became terrified and rushed madly about trying to get back to the start, but seeing themselves completely surrounded by the water they eventually stood still. Thus most of the elephants were successfully ferried over the Rhone. Unfortunately a few flung themselves in terror into the river but the water was shallow enough for them to wade, so, keeping their trunks above water, they were able to breathe and all safely made the passage although some of their mahouts were drowned.'

After the crossing of the Rhone, Hannibal faced the crossing of the Alps. It is one of the marvels of history that he succeeded in getting these mighty beasts, used to the tropical forest of Africa, over the mountains and through the snow and ice.

Charles Knight, describing it in 1844, writes:

'The ground was slippery with a recent fall of snow, and the fearful acclivities, even without this obstacle, were little suited to the elephant, the inhabitant of the plains. In fifteen days the passage was accomplished, but the army was reduced to twenty thousand foot and six thousand horse.

These mighty passes, through which neither the energies of war nor the quiet strength of commercial intercourse had created safe and practicable roads, saw their rugged pathways strewn with the carcasses of men and beasts who toppled over the fearful chasms, or perished by exhaustion and want of food.

'Great was the tumult there,
Deafening the din, when in barbaric pomp,
The Carthaginian, on his march to Rome,
Entered their fastnesses. Trampling the snows,
The war-horse reared, and the towered elephant
Upturned his trunk into murky sky,
Then tumbled headlong, swallowed up and lost,
He and his rider.'

Thus wrote Rogers in his *Italy*.

The number of elephants destroyed is not mentioned by the historians; many necessarily perished, but enough remained to constitute a powerful force, soon to be employed in the battles of the Ticinus and of the Trebia. It is difficult to imagine how these animals were conveyed at all through the tremendous passes of the Alps, without some mechanical contrivance. In the Roman invasion of Macedon, the consul Martius facilitated the descent of the elephants down a steep mountain by the construction of temporary bridges. It does not appear that Hannibal adopted any similar means, but relied upon that all conquering energy which, in its general influence upon his army, has rendered this celebrated passage of the Alps one of the most wonderful events of ancient history.

The historians minutely describe the powerful effects which the elephants produced in the battle of the Trebia. Livy records that the Gauls, who were the auxiliaries of the Romans, could not bear up against the fierceness of their assaults. Appian states that the Roman horses in this great battle could endure neither the sight nor the smell of the elephants (*c.f.* the account by Marco Polo of the terror of Nestardin's horses in the battle of Vochang). Silius Italicus, the poet of the Punic War, assigns the victory of Hannibal principally to his elephants.

In crossing the Apennines after the battle of Trebia, seven of these animals were starved to death. The small number remaining to Hannibal were probably still more reduced by subsequent fatigue, till at last, in passing the Arno, which was swollen by the mountain torrents, large numbers of men and horses perished; and of his elephants there only remained to Hannibal that 'Getulian beast' on which he himself rode. As Juvenal wrote (tr. Gifford):

> O for some master-hand the chief to trace,
> As through th'Etrurian swamps by rain increased
> Spoil'd of an eye, he flounced on his Getulian beast.

(It will be remembered that, like another commander 1300 years later, Hannibal lost an eye in battle.)

In a previous passage of the Po, the Carthaginian leader had advantageously employed his elephants, by forming them in a line across the shallow river, so that, the force of the current being broken by those bulky masses, his soldiers might pass through with comparative ease. Perdiccas put his elephants to a similar use in his unfortunate passage of the Nile near Memphis.

Silius Italicus describes the use of elephants at the battle of Cannae in 216 BC. The Romans are supposed to have attacked them with firebrands, setting fire also to the wooden towers on their backs; some of the terrified animals plunged into the river.

Neither Livy, Polybius nor Appian mentions this incident; nor, indeed, do they anywhere mention 'towers'. Contemporary coins do not generally show Hannibal's elephants with towers upon their backs, but it is hard to believe that they would be much use without 'castles' manned by slingers and archers. An imaginary picture of the battle of Zama in which Hannibal was finally defeated by Scipio Africanus, is published in John Ranking's *The Wars and Sports of the Mongols and Romans* in 1826 and shows numerous elephants with wooden towers on their backs, rushing all over the battlefield.

The surviving elephant which Hannibal himself rode was named 'Surus', the Syrian, and is described by Cato as the bravest of all the elephants.

So far as is known Hannibal's elephants were for the most part African forest elephants captured near the Atlas mountains. These were not more than eight feet tall and were no match for the bigger Indian elephants. Surus, however, as its name suggests, was probably an Indian elephant which had reached Carthage from Egypt and may have been a gift from Ptolemy who had acquired a number in his Syrian wars.

# Elephants conquer the Alps

Some commentators have argued that Hannibal's elephants *were* Indian from the fact that Polybius describes their drivers as Indoi (ἰνδοι), but it is believed that this was a general term used for the drivers, some of whom may have come from the East.

After the Battle of Cannae it is recorded that Hannibal caused a combat to take place between some of his Roman prisoners and an elephant. He promised liberty to any soldier who overcame the beast. One of them was lucky enough to kill the elephant single-handed. Hannibal released him but, with what the Romans would have described as Carthaginian treachery, he sent men after him and had him murdered, as he feared, so it is said, that if the soldier recounted his exploit in Rome, the Romans would lose their dread of his elephants.

It is not known whether the elephant slain on this occasion was Hannibal's own mount, Surus, but it seems unlikely that he would put Surus to this risk—which suggests that, contrary to other accounts, Surus was not the only elephant surviving in Hannibal's army at this time.

Silius Italicus describes a combat between a Roman soldier and an elephant at the Trebia in spirited verse, translated by Thomas Ross:

> For as
> The towered elephants attempt to pass,
> Into the flood with violence they fell
> (As when a rock, torn from its native hill
> by tempests, falls into the angry main);
> And Trebia, afraid to entertain
> Such monstrous bodies, flies before the beasts,
> Or shrinks beneath them, with their weight oppressed.
> But as adversity man's courage tries,
> And fearless valour doth to honour rise
> Through danger, stout Fibrenus doth disclaim
> A death ignoble, or that wanted fame;
> And cries, 'My fate shall be observed, nor shall
> Fortune beneath these waters hide my fall.
> I'll try if earth doth any living bear
> Which the Ausonian sword and Tyrrhean spear
> Cannot subdue and kill.' With that, he pressed
> His lance into the right eye of the beast,
> That, with blind rage, the penetrating blow
> Pursued; and tossing his mangled brow,
> Besmeared with reeking blood, with horrid cries
> Turns round, and from his fallen master flies;
> Then with their darts and frequent arrows all
> Invade him, and now dare to hope his fall.
> His immense shoulders and his sides appear
> One wound entire; his dusky back doth bear
> Innumerable shafts, that, like a wood,
> Still waving as he moved, upon him stood;
> Till, in so long a fight, their weapons all
> Consumed, he fell, death hasting through his fall.

# Earth-shaking beast

The Greek shall come against thee
　　The conqueror of the East.
Beside him stalks to battle
　　The huge earth-shaking beast,
The beast on whom the castle
　　With all its guards doth stand,
The beast who hath between his eyes
　　The serpent for a hand.
First march the bold Epirotes,
　　Wedged close with shield and spear;
And the ranks of false Tarentum
　　Are glittering in the rear.

The ranks of false Tarentum
　　Like hunted sheep shall fly;
In vain the bold Epirotes
　　Shall round their standard die;
And Apennine's grey vultures
　　Shall have a noble feast
On the fat and the eyes
　　Of the huge earth-shaking beast.

from 'The Prophecy of Capys', *Lays of Ancient Rome*, by Thomas Babington
Macaulay

# Julius Caesar forces the crossing of the Thames, 54 BC

Caesar was prevented from crossing the river by Cassivelaunus, the King of the Britons, who opposed him with a great press of cavalry and chariots. Now Caesar had in his train a most mighty elephant, a creature never before seen by the Britons. This animal he encased in iron chain mail and on its back he placed a great tower, manned by archers and slingers. Caesar then gave orders for his army to force the crossing.

The sight of so vast a creature such as they had never beheld before struck terror into the hearts of the British army. If the men were frightened, what of the horses? The Greeks had found by experience that horses could not stand up to an elephant even when it was unarmed and in a state of nature, so it is not surprising that the horses of Cassivelaunus could not bear to look upon an armed elephant and castle from which issued volleys of arrows and slingstones. So the Britons, horse, foot and chariots turned tail and fled. The Romans crossed the river without further trouble, the enemy having been terrrified out of their wits by a single beast.

from *Strategematum*, book VIII, by Polyaenus

**Note**

This is the only authority for the idea that Caesar used an elephant in his crossing of the Thames near Chertsey. There is no mention of the fact—if, indeed, it was a fact—in Caesar's *Commentaries*.

# O Elephant!

**After a latin epigram attributed to Petronius**

Most noble monster, huge and black as night,
O Elephant, whose tusks flash snowy white
And guard from all attack your writhing trunk,
Alive, your menace puts us in a funk.
Yet, when you kick the bucket, what we thought
Were only bones worth practically nought
Can bring much profit to humanity—
A mace to serve a Mayor's vanity,
A table's decorative centre-piece,
Or gaming counters, other things like these,
Or men in colours twain for draughts or chess—
All useful artifacts, or more or less—
Which proves that beasts which, living, terrify,
Become mere toys and knick-knacks when they die.

# Pepita's legacy

Imagine not, dear fellow, that I'm greedy;
Polonius is my friend—I know he's seedy,
But if he turns his toes up, he'll not leave
A penny-piece to me
For he has children three.
Why, even you, dear fellow, can't believe
That anyone would offer e'en a hen,
Sickly, blind, no use to mice or men,
In such a very idiotic scramble!
Not e'en for Dad a quail!
His kids enjoy th'entail.
Dear boy, give up the useless, stupid gamble.
Now, if some wealthy, childless dame, perhaps
Pepita, has a fev'rish cold, the chaps
Will have the porticos of churches stuffed
With votive plaques and prayers
From prophets and soothsayers,
Ostensibly for death to be rebuffed.

## Pepita's legacy

They'd kill a hundred beeves on her behalf
Or e'en a hundred elephants—you laugh?
Tis truth! But elephants you cannot buy;
Such beasts are not at home
In Italy or Rome;
In climate such as ours they mostly die
And well we know that elephants abide
In sunny lands where dusky folk reside.
Yet, if brought here, midst dark Rutulian trees
In Tuscany they dwell,
Where Turnus reigned. In dell
And glade they prowl as Caesar's self decrees.
They are not there for common mortals' joy;
Proud Caesar keeps them as a royal toy
To pleasure him as circus beasts, a fate
Their ancestors would ne'er
Have borne; they were aware
They served great Hannibal, a potentate
From Tyrian Carthage; Pyrrhus, too, who brought
His elephants to Italy and sought
To vanquish Rome—And Roman gen'rals, too,
Sent elephants to war;
Upon their backs they bore
Castles with cohorts, mighty deeds to do.
Blame not the greedy scroungers of bequests
Who fail an elephant to find; the breasts
Of characters like Croesus' self would swell
If they unto the altar
Could lead, with golden halter,
Ivory tuskers, whose most potent spell
Legacies win; what offering were sweeter
For such a lovely one as Dame Pepita!
Don't hesitate; such tricks as these employ
And soon you'll be Pepita's dearest boy!

after Juvenal, *Satire XII*

# Elephants and Kublai Khan

(Marco Polo dictated the account of his travels while he was a prisoner in Genoa, to another prisoner, one Rusticiano of Pisa. The manuscript was in French. There are between eighty and ninety different manuscripts in various languages, the most important being in the Bibliothèque Nationale in Paris.)

Kublai Khan was a grandson of Ghengis (or Jenghiz) Khan and the greatest of his successors. He eventually became sovereign of an Empire which stretched from Korea to the Arabian Desert. Our information about him comes chiefly from the writings of Marco Polo who was made much of by the great Khan. He arrived at the Khan's court at Shangtu not far from Pekin in 1275 with his father Nicolo and his uncle Maffeo. After many years of service they left Kublai's court to return to Venice; on their way, in 1294, they heard of Kublai's death.

Kublai came from northern Mongolia; Genghis had been born within territories now those of the USSR, and it was from these that he extended his dominions to stretch from the Pacific to the Black Sea.

Coming from the north as he did, Kublai did not employ elephants for war. In fact, elephants were not used for war by the Chinese. Yet we first hear of Kublai making use of elephants when he marched to subdue Nayan, a relative, who thought to overthrow Kublai.

Kublai collected a great army and when he met Nayan in battle, Marco Polo writes:

'Kublai took his station in a large wooden castle, borne on the backs of four elephants, whose bodies were protected with coverings of thick leather hardened by fire, over which were housings of cloth of gold. The castle contained many cross-bow men and archers, and on top of it was hoisted the imperial standard, adorned with representations of the Sun and Moon.'

Later when writing of Kublai Khan's hunting expeditions, he tells us:

'On account of the narrowness of the passes in some parts of the country where the Grand Khan follows the chase, he is borne upon two elephants only, and sometimes a single one, being more convenient than a greater number; but under other circumstances he makes use of four, upon the backs of which is placed a pavilion of wood, handsomely carved, the inside being lined with cloth of gold, and the outside covered with the skins of lions, a mode of conveyance which is rendered necessary to him during his hunting excursions, in consequence of the gout with which he is troubled.'

It is, however, when we come to the account of his struggle with the king of Mien and Bangala culminating in the battle of Vochang that we hear how Kublai's general Nestardin (a corruption of the Moslem name Nasr-eddin) dealt with the large number of elephants in the army of the king:

'When the king of Mien and Bangala, in India, who was powerful in the number of his subjects, in extent of territory, and in wealth, heard that an army of Tartars had arrived in Vochang, he took the resolution of advancing immediately to attack it, in order that by its destruction the Grand Khan should be deterred from again attempting to station a force upon the borders of his dominions.

'For this purpose he assembled a very large army, including a multitude of elephants (an animal with which his country abounds) upon whose backs were placed battlements or castles, of wood, capable of containing to the number of twelve or sixteen men in each. With these and a numerous army of horse and foot, he took the road to Vochang, where the Grand Khan's army lay and encamping at no great distance from it, intended to give his troops a few days of rest.

'As soon as the approach of the king of Mien, with so great a force, was known to Nestardin, who commanded the troops of the Grand Khan, although a brave and able officer, he felt much alarmed, not having under his orders more than twelve thousand men (veterans indeed, and valiant soldiers), whereas the enemy had sixty thousand, besides the elephants armed as has been described. He did not, however, betray any sign of apprehension, but descending into the plain of Vochang, took a position in which his flank was covered by a thick wood of large trees, whither, in case of a furious charge by the elephants, which his troops might not be able to sustain, they could retire, and from thence, in security, annoy them with their arrows.

'Calling together the principal officers of his army, he exhorted them not to display less valour on the present occasion than they had done in all their preceding engagements, reminding them that victory did not depend upon the number of men, but upon courage and discipline.

He represented to them that the troops of the king of Mien and Bangala were raw and unpractised in the art of war, not having had the opportunities of acquiring experience that had fallen to their lot; that instead of being discouraged by the superior number of their foes, they ought to feel confidence in their own valour so often put to the test; that their very name was a subject of terror, not merely to the enemy before them, but to the whole world, and he concluded by promising to lead them to certain victory.

'Upon the king of Mien's learning that the Tartars had descended into the plain, he immediately put his army into motion, took up his ground at the distance of about a mile from the enemy, and made a disposition of his force, placing the elephants in the front, and the cavalry and infantry, in two extended wings, in their rear, but leaving between them a considerable interval. Here he took his own station, and proceeded to animate his men and encourage them to fight valiantly, assuring them of victory, as well from the superiority of their numbers, being four to one, as from their formidable body of armed elephants, whose shock the enemy, who had never before been engaged with such combatants, could by no means resist.

'Then giving the order for sounding a prodigious number of warlike instruments, he advanced boldly with his whole army towards that of the Tartars, which remained firm, making no movement, but suffering them to approach their entrenchments.

'They then rushed out with great spirit in the utmost eagerness to engage but it was soon found that the Tartar horses, unused to the sight of such huge animals, with their castles, were terrified, and wheeling about endeavoured to fly; nor could their riders by any exertions restrain them, whilst the king, with the whole of his force, was every moment gaining ground.

'As soon as the prudent commander perceived this unexpected disorder, without losing his presence of mind, he instantly adopted the measure of ordering his men to dismount and their horses to be taken into the wood, where they were fastened to the trees. When dismounted, the men, without loss of time, advanced on foot towards the line of elephants, and commenced a brisk discharge of arrows, whilst, on the other side, those who were stationed in the castles, and the rest of the king's army, shot volleys in return with great activity; but their arrows did not make the same impression as those of the Tartars, whose bows were drawn with a stronger arm.

'So incessant were the discharges of the latter, and all their weapons (according to the instructions of their commander) being directed against the elephants, these were soon covered with arrows and suddenly giving way, fell back upon their own people in the rear, who were thereby thrown into confusion.

'It soon became impossible for their drivers to manage them, either by force or address. Smarting under the pain of their wounds, and terrified by the shouting of the assailants, they were no longer governable, but without guidance or control ran about in all directions, until at length, impelled by rage and fear, they rushed into a part of the wood not occupied by the Tartars. The consequence of this was, that from the closeness of the branches of large trees, they broke, with loud crashes, the battlements and castles that were upon their backs, and involved in the destruction those who sat upon them.

'Upon seeing the rout of the elephants the Tartars acquired fresh courage, and filing off by detachments, with perfect order and regularity, they remounted their horses, and joined their several divisions, where a sanguinary and dreadful combat was renewed. On the part of the king's troops there was no want of valour, and he himself was amongst the ranks entreating them to stand firm, and not to be alarmed by the accident that had befallen the elephants. But the Tartars, by their consummate skill in archery, were too powerful for them, and galled them the more exceedingly, from their not being provided with such armour as was worn by the former. The arrows having been expended on both sides, the men grasped their swords and iron maces, and violently encountered each other. Then in an instant were to be seen many horrible wounds, limbs dismembered, and multitudes falling to the ground, maimed and dying; with such effusion of blood as was dreadful to behold. So great also was the clangour of arms, and such the shoutings and the shrieks, that the noise seemed to ascend to the skies.

'The king of Mien, acting as became a valiant chief, was present wherever the greatest danger appeared, animating his soldiers, and beseeching them to maintain their ground with resolution. He ordered fresh squadrons from the reserve to advance to the support of those that were exhausted; but perceiving at length that it was impossible any longer to sustain the conflict or to withstand the impetuosity of the Tartars, the greater part of his troops being either killed or wounded, and all the

# Elephants and Kublai Khan

field covered with the carcasses of horses, whilst those who survived were beginning to give way, he also found himself compelled to take to flight with the wreck of his army, numbers of whom were afterwards slain in the pursuit.

'The losses in this battle, which lasted from the morning till noon, were severely felt on both sides; but the Tartars were finally victorious; a result that was materially to be attributed to the troops of the king of Mien and Bangala not wearing armour as the Tartars did, and to their elephants, especially those of the foremost line, being equally without that kind of defence, which, by enabling them to sustain the first discharges of the enemy's arrows, would have allowed them to break his ranks and throw him into disorder.

'A point perhaps of still greater importance is that the king ought not to have made his attack on the Tartars in a position where their flank was supported by a wood, but should have endeavoured to draw them into the open country where they could not have resisted the first impetuous onset of the armed elephants, and where, by extending the cavalry of his two wings, he might have surrounded them.

'The Tartars having collected their force, after the slaughter of the enemy, returned towards the wood into which the elephants had fled for shelter, in order to take possession of them, where they found that the men who had escaped from the overthrow were employed in cutting down trees or barricading the passages, with the intent of defending themselves. But their ramparts were soon demolished by the Tartars, who slew many of them, and with the assistance of the persons accustomed to the management of the elephants, they possessed themselves of these to the number of two hundred or more.

'From the period of this battle the Grand Khan has always chosen to employ elephants in his armies, which before that time he had not done. The consequences of the victory were, that he acquired possession of the whole of the territories of the king of Bangala and Mien, and annexed them to his dominions.'

Writing later of Zanzibar, Marco Polo describes how the natives of the island used elephants:

'They have no horses, but fight upon elephants and camels. Upon the backs of the former they place castles, capable of holding from fifteen to twenty men, armed with swords, lances and stones, with which weapons they fight. Previous to the combat they give draughts of wine to their elephants, supposing that it renders them more spirited and more furious in the assault.'

### Note

Some have argued that there is no evidence that the inhabitants of Zanzibar or the neighbouring coasts of Africa ever trained elephants for domestic or warlike use and that Marco Polo mixed up Zanzibar with possibly Ceylon. Mungo Park, the famous African explorer, however, agrees that as Hannibal used trained African elephants, it is quite reasonable to suppose the same applied to other parts of Africa.

The reference to wine may be compared with the account of Ptolemy Philopator in the *Third Book of the Maccabees* and the stimulation of the elephants with wine and frankincense.

Accounts taken from the travels of Marco Polo

# Akbar's elephants

Akbar, or to give him his full name, Jalal Ud-din Mohammed Akbar, was the greatest of the Mogul, or Mughal, Emperors. He lived from 1542 until 1605. At his death his dominions stretched from the Hindu Kush nearly to Hyderabad and from Bengal to Gujerat. He was enlightened and tolerant although an autocrat. He had a genius for administration and his rule was based on compromise. He was greatly interested in the study of comparative religion.

Most of the information about Akbar comes from the *Akbarnama*, compiled by Abu-l-Fazl Allami, Akbar's secretary of state and written on Akbar's order. That and the *Ain I Akbari*, the 'Institutes of Akbar' are the principal sources for the history of Akbar. In these Abu-l-Fazl describes Akbar's establishment of elephants, of which he had many thousands, and the use he made of them. The translation from the original Persian was made by H. Blochmann and H. S. Jarrett.

## The Imperial elephant stables

This wonderful animal is in bulk and strength like a mountain; and in courage and ferocity like a lion. It adds materially to the pomp of a king and to the success of a conqueror; and is of the greatest use for the army. Experienced men of Hindustan put the value of a good elephant equal to five hundred horse; and they believe, that when guided by a few bold men armed with matchlocks, such an elephant alone is worth double that number. In vehemence on one side, and submissiveness to the reins on the other, the elephant is like an Arab, whilst in point of obedience and attentiveness to even the slightest signs, it resembles an intelligent human being. In restiveness when full-blooded, and in vindictiveness, it surpasses man. An elephant never hurts the female though she be the cause of his captivity; he never will fight with young elephants, nor does he think it proper to punish them. From a sense of gratitude, he does his keepers no harm, nor will he throw dust over his body, when he is mounted, though he often does so at other times. Once an elephant, during the rutting season, was fighting with another. When he was in the height of excitement, a small elephant came in his way: he kindly lifted up the small one with his trunk, set him aside and renewed the combat. If a male elephant breaks loose during the rutting season, in order to have his own way, few people have the courage to approach him; and some bold and experienced man will have to get on a female elephant, and try to get near him and tie a rope round his foot. Female elephants, when mourning the loss of a young one, will often abstain from food and drink; they sometimes even die from grief.

The elephant can be taught various feats. He learns to remember such melodies as can only be remembered by people acquainted with music; he will move his limbs, to keep time, and exhibit his skill in various ways. He will shoot off an arrow from a bow, discharge a matchlock, and will learn to pick up things that have been dropped, and hand them over to the keeper. Sometimes they get grain to eat wrapped up in hay; this they hide in the side of their mouth, and give it back to the keeper, when they are alone with him.

The price of an elephant varies from a lak to one hundred rupees; elephants worth five thousand, and ten thousand rupees, are pretty common. There are four kinds of elephants:

1 *Bhaddar*. It is well proportioned, has an erect head, a broad chest, large ears, a long tail, and is bold, and can bear fatigue. They take out of his forehead an excrescence resembling a large pearl, which they call in Hindi *Gaj manik*. Many properties are ascribed to it.
2 *Mand*. It is black, has yellow eyes and is wild and ungovernable.
3 *Mirg*. It has a whitish skin, with black spots; the colour of its eyes is a mixture of red, yellow, black, and white.
4 *Mir*. It has a small head, and obeys readily. It gets frightened, when it thunders.

From a mixture of these four kinds are formed others of different names and properties. The colour of the skin of elephants is threefold: white, black, grey. Again, according to the three-fold division of the dispositions assigned by the Hindus to the mind, namely, *sat* benevolence, *raj* love of sensual enjoyment, and *tam* irascibility, which shall be further explained below, elephants are divided into three classes. *First*, such in which *sat* predominates. They are well proportioned, good-looking, eat moderately, are very submissive, do not care for intercourse with the female, and live to a very old age. *Secondly* such in whose disposition *raj* prevails. They are savage looking, and proud, bold, ungovernable, and voracious. *Lastly*, such as are full of *tam*. They are self-willed, destructive, and given to sleep and voraciousness.

The elephant, like man, lives to an age of one hundred and twenty years.

The Hindi language has several words for an elephant, as *hasti*, *gaj*, *pil*, *hat'hi*, etc. Under the hands of an experienced keeper, it will much improve, so that its value, in a short time, may rise from one hundred to ten thousand rupees.

The Hindus believe that the eight points of the earth are each guarded by a heavenly being in the shape of an elephant; they have curious legends regarding them. Their names are as follows:

| | | | |
|---|---|---|---|
| 1 *Airawata*, in the East | | 5 *Anjan*, West | |
| 2 *Pundarika*, South-east | | 6 *Puhpadanta*, North-west | |
| 3 *Báman*, South | | 7 *Sárbhabhúma*, North | |
| 4 *Kumada*, South-west | | 8 *Supratika*, North-east. | |

When occasions arise, people read incantations in their names, and address them in worship. They also think that every elephant in the world is the offspring of one of them. Thus, elephants of a white skin and white hairs are related to the first; elephants with a large head, and long hairs, of a fierce and bold temper, and eyelids far apart, belong to the second; such as are graceful, good-looking, black, and high in the back, are the offspring of the third; if tall, ungovernable, quick in understanding, short-haired, and with red and black eyes, they come from the fourth; if bright black, with one tusk longer than the other, with a white breast and belly, and long and thick fore-feet, from the fifth; if fearful, with prominent veins, with a short hump and ears, and a long trunk, from the sixth; if thin-bellied, red-eyed, and with a long trunk, from the seventh; and if of a combination of the preceding seven qualities, from the eighth.

A herd of elephants is called in Hindi *sahn*. They vary in number; sometimes a herd amounts to a thousand elephants. Wild elephants are very cautious. In winter and summer, they select a proper place, and break down a whole forest near their sleeping place. For the sake of pleasure, or for food and drink, they often travel over great distances. On the journey one runs far in front of the others, like a sentinel; a young female is generally selected for this purpose. When they go to sleep, they send out to the four sides of the sleeping place pickets of four female elephants, which relieve each other.

Elephants will lift up their young ones, for three or four days after their birth, with their trunks, and put them on their backs, or lay them over their tusks. They also prepare medicines for the females when they are sick or in labour pains, and crowd round about them. When some of them get caught, the female elephants break through the nets, and pull down the elephant-drivers. And when a young elephant falls into a snare, they hide themselves in an ambush, go at night to the place where the young one is, set it at liberty, and trample the hunters to death. Sometimes its mother slowly approaches alone, and frees it in some clever way. I have heard the following story from his Majesty. 'Once a wild young one had fallen into a pit. As night had approached, we did not care to pull it out immediately, and left it; but when we came next morning near the place, we saw that some wild elephants had filled the pit with broken logs and grass, and thus pulled out the young one.' Again, 'Once a female elephant played us a trick. She feigned to be dead. We passed her, and went onwards; but when at night we returned we saw no trace left of her.'

There was once an elephant in the Imperial stables, named *Ayáz*. For some reason, it had got offended with the driver, and was for ever watching for an opportunity. Once at night, it found him asleep. It got hold of a long piece of wood, managed to pull off with it the man's turban, seized him by the hair, and tore him asunder.

Many examples are on record of the extraordinary cleverness of elephants; in some cases it is difficult to believe them.

Kings have always shown a great predilection for this animal, and done everything in their power to collect a large number. Elephant-keepers are much esteemed, and a proper rank is assigned to such as have a special knowledge of the animal. Wicked, low men see in an elephant a means of lawlessness; and unprincipled evildoers, with the help of this animal, carry on their nefarious trade. Hence kings of former times never succeeded in suppressing the rebellious, and were thus disappointed in their best intentions. But His Majesty, though overwhelmed with other important matters, has been able, through God's assistance and his numerous elephants, to check those low but haughty men; he teaches them to desire submission, and bestows upon them, by wise laws, the blessings of peace.

His Majesty divided the Imperial elephants into sections, which he put in charge of honest Dároghahs. Certain elephants were also declared *kháçah*, i.e., appointed for the exclusive use of His Majesty.

G

## The classification of the Imperial elephants

His Majesty made a seven-fold division, based upon experience:

1 *Mast* (full blood)
2 *Shergir* (tiger-seizing)
3 *Sadah* (plain)
4 *Manjholah* (middlemost)

5 *Karha*
6 *P'handurkiya*
7 *Mokal*

## The servants of the elephant stables

1 *Mast* elephants. There are five and a half servants for each, *viz.*, *first*, a *Maháwat*, who sits on the neck of the animal and directs its movements. He must be acquainted with its good and bad properties, thus contribute to its usefulness. He gets 200 *dáms* per month; but if the elephant be *k'hutahar*, i.e. wicked and addicted to pulling down the driver, he gets 220d. *Secondly*, a *Bhoi*, who sits behind, upon the rump of the elephant, and assists in battle and in quickening the speed of the animal; but he often performs the duties of the *Maháwat*. His monthly pay is 110d. *Thirdly*, the *Met'hs*, of whom there are three and one-half, or only three in case of small elephants. A met'h fetches fodder, and assists in caparisoning the elephant. Met'hs of all classes get on the march four dáms daily, and at other times, three and a half.
2 For every *Shergir* there are five servants.
3 For every *Sadah*, there are four and a half servants.
4 For every *Manjholah*, there are four servants.
5 For every *Karha*, there are three and a half servants.
6 For every *P'handurkiya*, there are two servants.
7 For every *Mokal*, there are likewise two servants.
   *Female Elephants*, large ones have four servants.

## The Faujdár

His Majesty has appointed a Superintendent over every troop of ten, twenty, and thirty, elephants. Such a troop is called a *halqah*; the super-intendent is called *Faujdár*. His business is to look after the condition and the training of the elephants; he teaches them to be bold, and to stand firm at the sight of fire, and at the noise of artillery; and he is re-sponsible for their behaviour in these respects. When a Faujdár is raised to the dignity of a *Çadi* (a commander of one hundred), or higher, he has twenty-five elephants assigned to himself, the other Faujdárs, as *Bistis* (commanders of twenty) and *Dahbashis* (commanders of ten) being under his orders. The same order is followed from the *Dahbashis* up to the *Hazáris* (commanders of one thousand). The pay of officers above the *Çadi* is different. Some Faujdárs have been raised to the dignity of grandees of the court.

### The elephants for His Majesty's use (Kháçah)

There are one hundred and one elephants selected for the use of His Majesty. Their allowance of food is the same in quantity as that of the other elephants, but differs in quality. Most of them also get 5s. of sugar, 4s. of g'hi and half a *man* of rice mixed with chillies, cloves, etc.; and some have one and a half *man* of milk in addition to their grain. In the sugar-cane season, each elephant gets daily, for two months, 300 sugar-canes, more or less. His Majesty takes the place of the *Mahāwat*.

Each elephant requires three *bhois* in the rutting season, and two, when cool. Their monthly wages vary from 120 to 400d., and are fixed by His Majesty himself. For each elephant there are four *Met'hs*. In the *Halqahs*, female elephants are but rarely told off to accompany big male ones; but for each *kháçah* elephant there are three, and sometimes even more, appointed. First class big female elephants have two and one-half met'hs; second class do., two; third class do., one and one-half; for the other classes, the same as in the *Halqahs*.

As each *Halqah* is in charge of one of the Grandees, so is every *kháçah* elephant put in charge of one of them. Likewise, for every ten *kháçah* elephants, a professional man is appointed, who is called *Dahaidar*. They draw twelve, ten, and eight rupees *per mensem*. Besides, an active and honest superintendent is appointed for every ten elephants. He is called *Naqib* (watcher), and has to submit a daily report, when elephants eat little, or get a shortened allowance, or in cases of sickness, or when anything unusual happens. He marks a horse, and holds the rank of an *Ahadi*. His Majesty also weekly dispatches some of the servants near him, in the proportion of one for every ten elephants, who inspect them and send in a report.

### The manner of riding Kháçah-elephants

His Majesty, the royal rider of the plain of auspiciousness, mounts on every kind of elephants, from the first to the last class, making them, notwithstanding their almost supernatural strength, obedient to his command. His Majesty will put his foot on the tusks, and mount them even when they are in the rutting season, and astonishes experienced people.

They also put comfortable turrets on the backs of swift-paced elephants, which serve as a travelling sleeping apartment. An elephant so caparisoned, is always ready at the palace.

Whenever His Majesty mounts an elephant, a month's wages are given as a donation to the Bhois.

### The muster of elephants

The beginning of the musters is made with this animal. The *Kháçah* elephants with their furniture and ornaments are the first which are daily brought before His Majesty, namely ten on the first day of every solar month. After this, the *Halqah* elephants are mustered according to their number. On Tuesdays from ten to twenty are mustered. The Bitikchi, during the muster, must be ready to answer any questions as to the name of each animal (there are more than five thousand elephants, each having a different name. His Majesty knows to which section most of the elephants belong—ten elephants form a section of ten (*dahai*), and are in charge of an experienced officer); as to how each elephant came into the possession of His Majesty; the price; the quantity of food; the age of the animal; where it was born; the period of heat, and the duration of that state each time; the date when an elephant was made *kháçah*; its promotion in the *halqahs*; the time when the tusks are cut; how many times His Majesty has mounted it; how many times it was brought for riding out; the time of the last muster; the condition of the keepers; the name of the Amir in charge. For all other elephants eight things are to be reported, *viz.*, the change of its name; the repetition of it; its price; how it came into the possession of His Majesty; whether it is fit for riding, or for carrying burdens; its rank; whether it has plain furniture or not; which rank the Faujdár has assigned to it. The rule is, that every Faujdár divides his elephants into four classes, separating those that are best from those that are worst, whether they are to remain with him, or whether he has to give some to other Faujdárs.

Each day five *tahwili* (transferable) elephants are inspected by an experienced man. The following custom is observed: When new elephants arrive for the government, they are handed over in fifties or hundreds to experienced officers, who fix their ranks. Such elephants are called *Tahwili* elephants. When His Majesty inspects them, their rank is finally settled, and the elephants are transferred to the proper sections. Every Sunday one elephant is brought before His Majesty, to be given away as a present to some deserving servant. Several *halqahs* are set apart for this purpose. The rank of the *kháçah* elephants formerly depended on the number of times they had been inspected by His Majesty; but now their precedence is fixed by the number of times His Majesty has mounted them. In the *halqahs* the precedence of elephants is determined by the price. When all elephants have been mustered, the kháçah elephants are again examined, ten every day. Then come the elephants of the princes, who mostly march them past themselves. After them come the halqahs. As they are arranged in sections according to the price, some elephants have, at every muster, their value either enhanced or lowered, and are then put among their equals. For this reason, many Faujdárs are anxious to complete their sets, and place themselves for this purpose in a row at the time of the musters. His Majesty then gives the elephants to whomsoever he likes. If the number of the elephants of any Faujdár is found correct, some more are put in his charge; for such officers are thought of first. Faujdárs, whose elephants are found to be lean, are preferred, in making up the complements, to such as bring less than their original number. Each Faujdár receives some, provided he musters all his elephants. The Mushrif (accountant) receives orders where to keep the elephants.

The elephants of the grandees also, though not belonging to the fixed establishment, are almost daily brought before His Majesty, who settles their ranks, and orders them to be branded with a peculiar mark. Elephants of dealers are also brought before His Majesty, who fixes their rank and value.

## Elephant-hunts

There are several modes of hunting elephants:
1 *K'hedah.* The hunters are both on horseback and on foot. They go during summer to the grazing places of this wonderful animal, and commence to beat drums and blow the pipes, the noise of which makes the elephants quite frightened. They commence to rush about, till from their heaviness and exertions no strength is left in them. They are then sure to run under a tree for shade, when some experienced hunters throw a rope, made of hemp or bark, round their feet or necks, and thus tie them to the trees. They are afterwards led off in company with some trained elephants, and gradually get tame. One-fourth of the value of an elephant thus caught is given to the hunters as wages.
2 *Chor k'hedah.* They take a tame female elephant to the grazing place of wild elephants, the driver stretching himself on the back of the elephant, without moving or giving any other sign of his presence. The elephants then commence to fight, when the driver manages to secure one by throwing a rope round the foot.
3 *Gad.* A deep pit is constructed in a place frequented by elephants, which is covered up with grass. As soon as the elephants come near it, the hunters from their ambush commence to make a great noise. The elephants get confused, and losing their habitual cautiousness, they fall rapidly and noisily into the hole. They are then starved and kept without water, when they soon get tame.
4 *Bar.* They dig a ditch round the resting place of elephants, leaving only one road open, before which they put up a door, which is fastened with ropes. The door is left open, but closes when the rope is cut. The hunters then put both inside and outside the door such food as elephants like. The elephants eat it up greedily; their voraciousness makes them forget all cautiousness, and without fear they enter at the door. A fearless hunter, who has been lying concealed, then cuts the rope, and the door closes. The elephants start up, and in their fury try to break the door. They are all in commotion. The hunters then kindle fires and make much noise. The elephants run about till they get tired, and no strength is left in them. Tame females are then brought to the place, by whose means the wild elephants are caught. They soon get tame.

From times of old, people have enjoyed elephant hunts by any of the above modes; His Majesty has invented a new manner, which admits of remarkable *finesse.* In fact, all excellent modes of hunting are inventions of His Majesty. A wild herd of elephants is surrounded on three sides by drivers, one side alone being left open. At it several female elephants are stationed. From all sides, the male elephants will approach to cover the females. The latter then go gradually into an enclosure, whither the males follow. They are now caught as shown above.

## The names of the King's elephants

The names of the chief elephants on which the king rides, are as follows:

| | |
|---|---|
| Aurang-gaj | Throne-elephant, the Captain of all the Elephants |
| Khaliq-dad | Creator-given |
| Maimun-mubarak | Highly Sedate |
| Khuda-dad | God-given |
| Sarv-sairat | Pretty Artist |
| Rel-kasha | The Worker |
| Dil-pasand | Heart's Friend |
| Bakht-Bahadur | Valiant with the Cut Ear |
| Yak-danta | One-tusked |
| Kabra (Hindi) | Enamelled Head (or Speckled) |
| Mudam-mast | Ever bold |
| Sada-mast | Always Drunk |
| Nimtao | Expert |
| Dil-kusha | Heart-opener |
| Baba-bakhsh | Father's Gift |
| Nek-bakht | Handsome |
| Maknah | Tuskless |
| Kamari | Short (in back) |
| Buland | Tall |
| Sarila | Polished |
| Latif | Exquisite |
| Nar Singh | Male Lion |
| *Kh*ub-rau | Fine Mover |
| Fath Mubarak | Fortune of Victory |
| Dil-Diler | Heart of Hearts |
| Shah-inayat | Royal Gift |
| Inayat-bakhsh | Gift of Grace |
| Allah-bakhsh | God-protected |
| Fath-nusrat | Victor Victorious |
| Da,im-shukok | Ever Great |
| Dilasa-sairat | Polished Face |
| Fath-jang | Victory in War |
| Fath-lashkar | Army Conqueror |
| Ran-jit | Overcomer in War |
| Dal-singar | Army Ornament |
| Lashkar-sobha | Army Beauty |
| Dushman-kush | Enemy-treader |
| Kala-pahar | Black Mountain |
| Ghussah-war | Industrious |
| Kashawar-kasha | Faithful Worker |
| Zalzalah | Earth-shaker |
| *Kh*uni | The Slayer |
| *Kh*auf-nak | Frightener |
| Madan-mohan | Heart-ravisher |
| Maha-mohan | Amorous |
| Uttam | Exquisite |

| Bagh-mar | Lion-slayer |
|---|---|
| Pur-i-zor | Full of Strength |
| Mah-ru | Moon-faced |
| Sitara | Star |
| *Ka*shawar-*gh*arur | The Proud |
| Sundar-gaj | Good Name |
| Pae-ta*kh*t | Foot of the Throne |
| Atashi | Burning |
| Nur | Dawn |
| La'l | Ruby |
| Hira | Diamond |
| *Kh*ush-raftar | Good Mover |
| Tez-rau | Quick Walker |
| Manik-surat | Pearl-like |
| Baghela | Lion's Whelp |
| Da,im-nasr | Always Advancing |
| Chand-kunwar | Good Ball |
| Qila'h-shikan | Fortress-destroyer |
| Koh-shikan | Mountain-destroyer |
| *Kh*ush-sakil | Supreme Beauty |

The greater number of these names are Hindu. Gas (gaj) means an elephant, and although several slaves, of one and the other sex, have similar names, one must not be astonished, for the king gives these names according to his fancy or some aptitude he detects in these animals.

## The training and use of elephants

Usually the king has one hundred very tall elephants which he uses himself, and there are also female elephants, on whom he does not disdain to ride. All the elephants he rides are trained to stand fire of both artillery and musketry, of rockets, and other fireworks. This is done so that when they come across such things they may not be afraid. Others are taught not be frightened of tigers or of lions, so that they may be used in hunting. To teach them, they take a tiger-skin or lion-skin, and stuff it with straw. Then, just as if it were alive, they move it here and there by a rope. The driver encourages the elephant, and urges him towards the dummy, which with feet and trunk he tears to pieces. The elephants are well looked after; they are given spirits to drink to increase their courage in a fight. It is the rule that there shall always be one elephant on sentry duty day and night on the river bank, stationed within a little gateway just underneath the royal seat.

Among these animals is one stronger and taller than the rest which bears the title of 'General of the Elephants'. When he appears at court he is very richly caparisoned, and attended by a number of other elephants, by flutes, trumpets, cymbals, and flags, all of which makes a grand show. The chief elephants have every day for their ration each one hundred and sixty-five pounds of food-stuff—namely, flour, rice, meat, butter, fine spices and thirty pounds of sugar-cane. This is in addition to straw, grass, and leaves, for which they have twenty-five rupees a day. To wait on each elephant there are ten servants—that is, two drivers to ride on and direct him; two to fix on his chains; two men with spears; two for the fireworks and to assist the others if necessary; one to remove the dung, and another to give him water for drinking and cooling himself. All these men are paid out of the twenty-five rupees a day allotted to the elephant, and these attendants have each four rupees a month, besides what they can steal from the elephant's food.

In addition to the above elephants there are fourteen hundred others that are employed to carry the queens, princesses, and the prince's concubines, the tents, the baggage, and the kitchen utensils. The strongest of all, who have no tusks, draw the heavy artillery over difficult ground and perform such-like duties. The lowest among them has three rupees a day and three servants. All the elephants move with bells attached to their body, serving to warn the passers-by and give them time to move and get out of the way; for when an elephant runs, or merely walks, he does not stop like a horse would.

When the king makes them (the elephants) fight, the wives of the drivers remove their ornaments, smash their bracelets, and put on mourning, just as if they were widows. If their husbands come back alive they give a great feast, just as if newly married; for in these encounters and combats the drivers put their lives in great jeopardy, as I have seen several times. Moreover, though these animals are enormously strong, they do not have long lives, for often they fall suddenly to the ground and die in a short time. For, once they have fallen down, there is no hope of getting them up again; that is why they remove their tusks and leave them where they are.

28  Arms of Sir Andrew Fountaine, 1753; Narford, Norfolk

29  Elephant and castle; 13th-cent. floor tile, Dunkeswell Abbey (Holy Trinity), Devon

30  Elephant and castle; 15th-cent. misericord, Beverley, St Mary

31 Brass on tomb of Dame Margaret Vernon, 1467; Tong Church, Salop

32 Detail from Corbet tomb
33 Corbet tomb, 1567; Moreton Corbet Church, Salop

34 Battle scene with elephants and pigs

35 Elephant presented to Henry III, 1255

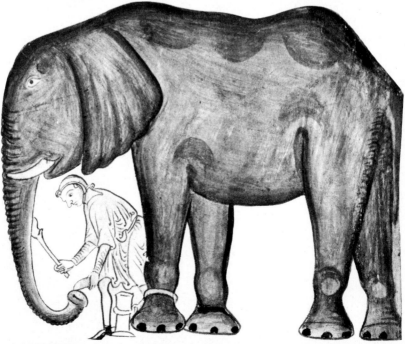

36 (*overleaf*) Battle scene from *Romance of Alexander*, 1463; done for Charles the Bold

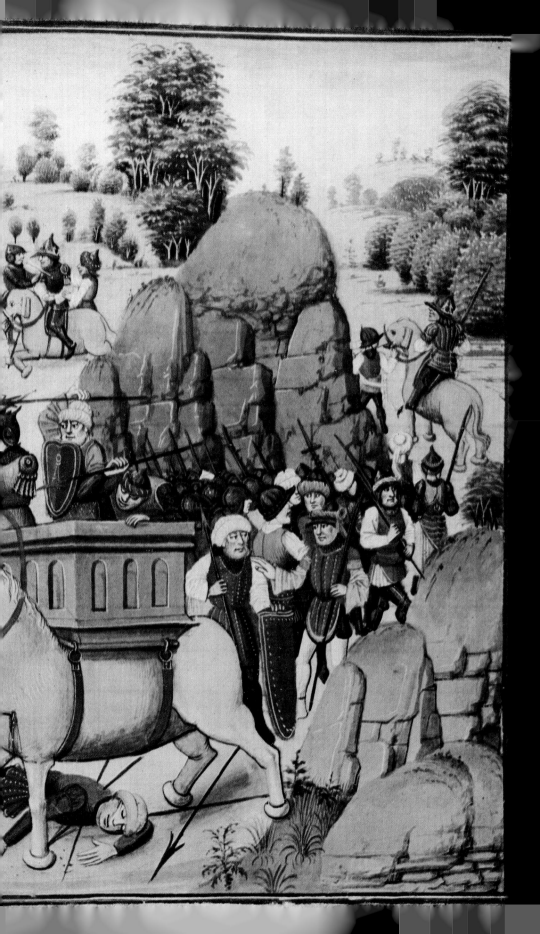

37 (*opposite*) Detail from Indian (Mughal) ivory and ebony chest

38 Elephant and Adam on ivory cabinet from Ceylon; *c.* 1700

39 Siculo-Arabic ivory drinking horn; 11th or 12th cent.

# Some elephant tales

### The boy in the tree

There was a youth who was a great hunter. Leaving his companions, he penetrated far into the forest, and close to a river he met an elephant. Seeing the danger to his life if he were pursued, he climbed on to a large tree. Coming after the youth, the elephant, in the hope of seizing him, broke off branches and tried hard to knock the tree down. Finding this impossible, it trumpeted loudly, whereupon there came up a female elephant blind of one eye. The two together recommenced pushing at the tree to uproot it. Seeing that the tree did not move, they began to strike at the roots with their feet. But the earth was too hard, and the female was left on guard at the foot of the tree while the male went to the river as fast as he could go to fetch water in his trunk. He emptied it at the foot of the tree and began to strike, so that the tree shook. The poor youth was in a great fright, realizing his danger; but noticing that the female was one-eyed, when the male elephant went for more water the youth hastily descended from the tree on the side of her blind eye and scrambled up a larger tree, whence he watched what they were doing, still somewhat perturbed. The two elephants worked at the tree till they had uprooted it. When they failed to find the youth, the male broke off a branch and gave the female a sound beating, and pursuing her, they disappeared. The elephant had continued its efforts from eight o'clock in the morning until two in the afternoon. The youth awaited nightfall, and then set out to find his companions. From that time forth he never attempted again to follow the chase.

### Shepherd-boy becomes King

They say that formerly there died a King of Arakan without leaving a successor, at a time when the nobles were in discord and each one wished himself to become king. In the end they decided to let the chief royal elephant loose outside the city, and he who should return mounted on it would be made king. After three days the elephant appeared in front of the royal palace with a boy upon his back. The lad was the son of a shepherd; but he was accepted as king.

### The elephant and the wood-cutter

It is also said that there was a man whose only livelihood was the sale of wood, which he brought in person from the forest. Going one day on this business, he found a great stack of wood. He was quite astonished at the quantity collected between one day and the next, yet no one else went to collect wood at that spot. When he arrived opposite the wood-pile to bind his bundle, there suddenly came out an elephant who had been hiding behind it, and had collected all the wood. It seized him without hurting him, and lying down on the ground, it showed him one of its feet, in which a great thorn had stuck. The wood-cutter understood that it wanted help, and plucked out the thorn for him. The

H

elephant rose and moved a pace or two, and tried if his foot still hurt him; then, going to the heap, laid hold with his trunk of a quantity of wood, and went off along the road to the man's home. Seeing that the elephant was doing him service, he followed. It went with him to a certain point and deposited the wood on the ground; then, raising its trunk, it stood before the man a moment or two in sign of gratitude, and departed. The wood-cutter went home with his bundle. Next day he went out to his work as usual, and at the same place where he had parted from the elephant he found a large quantity of wood placed there by it. Ever afterwards it left wood at the same spot, and the man was saved the trouble of a long journey for it.

## The elephant's 'steady'

Among the many elephants owned by the King of Gulkandah, he had one very lofty and superb animal, which the king valued most highly. This elephant formed a great affection for a young girl who lived close to its stable; and every time the elephant was fed with various kinds of grain, cooked food, and sugar-cane, it threw a portion with its trunk to the girl. She, being used to the elephant, would go up to him fearlessly, and would walk beneath him and between his legs without being hurt. The older she grew, the greater was the elephant's affection.

Aurangzeb heard that the King of Gulkandah had this fine elephant; and as he was accustomed to demand all that was best in that kingdom, he directed the king to send it. Unable to make denial, the king ordered the elephant to be sent. When it saw itself outside the city, and knew it was going a long journey, it got out of hand and would not obey the drivers, but returned to its stable. Whenever they began the journey, the same thing occurred. In time they recognised that he would not start, through the affection he bore to the child. On being assured of this, they reported to the king. Orders were given to send the girl with him, also her parents, and then he proceeded on his way without any difficulty. On reaching the Mogul's court the king was told of the affair, and he granted pay for the girl and her parents. The girl when she grew up drove this elephant, and it obeyed her without hesitation.

## A grateful elephant

These animals are most grateful, and recognise any benefit done them; they also feel an injury, and when the opportunity arises take a cruel revenge. This have I seen suffered by many an elephant-driver for the ill-treatment he had been guilty of, some because of stealing their food and not giving them their full rations, others for having without cause struck and abused them. It happened to me once that I was attending a princess, entering and issuing by a great courtyard, where I saw collected together her horses and elephants. On my leaving, the princess presented me with some betel leaf. I passed near an elephant, and holding out my hand, offered it the betel leaf. It put out its trunk, took it, placed it in its mouth and ate it. Every time I came out of the palace it recognised me, and put out its trunk, and I made over to it all the betel I had received. In a short time the princess recovered, and I went no more to the house. A year afterwards I was passing through the city with some horsemen in my train, when an elephant approached me with its trunk raised, and followed me. I cried out angrily to the driver to keep his elephant under control. He answered that the elephant knew me again and wanted betel leaf, to which he had become accustomed on my visits to the princess's house.

## A delicate attention

One day, coming from the palace, I passed through a street, where I saw many elephants collected before the door of Momencan (Mumin Khan), the official in charge of them. He was seated at the door of his mansion and seeing me, called to me. I got down from my horse and walked between the elephants, which stood very close to each other. Near the door the space was very narrow, and I could hardly pass. I put my hand on the trunk of a small female elephant to make it give way. It could not move aside, and without my imagining such a thing, it suddenly put its trunk between my legs and deposited me lightly in a shop close by, which was full of gurguris (pottery pipe-heads), from which the Mahomedans smoke tobacco, and as I subsided I heard a great disturbance of cooking-pots, gurguris, and other crockery; though put out at finding myself in such a state, without any turban on my head, I was not hurt in any way. The female elephant put her trunk into her mouth and trumpeted loudly. This was to show she was in fault, but that the crowded position in which she found herself had forced her to take such a course.

## Chastiser of elephants

When Mahabat Khan was governor of Gujarat, he kept many elephants. Among them were some very choice, large, and handsome. The driver in charge of the chief of these elephants (its name was Zalzalah—that is, 'Earthquake') bore a grudge against a greengrocer. To revenge himself, he went past the man's shop, and, halting the elephant, gave it a sign. It set to work with its trunk and scattered the whole of the goods in all directions—radishes, turnips, garlic, onions, lemons, and so forth.

In the confusion, a bull belonging to the vegetable-seller, which had been tied up close by, broke its rope and pursued the elephant, prodding it between the legs from behind with its horns. The elephant, not accustomed to such unusual attentions, was terrorized, and without waiting for more, broke into flight, the bull after him. The driver, looking on it as a point of honour, made the elephant pull up and face the foe. Upon this, the bull also halted, and began to paw the ground with his fore-feet, raising a great dust, and bellowing at the same time. This caused the elephant to be still more frightened. It turned and fled; the bull, overtaking it, renewed the attack with its horns. In this way it pursued, until it had ejected the elephant from the city, to the great admiration of the people, who ran to see this singular sight.

Informed of the facts, Mahabat Khan ordered into his presence the bull and the elephant to see this curious thing himself. As soon as the bull saw the elephant, it did as before. Mahabat Khan, too, feeling his honour at stake, wanted the elephant to kill the bull. He ordered other elephants to be called in. One after another made the attempt, but still the bull remained victor. The reader must understand that when the bull saw the elephant approach, he went to attack him, and raising a great deal of dust with his feet, deceived the elephant. In this cloud of dust the bull suddenly got behind the elephant and used its horns. In this way it overcame the elephant. Finding the bull so violent, Mahabat Khan kept it, and gave a present to its owner of two hundred rupees, and he used it to punish any mad elephants that had broken their chains and caused injuries. I saw once, as I was passing along in the city of Lahore, an elephant break its chain, and the elephant-men could not catch it. They let loose the bull, and it, by its cleverness and the use of its horns, drove the elephant back to its place. Mahabat Khan was so pleased with this bull that he gave it the name of 'Chastiser of Elephants'.

## The reluctant executioner

I could extend my remarks to greater length on the instinct of these animals, but that would carry me too far, and therefore I will conclude my account with an unusual event occurring in the Island of Ceylon. The king of that island was angry with one of his nephews for some trick he had played. He ordered him to be put to death in his own presence by a mad elephant. The elephant advanced towards the victim. The latter cried out at once to the animal, and told it not to kill him. The elephant recognized the voice, because the man had formerly ridden on it, and drew back, raising its trunk as a mark of politeness and respect.

At this the king grew angry with the driver, and commanded him to drive the beast forward once more. The victim began to cry out again, saying he relied upon him not to kill him. On seeing that the elephant did not mean to obey, the king stood up and shouted to it; all the same, it did not obey his orders. 'Kill,' said he, 'this traitor forthwith, for such is my will.' At this the elephant, finding itself forced by the king's orders, put his trunk into his mouth, and, shutting his eyes, rushed as quickly as possible at the unfortunate being, without touching him with his trunk or his tusks. These are the members with which they are accustomed to kill anyone. But in spite of that it did not fail to take the man's life by crushing him under its feet.

from the *Storia do Mogor*, or Mogul India 1653-1708 by N. Manucci, tr. by W. Irvine

# The fate of Middlemas

Richard Middlemas was an illegitimate child left in the charge of Gideon Gray, surgeon of the village of Middlemas. Eventually he and Janet, the surgeon's daughter, fell in love. But Richard is a restless scoundrel. He goes to India hoping to make his fortune. There he comes under the influence of the Begum Mootee Mahal, alias Madame Montreville. Between them they hatch a plot to lure poor Janet to India, ostensibly to marry Richard, in fact, to be handed over to the Zenana of Tippoo Sahib.

The plot is foiled by Adam Hartley who was a pupil of Surgeon Gray and is himself in love with Janet. Dr Hartley wins favour with Hyder Ali, father of Tippoo; the latter who has promised Richard all sorts of power and honours in return for Janet, is suddenly confronted by his father Hyder Ali. Hyder Ali hands Janet over to Adam Hartley (who escorts her to her home in Scotland), but declares to Tippoo:

'For thee, Tippoo, I am not come hither to deprive thee of authority or to disgrace thee before the Durbar. Such things as thou hast promised to this Feringi, proceed to make them good. The sun calleth not back the splendour which he lends to the moon; and the father obscures not the dignity which he has conferred on the son. What thou hast promised, that do thou proceed to make good.'

The ceremony of investiture was therefore recommenced, by which Prince Tippoo conferred on Middlemas the important government of the city of Bangalore, probably with the internal resolution, that since he himself was deprived of his fair European, he would take an early opportunity to remove the new Killedar from his charge; while Middlemas accepted it with the throbbing hope that he might yet outwit both father and son. The deed of investiture was read aloud—the robe of honour was put upon the newly created Killedar, and a hundred voices, while they blessed the prudent choice of Tippoo, wished the governor good fortune, and victory over his enemies.

A horse was led forward, as the Prince's gift. It was a fine steed of the Cuttyawar breed, high-crested with broad hind-quarters; he was of a white colour, but had the extremity of his tail and mane stained red. His saddle was red velvet, the bridle and crupper studded with gilded knobs. Two attendants on lesser horses led this prancing animal, one holding the lance, and the other holding the long spear of their patron. The horse was shown to the applauding courtiers, and withdrawn, in order to be led in state through the streets, while the new Killedar should follow on the elephant, another present usual on such an occasion, which was next made to advance, that the world might admire the munificence of the Prince.

The huge animal approached the platform, shaking his large wrinkled head, which he raised and sunk, as if impatient, and curling upwards his trunk from time to time, as if to show the gulf of his tongueless mouth. Gracefully retiring with the deepest obeisance, the Killedar, well pleased the audience was finished, stood by the neck of the elephant, expecting the conductor of the animal would make him kneel down, that he might ascend the gilded howdah, which awaited his occupancy.

'Hold, Feringi,' said Hyder. 'Thou hast received all that was promised thee by the bounty of Tippoo. Accept now what is the fruit of the justice of Hyder.'

# The fate of Middlemas

As he spoke, he signed with his fingers, and the driver of the elephant instantly conveyed to the animal the pleasure of the Nawaub. Curling his long trunk around the neck of the ill-fated European, the monster suddenly threw the wretch prostrate before him, and stamping his huge shapeless foot upon his breast, put an end at once to his life, and his crimes. The cry which his victim uttered was mimicked by the roar of the monster, and a sound like a hysterical laugh mingling with a scream, which rang from under the veil of the Begum. The elephant once more raised his trunk aloft, and gaped fearfully.

from *The Surgeon's Daughter* by Sir Walter Scott

# Elephants and Mecca

1 The following is the story of the defeat of Abraha, in the year of the elephant (the year of the birth of the Prophet), recorded in the chapter of the elephant in the Koran:

In the year of Our Lord 571, I, Abraha, King of the Yemen and governor at Sana appointed by the King of Abyssinia, determined to invest the city of Mecca and destroy the Ka'aba, detesting the Sabinianism [1] of the Arabs. At that time the guardianship of the great temple of Mecca was entrusted to Abou-Thaleb, grandfather of Mohammed. I set out with a strong force and marched through South Arabia. I myself rode upon a powerful elephant which unhappily had the ill-omened name of Mahmud.

My campaign was dogged by misfortune and I lost many men and many elephants. At last my army was within sight of Mecca and I felt that I was about to strike a great blow for the true Christian religion. I was not to know then that a great prophet was to arise and spread an Islamic religion through the land. The name of my elephant was the same as that of the prophet who was born at the very time of my expedition.

As we approached Mecca, myself leading the host upon Mahmud, the Arab guide whispered some words into my elephant's ear. Mahmud stopped his march and knelt in the way. The other elephants did likewise and the whole force was brought to a halt.

My officers and I endeavoured to persuade Mahmud to resume his march towards Mecca but he would not and my army began to murmur and to say that they would not themselves march on Mecca against the elephant's will. Turning Mahmud away from Mecca, the elephant rose obediently ready to proceed but even when by stratagem I moved in a circle again facing Mecca, Mahmud would not.

At this moment a vast cloud of small birds arose from the sea and flew over the army. Each bird had three pebbles, [2] one in each claw and one in its beak. These they let fall upon the army and all my men and my elephants were killed thereby. I alone survived and told this tale on my deathbed at Sana, whither I had escaped.

## 2 Abu-'Abd-Allah al-Kalamis is rescued by an Elephant

It is but lately that I took ship from Balsorah on pilgrimage to Mecca as I coveted the title of Hajji. All went well and we sailed down the Persian Gulf praying and chanting.

As the vessel was passing between Aden and the island of Socotra, a great tempest arose and all on board thought that the end had come.

But I, Abu-'Abd-Allah al-Kalamis, prayed to Allah. And Allah put these words into my mouth. 'From now will I never eat of the flesh of an elephant.' And I knew not why I said these words.

Now it happened that presently the ship was wrecked upon the barren

1. Sabinianism = Star worship.
2. Some commentators have said that the hail of pebbles was an allegorical manner of stating that smallpox was brought from Africa into Arabia by an Abyssinian army which was itself exterminated by the disease.

coast of Africa between Perim and Jeddah. My companions and I who gained the shore made certain that we had escaped drowning only to starve to death. Miraculously there appeared an elephant's child and my friends did kill it and they ate of its flesh. But I would not. And in the night the mother of the elephant child came and trampled my companions to death but me she left in peace as I smelt not of her child and she raised me with her trunk on to her back and took me for many days and left me near a village. And there I lay until the people found me all but dead from starvation and thirst and brought me back to life. And I Abu-'Abd-Allah al-Kalamis gave thanks to Allah.

Knights attacking elephant

# The reverent elephant

Trampling his path through wood and brake,
And canes which crackling fall before his way,
And tassel-grass, whose silvery feathers play
O'ertopping the young trees,
On comes the Elephant, to slake
His thirst at noon in yon pellucid springs.
Lo! from his trunk upturn'd, aloft he flings
The grateful shower; and now
Plucking the broad-leaved bough
Of yonder plane, with wavy motion slow,
Fanning the languid air,
He moves it to and fro.
But when that form of beauty meets his sight,
The trunk its undulating motion stops,
From his forgetful hold the plane-branch drops,
Reverent he kneels, and lifts his rational eyes
To her as if in prayer;
And when she pours her angel voice in song,
Entranced he listens to the thrilling notes,
Till his strong temples, bathed with sudden dews,
Their fragrance of delight and love diffuse.

from *The Curse of Kehama* by Robert Southey

# Cupid's elephant

The human race has, with the exception of Mr Bernard Shaw, no rival among its vegetarian teetotallers to compare for wisdom and longevity with elephants. Whatever the task at which they are called upon to lend a trunk, they lay on, unfortified by petrol coupons, enough willing horse power to drive a tractor. Give these Admirable Crichtons of the animal world a stack of teak and they shove it around with a will. Offer them, at the other extreme, a crumb, well outside the wooden bars of their home at the zoo, and, deftly and patiently, they angle for it and steer it down their capacious throats. Mr Strachey, if he ever finds time to watch them, must wish we all received as thankfully the small mercies of his meat ration. The good they do has, hitherto, stopped short of restoring harmony in unhappy families, but, as our Colombo Correspondent shows this morning, this much needed art is within reach of their benevolent versatility.

A female of the species, having grown fond of her owner's bride, pined and refused food and work when the lady, following a convention of discord among the newly wedded, went home to mother. The grief of this family-loving animal next found positive expression. The truant was tracked down, reproachfully trumpeted at, caressed with an appealing trunk, and brought back to her husband. Welfare workers, in arms against a sea of matrimonial troubles, will welcome this powerful new recruit. They will remember how marked is an elephant's affection for children and how it strolls, as gentle as a lamb, giving pick-a-backs through the long summer afternoons.

If every youth and maiden, before they went to the altar, found an elephant among their wedding presents, it would evidently prove a tower of strength as a mascot against hasty breakages. A spouse brimful with self-pity over alleged mental cruelty, would look into those little, shrewd, twinkling eyes or lean against that comfortable massive bulk and begin to wonder whether life was really quite so bad after all.

Modern houses and flats are the main obstacle to the success of an elephant-in-every-home campaign. Some marriages must begin in premises less spacious than an ivory tower and landlords, who so often strain at cats and dogs, might refuse to swallow an elephant. They might, in defence of obstruction, point out that the only case of a married couple of elephants having their affairs publicized appears at first sight somewhat unfortunate. When Jumbo said in the old song to Alice, I love you, Alice said to Jumbo I don't believe you do or you wouldn't have gone to Yankee-land and left me at the Zoo. This plea is inadmissible, for the journey was on business. Poor Jumbo, as a patriotic pachyderm, should have hit back with I could not love thee half so much, loved I not dollars more. If full-grown bulls or cows are asking too much, then at least communal crêches might be provided by housing authorities for baby elephants. Cupid needs in these unsettled days all available help, and he or she would be a hard-boiled injured party to a tiff who, having poured out woes before that tribunal, did not end with a smile and a murmur of oh! unarm Eros, may be it was my fault.

from *The Times* 31 May 1949

# The blind men and the elephant

It was six men of Indostan
To learning much inclined,
Who went to see the Elephant
(Though all of them were blind),
That each by observation
Might satisfy his mind.

The *First* approached the Elephant,
And happening to fall
Against his broad and sturdy side,
At once began to bawl:
'God bless me! but the Elephant
Is very like a wall!'

The *Second*, feeling of the tusk,
Cried, 'Ho! what have we here
So very round and smooth and sharp?
To me 'tis mighty clear
This wonder of a Elephant
Is very like a spear!'

The *Third* approached the animal,
And happening to take
The squirming trunk within his hands,
Thus boldly up and spake:
'I see,' quoth he, 'the Elephant
Is very like a snake.'

The *Fourth* reached out his eager hand,
And felt about the knee.
'What most this wondrous beast is like
Is mighty plain,' quoth he;
''Tis clear enough the Elephant
Is very like a tree!'

The *Fifth*, who chanced to touch the ear,
Said: 'E'en the blindest man
Can tell what this resembles most:
Deny the fact who can,
This marvel of an Elephant
Is very like a fan!'

The *Sixth* no sooner had begun
About the beast to grope,
Than, seizing on the swinging tail
That fell within his scope,
'I see,' quoth he, 'the Elephant
Is very like a rope!'

# The blind men and the elephant

And so these men of Indostan
Disputed loud and long,
Each in his own opinion
Exceeding stiff and strong,
Though each was partly in the right,
And all were in the wrong!

      MORAL
So, oft in theologic wars,
The disputants, I ween,
Rail on in utter ignorance
Of what each other mean,
*And prate about an Elephant*
*Not one of them has seen!*

A Hindu fable by John Godfrey Saxe

**Note**

*The Blind Men and the Elephant* occurs in the Udāna, a Canonical Hindu Scripture.

# Zoo and circus elephants

*What is bigger than an elephant? But this is also become man's plaything, and a spectacle at public solemnities; and it learns to skip, dance and kneel.*

*Plutarch,* On Fortune

Both the ancient and modern, and the Eastern and Western worlds have used elephants for entertainment in zoos, menageries and circuses. Among the earliest zoo elephants recorded are those which the Syrian king, Assur-nasi-pal II captured in Syria itself in the ninth century BC, at which period there were still wild elephants to be found in that country.

The Romans were the first to display elephants in circuses in Europe and it is recorded by Pliny and others that Metellius in 251 BC brought to Rome elephants which he had captured from the Carthaginians at the Battle of Palermo. From then on the elephants often appeared in Triumphs held in Rome. Their first appearance as combatants in a circus was when they were introduced by the consuls Cornelius Scipio Nasica and C. Lentulus in about 131 BC. The combats took place between armed men and elephants, lions and bears, and Livy recounts how the consuls let loose sixty-three lions, forty bears and a great number of elephants in the circus. Ranking, commenting on this, remarks:

> These were bloody battles, but the Romans delighted in bloodshed. They thereby kept up that martial spirit, which made them superior to all other nations.

Pompey, too, loved to display animals in the circus at Rome, hoping to win the hearts of the populace by the magnificence of his shows. He brought a number of elephants from Africa. For his Triumph he directed that his chariot should be drawn by four elephants but found to his chagrin that the arch through which they had to pass was not wide enough and he had to be content with horses as usual.

'At the opening of his theatre,' says Ranking, 'Pompey exhibited a variety of games, and battles with wild beasts, in which five hundred lions were slain in five days. Eighteen elephants fought with one another, then with gladiators; and lastly, with Getulian archers, who were hunters of wild elephants. Some were killed, when the survivors grew mad and made terrible and furious efforts to break the iron grating which separated them from the spectators. Fear seized the assembly. It was soon turned into compassion for the poor animals. The elephants lifted up their trunks to heaven, as if to call on the Gods to witness the perfidiousness of men; and the people concluded they had been forced on board ship, after a promise that their lives should be saved; for the Romans fancied that the elephants had reason and understood the language of men though they could not answer them.'

However, the entertainments in Rome were not all brutal. Suetonius tells us of a Roman knight during the reign of Nero, who rode along a rope upon an elephant and there are a number of accounts of elephants able to dance and to keep time with music. Indeed the Romans appear to have become as skilful in taming and instructing elephants as the

Eastern races. It is interesting that in a miniature in MS. 10 E.4 in the BM the elephant with castle and several occupants is walking down a rope garnished with leaves (plate 14).

Every emperor or successful commander vied with his rivals in putting on shows, and besides elephants and lions there were exhibited or slaughtered bears, tigers, ostriches, hyenas, hippopotamuses, rhinoceroses, panthers, zebras and even turtles; well might Juvenal write of *panem et circenses*:

> And those who once held unresisted sway
> Gave armies, empires, everything away,
> For two poor claims have long renounced the whole,
> And only ask—the circus and the dole.

While elephants cannot have enjoyed the brutal combats in which they were made to indulge, there are many stories of their delight in taking part in public performances. Aelian tells how the elephants of Germanicus used to perform a ritualistic or modulated dance. Some writers, have, however, declared that elephants are tone deaf. The surgeon, Sir Everard Home, who carried out an exhaustive anatomical examination of the elephant's ear, maintained that its structure precluded the animal from having any appreciation of music. He persuaded Mr Broadwood to take one of his pianos down to Exeter 'Change (Corn Exchange) and play it to the elephant there. When what he terms 'acute' notes were sounded the elephant paid no attention. 'Grave' (presumably bass) notes, however, interested the elephant greatly and the animal tried hard to discover where the sounds came from.

Mr C. Knight in his book on the elephant tells of a series of experiments carried out in 1748 at the Jardin des Plantes in Paris on a male and female. The results were given in the periodical *Décade Philosophique* from which it appears that 'the tender air of "Charmante Gabrielle" plunged them into a species of voluptuous languor' while 'the lively movement of "Ça ira" roused them to an extraordinary state of excitement.'

It was during the eighteenth century, that the modern type of circus came into being, Astley's being the first to win world fame. This circus was formed near the site of the present Waterloo Station in London in 1768. The circus developed rapidly in both Europe and America. It is reported that an elephant named Mademoiselle Jeck, famed on the Continent, gave regular performances at Astley's (although Sanderson states that 1827 was the first year in which an elephant appeared in a public show in England). The first circus elephant to appear in America was imported into the United States from Bengal by Captain Jacob Crowninshield in 1796, and was shown all over the States, where it became well known.

It was, however, in the latter half of the nineteenth century that the circus came into its own. The Sells Brothers in America, Lord George Sanger in Britain, Hagenbeck in Germany, were among the well-known names of circus owners. The Sells brothers' circus came to be known as the 'The Seven Elephant Show', the elephants parading in time to music, the leader holding high in his trunk a betighted and bespangled young woman while the other six elephants followed, forelegs upon the behind of the elephant in front.

This show had a wide appeal but did not approach some of the shows with trained elephants which appeared in Rome many centuries before. It is recorded by Aelian that in one of these, twelve highly trained elephants came into the theatre and gave a display of marching in figure and scattering flowers from side to side. After the performance attendants placed large couches as for dinner, spread a banquet on tables of ivory and cedar, all the plates and vessels being of gold or silver. The twelve elephants then came in, six of them dressed as men and six as women, and disposed themselves on the couches and proceeded decorously to feed themselves with their trunks.

There are countless stories of circus elephants, many of them similar. Sanderson tells a sad but intriguing story about a poor circus elephant which came to a bad end in a town in New England about 1800. Two irresponsible teenagers conceived the idea of having an elephant hunt. They hid themselves with their guns beside the road along which the elephant would pass when the circus was on the move to its next stance. As the elephant passed, the two youths shot it. Elephant hunters know that it is hard to direct one's bullet into a mortal part of the elephant. Unhappily, the boys' bullets pierced the animal's heart and killed it.

The proprietor of the circus elephant managed to trace the boys and brought them before a Justice of the Peace. The J.P.'s judgment, doubtless recorded in the judicial records of the state concerned, is given by Sanderson in these words:

> 'I hev examined the law purty therewly in this case. The laws of this state provides proper penalties for all them that maliciously, or wilfully, or with malice aforethought kills or cripples up of a hoss, or a keow, or a hog, but there ain't a word abeout killin' a elerphant. What's more, a elerphant is a dangersome varmint that hain't got no bizness a-running eround the country a-skeerin' of hosses an' a-frightenin' wimming an' children. Under them circumstances, I reckon I'll hev to turn the defendents loost.'

There is much foolishness talked by the well-meaning sentimentalists about imaginary cruelties perpetrated on circus animals in their training. Others feel it an indignity to an animal to teach it to perform clever tricks. But there is no doubt that the trainers and keepers are devoted to their charges. The animals and their trainers become a team the members of which respect and support each other.

Gosta Kruse's book *Trunk Call* is full of delightfully told incidents of his experiences as an elephant-trainer. Most of the stories prove conclusively that however intelligent the elephants may be, however humanly they seem to think, they still behave like animals.

Kruse tells one such charming story about an elephant called Susila. Susila was going on an overnight journey by rail and Kruse asked a new groom whom he had hired to travel with her and the other elephants and to sleep in their van. On their arrival in their new town there was a lot to arrange and Kruse hurried down to the station in the early morning to help the groom to get them ready. There was no sound from the van and no sign of the groom being about. At last the groom was roused up in the van dressed only in his vest and pants.

Excusing himself he said: 'I'm sorry, Mr Kruse, but the elephants have eaten my shoes, my trousers and my shirt and before I went to sleep I put my watch in my shoes for safety and it's vanished too!'

In spite of it the elephants were perfectly well and the following day Susila delivered the watch in the usual manner; it was still ticking.

The most famous circus elephant was, without doubt, Jumbo, who started public life in the Jardin des Plantes in Paris. From there he moved, in exchange for a rhinoceros, to the zoo in London; later still he joined the circus of Mr Barnum in America who bought him for £2000 when he had become too bad tempered to be entrusted with carrying children for rides.

In the next stall in the zoo in London there was placed a female elephant from the Sudan named Alice (captured by an Italian of the interesting name of Casanova). Alice and Jumbo—who was himself a very large African gentleman—became close friends. Jumbo had come to the zoo in June 1865. He became immensely popular and when in January 1882 people read in *The Times* that Jumbo had been sold to Barnum and was going to America, the storm broke. The Zoological Society was roundly blackguarded and letters objecting to the deal poured in. The papers and journals were filled with cartoons showing Jumbo and Alice in tears at the thought of parting. Barnum too was besieged with appeals, the crowning idiocy coming from the *Daily Telegraph*. The Editor sent Barnum the following telegram:

P. T. Barnum, New York.—Editor's compliments. All British children distressed at elephant's departure. Hundreds of correspondents beg us to inquire on what terms you will kindly return Jumbo. Answer prepaid, unlimited. *Le Sage*

Barnum, who had evidently a sardonic sense of humour, replied:

My compliments to editor *Daily Telegraph* and British nation. Fifty millions of American citizens anxiously awaiting Jumbo's arrival. My forty years' invariable practice of exhibiting best that money could procure, makes Jumbo's presence here imperative. Hundred thousand pounds would be no inducement to cancel purchase . . .

In December next I visit Australia in person with Jumbo and my entire mammoth combination of seven shows, *via* California, thence through Suez Canal. Following summer to London. I shall then exhibit in every prominent city in Great Britain. May afterwards return Jumbo to his old position in Royal Zoological Gardens. Wishing long life and prosperity to the British nation, 'The Daily Telegraph', and Jumbo, I am the public's obedient servant, *P. T. Barnum*

To this answer, the *Telegraph* referred in the following editorial:

Jumbo's fate is sealed. The disappointing answer from his new American proprietor, which we published yesterday, proves too clearly that there is nothing to expect from delicacy or remorse in that quarter. Moved by the universal emotion which the approaching departure of

40  Battle scene from *Romance of Alexander*; 15th cent.

41  Elephants presented to Alexander

42 Ivory elephant and howdah

43 Ivory figure of Ganesha

44 Carthaginian and Latin coins

45 Elephant on *Tissu de Soie*, from Charlemagne's tomb

46 Elephant fighting lion; Elephant Terrace, Angkor Thom, Cambodia; 12th cent.

ایرچ دراوج فتح مسعی وحی و تعذو است کرار ساختہ پسپان نین رشد آباد
و ارنیشران نامی ارمین کردرت سپیدہ شیدہ رہ باد آمدون کان و ہر دوبی عظم
بون دگر پس پیدہ دافقان درگ نامی درجنگ جبہ جابان فی عدر و پس پس آپسا
انعافل فی لعث لانج بین پس سابن و قا عدون اجم کست راری وقت
گفتوم فرد رہا لہذہ دست و مرگ کرکرگرو آورد و دیو مترت بافت نہ آبارش می ابست
داد و ولیاست لندی

51 Elephants confronted by iron horses

52 Rustum killing mad elephant

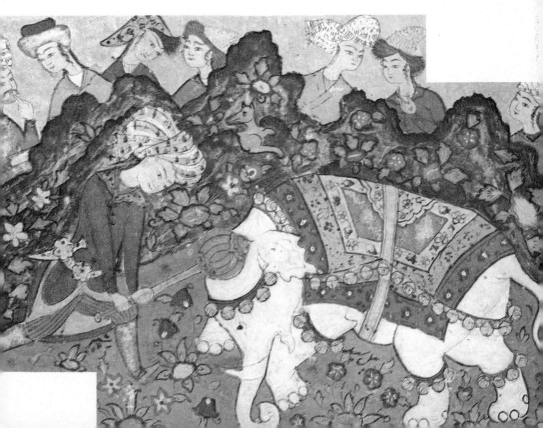

53 Campanian Etruscan plate with war elephant and baby elephant; 3rd cent. BC

54 Animals coming out of the Ark; 16th-cent. Limoges plate

London's gigantic friend had aroused, we communicated with Mr Barnum, indicating that 'money was no object' if he would only listen to the entreaties of the English children, and let the Royal Zoological Council off their foolish bargain. The famous showman replied—as all the world now knows—in tones of polite but implacable decision. He has bought Jumbo, and Jumbo he means to have; nor would 'a hundred thousand pounds' be any inducement to cancel the purchase. If innumerable childish hearts are grieving here over the loss of a creature so gentle, vast, and sensible, 'fifty millions of American citizens', Mr Barnum says, are anxiously waiting to see the great elephant arrive in the States. Then to increase the general regret, the message depicts the sort of life which poor Jumbo has before him. No more quiet garden-strolls, no shady trees, green lawns, and flowery thickets, peopled with tropical beasts, bright birds, and snakes, making it all quite homely. Our amiable monster must dwell in a tent, take part in the routine of a circus. Mr Barnum announces the intention of taking his 'mammoth combination of seven shows' round the world, *via* California, Australia, and the Suez Canal. Elephants hate the sea. They love a quiet bath as much as any Christians; but the indignity and terror of being slung on board a ship, and tossed about in the agony of sea-sickness, which is probably on a scale with the size of their stomachs, would appear to them worse than death. Yet to this doom the children's 'dear old Jumbo' is condemned; and it is enough, if he knew of it, to precipitate that insanity which his guardians have pretended to fear. It is true Mr Barnum holds out hopes that we may some day see again the colossal form of the public favourite. In the summer of 1883 he proposes to bring the good beast back to England, exhibiting him in 'every prominent city'; and the message adds, 'I may afterwards return Jumbo to his old position in the Royal Zoological Gardens'. There is a gleam of consolation in this, which we would not darken by any remarks upon the great showman's ironclad inflexibility; but what will be the mental and physical condition of our immense friend when bereavement, sea-sickness, and American diet shall have ruined his temper and digestion, and abolished his self-respect? There will be a Yankee twang in his trumpeting; he will roll about on his 'sea-legs', with a gait sadly changed from the substantial swing so well known; and Alice herself will hardly know him.

We fear, however, that Jumbo will never come back to her and us alive. His mighty heart will probably break with rage, shame, and grief; and we may hear of him, like another Samson, playing mischief with the Philistines who have led him into captivity, and dying amid some scene of terrible wrath and ruin. We hope Mr Barnum fully realizes what ten tons and a half of solid fury can do when it has a mind.

Scores of children wrote, some to Barnum, some to the zoo. One of them, Gertrude Cox, wrote as follows:

9 Dingle Hill, Liverpool, March 7
Dear Mr Barnum, Please do not take Jumbo to America. I think it

55   Indian watercolour: Tiger attacks Elephant
56   Ceremonial elephant painted on mica

will be cruel if you do take him when he begs so hard not to be taken. There are plenty of other elephants—will not one of them do for you instead?—one that does not mind going. If you will only let Jumbo stay, I am sure the English children will thank you; and I do not think the people in America can be so cruel as to wish to have him when it makes him so unhappy to leave England. *Gertrude Cox.*

Others wrote over pseudonyms such as 'one of Jumbo's sincere friends', and 'a young English girl'.

Many of the letters referred to Jumbo's angelic temper, but this alas, had become so frayed that the Zoological Society had decided that they would have to get rid of him.

To Miss Nichols and her companions, ninety pupils of a school in the Edgware Road in London, who had memorialized him on the subject, the secretary to the Zoological Society replied in the following letter:

Zoological Society of London, 11 Hanover Square, W.   March 2, 1882

Dear Friends, Your petition has been duly received, but I fear we shall not be able to assent to your request. We must ask you to believe that our experienced superintendent knows better what elephants are suitable to be kept in the Society's Gardens than you do. There are still three elephants left in the gardens, upon which we hope you will have many rides in future.

Yours faithfully, P. S. Sclater, Secretary to the Society

Richard Carrington in telling the story of Jumbo remarks that his departure to America was 'too sombre a theme for music-hall quips'. One classicist remarked, following Thucydides on the sufferings of the Athenian prisoners in the quarries of Syracuse, that if Jumbo did not come back from the States the children of England would have τα κατα δακρυα πεπονθετες—'suffered things too deep for tears'.

Music-hall songs were not lacking and the most famous of these, written by G. H. Macdermott and composed by E. T. Symons, is not unknown today.

In spite of all the frenzied efforts by admirers, Jumbo went to America. He sailed in the *Assyrian Monarch*—not an unsuitable name—on 25 March, 1882. He was seen off with buns, oysters and champagne. Alas, on 13 September, 1885, after the final performance of the circus, in St Thomas, Canada, Jumbo and another elephant named Tom were marching over the railway track to reach their cars guided by Scott, the former's trainer, when a heavy freight train came along the line from the east. The headlight was not seen until the train was within five hundred yards of the animals, and was not expected, as the railroad officials had assured the men that a train was not due for an hour. Signals were given as soon as possible, and the brakes were put on; while the elephants fled up the track, led by Scott, who stood by them to the last: but the heavy train could not be stopped, being on a down grade; and with a thundering roar it came on, striking the clown elephant, and hurtling him into a ditch, then crashing into the ponderous Jumbo, the contact stopping the train, and derailing the engine and two cars.

The unfortunate Jumbo was struck in the hind-legs; and it is said, as he felt the cow-catcher, he gave a loud roar, turned and fell; the first car passing along his back, and inflicting wounds from which he died in fifteen minutes.

His stuffed body is in Tufts University, Boston; his skeleton is in the American Museum of Natural History in New York.

Elephant in chain armour: coin from Cuperus

# The Duke's elephant

'Oh, Duke, I see my husband getting restive. This has been a wonderful party, but as you know it's to-morrow we sail.'

'I know, I know. You must have a lot to do. I wonder how you'll like Government House. I expect that it's less primitive than when I was there. I confess I found the endless ceremonial pretty trying. However, you've got a good staff. That young nephew of mine's not such a scatterbrain as he'd have you believe.'

'He's a nice boy and we're so grateful to you for sending him to us. I wonder what we can send you from India for your villa at Chiswick as a little thank-offering?'

'Ah, Jane, you mustn't think of such a thing. After all, it is you and your husband who are doing me a kindness in taking the young man off my hands—unless, of course,' the Duke added as an afterthought, with a twinkle, 'you care to send me one of your elephants!'

'We must see what we can do,' said Lady Jane, laughing.

The Duke of Devonshire—for he it was—completely forgot this conversation and it was not until several months had passed that it recurred to his mind. He was breakfasting in the morning-room at Chiswick with his wife when the butler, Hansard, came rather hurriedly into the room.

'I beg your pardon, Your Grace,' he said looking at the Duke and then glancing uneasily towards the Duchess. 'A person is delivering an animal.'

The Duchess burst out laughing.

'Whatever do you mean, Hansard?' she asked. 'Is my poor old bitch Julie having her puppies?'

'No, Your Grace,' said Hansard shakily to the Duchess, looking askance at the Duke. 'A man—two men—have brought an animal to the door. They say they were instructed to bring it to your Grace.'

'Animal?' exclaimed the Duke. 'What sort of an animal, in Heaven's name?'

The butler looked about with frightened eyes.

'I fear it's an—an elephant, Your Grace.'

'A *what?*'

'An elephant, Your Grace.'

Their Graces hurried to the window. It was but too true. They saw a large elephant backing out of a Carter Paterson furniture van in the courtyard. An Indian was superintending the unloading and saying cooing things to the elephant in Hindustani.

'This must be Jane's doing,' said the Duke grimly. 'I never imagined she would take me seriously.' He hurried to the door.

'Come on, Hansard! Help me to deal with this. Get hold of Stewart and tell him to collect two or three under-gardeners.'

Fanciful? Well, it is more or less what happened.

The elephant having arrived at the Duke's villa at Chiswick was housed in a large and comfortable house. Rapidly it—or rather she— became devoted to the head-gardener who became her keeper. When he came along in the morning and called to her, she would come out and pick up a broom and pail. She would do whatever he told her, sweeping the paths, or the lawn, or following him carrying the pail full of water. Sometimes she would bring her master's gloves.

She used to be rewarded with a carrot, or, if she was thirsty, with a bottle of soda-water. This she would open, extracting the cork by holding the bottle to the ground with her foot at an angle of forty-five degrees and working the cork out with her trunk. She would then draw the contents into her trunk, hand—or perhaps one should say 'trunk'—the bottle back to the keeper and then squirt the liquid down her throat.

The gardener used to ride on her like an Indian Mahout. She had a backcloth on her back and when he got down he would tell the elephant to put away the cloth. The elephant then twitched her back until the cloth fell to the ground, when she smoothed it out with her trunk, folded it into a neat square and, with an accurate cast, threw it on to her head. She then marched back to her house for the night.

This elephant is said to have died in 1829 at the age of twenty-one, no great age for an elephant.

(Based on fact)

# Dis Merci

'It is time, Jacques, that we named this elephant. Elephants have always had names and the public visiting the *Jardin des Plantes* expect to address the animals they come to see by name.'

'Well, *Monsieur le Directeur*, this elephant already has a name. She is called Gretchen. Herr Böhme, who brought us this elephant from the Congo, gave her this name. He had intended to call her "Reine", after the Queen of the Belgians, but the authorities said that King Leopold would not be pleased. So Herr Böhme called her Gretchen after his niece.'

'Come, come, Jacques; we can't have a Gretchen in the *Jardin des Plantes*. What about Josephine? After all, Napoleon wanted a memorial elephant erected in the *Place de la Bastille*.'

'We could name the elephant Hannibal, *Monsieur le Directeur*. It came from Africa.'

'Nonsense, Jacques; it's a lady. What about Du Barry?'

'Oh, Monsieur, I'm sure this is a virtuous elephant! Offer her this bottle of Beaujolais.'

The elephant took the bottle from *Monsieur le Directeur*, delicately extracted the cork, and sucking the wine into her trunk, squirted it down her throat with every appearance of satisfaction.

'Now, *Mademoiselle, dis Merci!*'

The elephant bowed her great head to the director and gave two contented little grunts like a well-fed pig.

'You see, *Monsieur le Directeur*, she says thank you, like a real lady.'

'Good, Jacques; henceforward she shall be called "Dis Merci".'

Dis Merci had a happy temperament and led a pleasant life in the *Jardin des Plantes*. All Paris came to see her and give her tit-bits. Among those who visited her was one Pidcock who had a menagerie in Exeter. Dis Merci took a great fancy to Pidcock and he to her. They had long confabulations together in a language only understood by each other. Pidcock would present Dis Merci with a bottle of wine and, taking one for himself, he and she would drink together, for all the world like two old cronies in a café, the bystanders watching Dis Merci with great delight.

Pidcock spent a month wooing Dis Merci. From time to time Jacques or the Director would come and join them, when Pidcock would tell Dis Merci to offer them a drink; whereupon Dis Merci would, quick as lightning, seize Pidcock's bottle in her trunk and present it to the Director, holding on to it until the Director said '*À votre santé, Mademoiselle!*' and took a drink, when Dis Merci would release the bottle and pick up her own. The beholders were charmed by the performance.

During this period Dis Merci made the acquaintance of an elderly Englishwoman, Madame Delavallade, the wife of a Parisian businessman. Madame Delavallade lived near the *Jardin des Plantes* and acquired the habit of calling upon Dis Merci almost every day with some delicacy, even, occasionally, a small bottle of cognac, which she brought in a basket. The elephant would put out her trunk—or 'hand', as it used to be called by the ancients—and then feel in the basket for the dainty or bottle. If it was a bottle she would delicately extract the cork, suck up the liquid and squirt it into her mouth, after which she would bow to Madame Delavallade and utter her two little grunts as thanks.

Eventually Pidcock acquired Dis Merci and took her to Exeter where she entered his menagerie, living a life of ease, entertaining the populace and enjoying the company of Pidcock. The latter used to drink gin or some other spirituous liquor in the evening in the company of Dis Merci and it was his habit to offer the first glass to Dis Merci. One evening, however, he suddenly felt it was time to take the first glass himself.

'You,' he said to the elephant, 'You have been served first long enough. It is my turn now.'

He drank his glass and then offered one to the elephant. But Dis Merci was deeply offended and refused to drink and it is related that she would never drink with Pidcock again.

One day, years later, while in the Exeter 'Change Menagerie, Dis Merci suddenly became wildly excited. Her keeper—Pidcock had left—looked about, but all he could see was a little old lady slowly walking along the path which passed Dis Merci's home, with a basket over her arm. She stopped and put out her hand. Dis Merci put out her trunk and to the keeper's astonishment the two shook hands. The elephant then felt in the basket, found a bottle of cognac, pulled the cork, sucked up the contents and squirted them down her throat with obvious enjoyment. Then she gave her two little grunting 'thank-yous' and bowed her head. Her visitor was, of course, Madame Delavallade, now a widow and come to live in her native Exeter. Dis Merci had from afar recognized her friend. Madame Delavallade came regularly to see Dis Merci. It is not related how long their friendship lasted, but clearly the two ladies greatly enjoyed each other's company. Pidcock had, alas, been expunged from Dis Merci's memory.

# Le rat et l'éléphant

Se croire un personnage est fort commun en France:
    On y fait l'homme d'importance,
    Et l'on n'est souvent qu'un bourgeois.
    C'est proprement le mal françois.

La sotte vanité nous est particulière.
Les Espagnols sont vains, mais d'une autre manière:
    Leur orgueil me semble, en un mot,
    Beaucoup plus fou, mais pas si sot.
    Donnons quelque image du nôtre,
    Qui sans doute en vaut bien un autre.

Un rat des plus petits voyoit un éléphant
Des plus gros, et railloit le marcher un peu lent
    De la bête de haut parage,
    Qui marchoit à gros équipage.
    Sur l'animal à triple étage,
    Une sultane de renom,
    Son chien, son chat et sa guenon.

Son perroquet, sa vieille, et toute sa maison,
    S'en alloit en pèlerinage.
    Le rat s'étonnoit que les gens
Fussent touchés de voir cette pesante masse:
Comme si d'occuper ou plus ou moins de place
Nous rendoit, disoit-il, plus ou moins importants.
Mais qu'admirez-vous tant en lui, vous autres hommes?
Seroit-ce ce grand corps qui fait peur aux enfants?
Nous ne nous prisons pas, tout petits que nous sommes,
    D'un grain moins que les éléphants
    Il en auroit dit davantage;
    Mais le chat, sortant de sa cage,
    Lui fit voir en moins d'un instant
    Qu'un rat n'est pas un éléphant.

from *Fables*, by La Fontaine

# The elephants of Ava

The city of Rangoon was first occupied by the British in 1824 at the beginning of the first Burmese war. The war ended in 1826 when the British appointed a Civil Commissioner to reside in Rangoon. The Civil Commissioner, John Crawfurd, had resided in Rangoon for six months, when he received instructions to proceed on an embassy to the Burmese Government at Ava, the capital of Burma. The story of the mission is told by John Crawfurd in a detailed journal in which life in Burma and the customs of the court at Ava are described. As frontispiece to the journal there is a splendid picture of a white elephant. At that time there was only one white elephant at Ava and this had been captured in 1806, but while Crawfurd was at the Court a wild one was reported to have been seen in the country. Crawfurd, having explained that in Burma the white elephant is not in fact an object of worship, but that the Court and people would consider it as peculiarly inauspicious to *want* a white elephant, writes as follows:

'While we were at Ava, a report was brought that a white elephant had been seen; but it was stated, at the same time, that its capture and transport on a sledge over the cultivated country would be accompanied by the destruction of ten thousand baskets of rice. His Majesty is said to have exclaimed more with the enthusiasm of an amateur than the consideration of a patriot King, "What signifies the destruction of ten thousand baskets of rice, in comparison with the possession of a white elephant?" and the order was given for the hunt. . . . When the present elephant was taken, the event was considered a joyous one; and the late King, who was fond of money, taking advantage of the circumstance, issued an order to the tributaries and chiefs, to ask pardon of the white elephant (Ka-dau), accompanied of course by the usual presents which his Majesty deposited in his coffers.

'The establishment of the white elephant is very large: he has his Wun, or Minister; his Wun-dauk, or deputy to that officer; his Saregyi, or Secretary, etc., with a considerable endowment for his maintenance. In the late reign, Sa-len, one of the finest districts in the kingdom, was the estate of the white elephant.

'All the elephants of the kingdom, tame or wild, are considered royal property; they are a royal monopoly; but the King, as a mark of special favour, gives the use of them to his wives, concubines, brothers, sons and occasionally, but rarely, to some of the highest dignitaries of the Government. Everyone who takes an elephant must deliver it to the King; and the killing of even a wild elephant is deemed an offence punishable by a heavy fine; it is done notwithstanding, both on account of the ivory and the flesh, which last is eaten by the Burmans, after being dried in the sun, when, to save the penalty, it passes under the name of buffalo beef. The King, I am told, is possessed, in all, of about one thousand elephants, divided into two classes; those which are thoroughly broken and tamed, consisting principally of males; and those that are employed as decoys, all females, and in a half wild state. They are under two chiefs: that of the first called the Senwun, or Elephant Governor;

and that of the second, the Aok-ma, or Aong-ma-wun; words which signify "governor of female decoys".

'If man has been called the wisest of animals, because he possesses hands, the elephant may, with as much truth, be called the wisest of quadrupeds, because he possesses a trunk. But for this instrument, and its great strength, I think it would be doubtful whether it would be ranked higher in intellectual endowments than a despised animal of the same natural family—the hog.'

# The white elephant

In 1862 the King of Siam, H. M. Somdetch P'hra Paarmendr Maha Mongkut, engaged Mrs Anna Leonowens, an English lady, as governess to his children. Mrs Leonowens spent six years at the Siamese court and has left a fascinating account of her experiences and of the life and customs of Siam. One chapter of her book is devoted to a description of the place of the White Elephant in the religion and the ceremonial of the country. Here is her account:

'It is commonly supposed that the Buddhists of Siam and Birmah regard the Chang Phoouk, or white elephant, as a deity, and worship it accordingly. The notion is erroneous, especially as it relates to Siam. The Buddhists do not recognise God in any material form whatever, and are shocked at the idea of adoring an elephant. Even Buddha, to whom they undoubtedly offer pious homage, they do not style 'God', but on the contrary maintain that, though an emanation from a 'sublimated ethereal being', he is by no means a deity. According to their philosophy of metempsychosis, however, each successive Buddha, in passing through a series of transmigrations, must necessarily have occupied in turn the forms of white animals of a certain class—particularly the swan, the stork, the white sparrow, the dove, the monkey, and the elephant. But there is much diversity and obscurity in the views of their ancient writers on this subject. Only one thing is certain, that the forms of these nobler and purer creatures are reserved for the souls of the good and great, who find in them a kind of redemption from the baser animal life. Thus almost all white animals are held in reverence by the Siamese, because they were once superior human beings, and the white elephant, in particular, is supposed to be animated by the spirit of some king or hero. Having once been a great man, he is thought to be familiar with the dangers that surround the great, and to know what is best and safest for those whose condition in all respects was once his own. He is hence supposed to avert national calamity, and bring prosperity and peace to a people.
　'From the earliest times the kings of Siam and Birmah have anxiously sought for the white elephant, and having had the rare fortune to procure one, have loaded it with gifts and dignities, as though it were a conscious favourite of the throne. When the governor of a province of Siam is notified of the appearance of a white elephant within his bailiwick, he immediately commands that prayers and offerings shall be made in all the temples, while he sends out a formidable expedition of hunters and slaves to take the precious beast, and bring it in in triumph. As soon as he is informed of its capture, a special messenger is despatched to inform the king of its sex, probable age, size, complexion, deportment, looks, and ways; and in the presence of his Majesty this bearer of glorious tidings undergoes the painfully pleasant operation of having his mouth, ears, and nostrils stuffed with gold. Especially is the lucky wight—perhaps some half-wild woodsman—who was first to spy the illustrious monster munificently rewarded. Orders are promptly issued to the woons and wongses of the several districts through which he must pass to prepare to receive him royally, and a wide path is cut for him through the forests he must traverse on his way to the capital.

Wherever he rests he is sumptuously entertained, and everywhere he is escorted and served by a host of attendants, who sing, dance, play upon instruments, and perform feats of strength or skill for his amusement, until he reaches the banks of the Meinam, where a great floating palace of wood, surmounted by a gorgeous roof and hung with crimson curtains, awaits him. The roof is literally thatched with flowers ingeniously arranged so as to form symbols and mottoes, which the superior beast is supposed to decipher with ease. The floor of this splendid float is laid with gilt matting curiously woven, in the centre of which his four-footed lordship is installed in state, surrounded by an obsequious and enraptured crowd of mere bipeds, who bathe him, perfume him, fan him, feed him, sing and play to him, flatter him. His food consists of the finest herbs, the tenderest grass, the sweetest sugar-cane, the mellowest plantains, the brownest cakes of wheat, served on huge trays of gold and silver; and his drink is perfumed with the fragrant flower of the *dok mallee*, the large native jessamine.

'Thus, in more than princely state, he is floated down the river to a point within seventy miles of the capital, where the king and his court, all the chief personages of the kingdom, and a multitude of priests, both Buddhist and Brahmin, accompanied by troops of players and musicians, come out to meet him, and conduct him with all the honours to his stable-palace. A great number of cords and ropes of all qualities and lengths are attached to the raft, those in the centre being of fine silk (figuratively, 'spun from a spider's web'). These are for the king and his noble retinue, who with their own hands make them fast to their gilded barges; the rest are secured to the great fleet of lesser boats. And so, with shouts of joy, beating of drums, blare of trumpets, boom of cannon, a hallelujah of music, and various splendid revelry, the great Chang Phoouk is conducted in triumph to the capital.

'Here in a pavilion, temporary but very beautiful, he is welcomed with imposing ceremonies by the custodians of the palace and the principal personages of the royal household. The king, his courtiers, and the chief priests being gathered round him, thanksgiving is offered up; and then the lordly beast is knighted, after the ancient manner of the Buddhists, by pouring upon his forehead consecrated water from a chank-shell.

'The titles reserved for the Chang Phoouk vary according to the purity of the complexion (for these favoured creatures are rarely true albinos—salmon or flesh-colour being the nearest approach to white in almost all the historic 'White elephants' of the courts of Birmah and Siam) and the sex; for though one naturally has recourse to the masculine pronoun in writing of a transmigrated prince or warrior, it often happens that that prince or warrior has, in the medlied mask of metempsychosis, assumed a female form. Such, in fact, was the case with the stately occupant of the stable-palace at the court of Maha Mongkut; and she was distinguished by the high-sounding appellation of Mââ Phya Seri Wongsah Ditsarah Krasâat—'August and Glorious Mother, Descendant of Kings and Heroes'.

'For seven or nine days, according to certain conditions, the Chang Phoouk is fêted at the temporary pavilion, and entertained with a variety of dramatic performances; and these days are observed as a general holiday throughout the land. At the expiration of this period he is conducted with great pomp to his sumptuous quarters within the precincts of the first king's palace, where he is received by his own court of officers, attendants and slaves, who install him in his fine lodgings, and at once proceed to robe and decorate him. First, the court jeweller rings his tremendous tusks with massive gold, crowns him with a diadem of beaten gold of perfect purity, and adorns his burly neck with heavy golden chains. Next his attendants robe him in a superb velvet cloak of purple, fringed with scarlet and gold; and then his court prostrate themselves around him, and offer him royal homage.

'When his lordship would refresh his portly person in the bath, an officer of high rank shelters his noble head with a great umbrella of crimson and gold, while others wave golden fans before him. On these occasions he is invariably preceded by musicians, who announce his approach with cheerful minstrelsy and songs.

'If he falls ill, the king's own leech prescribes for him, and the chief priests repair daily to his palace to pray for his safe deliverance, and sprinkle him with consecrated waters and anoint him with consecrated oils. Should he die, all Siam is bereaved, and the nation, as one man, goes into mourning for him. But his body is not burned; only his brains and heart are thought worthy of that last and highest honour. The carcass, shrouded in fine white linen, and laid on a bier, is carried down the river with much wailing and many mournful dirges, to be thrown in the Gulf of Siam.

'In 1862 a magnificent white—or, rather, salmon-coloured—elephant was 'bagged', and preparations on a gorgeous scale were made to receive him. A temporary pavilion of extraordinary splendour sprang up, as if by magic, before the eastern gate of the palace; and the whole nation was wild with joy; when suddenly came awful tidings—he had died!

'No man dared tell the king. But the Kralahome—that man of prompt expedients and unfailing presence of mind—commanded that the preparations should cease instantly, and that the building should vanish with the builders. In the evening his Majesty came forth, as usual, to exult in the glorious work. What was his astonishment to find no vestige of the splendid structure that had been so nearly completed the night before. He turned, bewildered, to his courtiers, to demand an explanation, when suddenly the terrible truth flashed into his mind. With a cry of pain he sank down upon a stone, and gave vent to an hysterical passion of tears; but was presently consoled by one of his children, who, carefully prompted in his part, knelt before him and said: 'Weep not, O my father! The stranger lord may have left us but for a time.' The stranger lord, fatally pampered, had succumbed to astonishment and indigestion.

'A few days after this mournful event the king read to me a curious description of the defunct monster, and showed me parts of his skin preserved, and his tusks, which in size and whiteness surpassed the finest I had ever seen. 'His (that is, the elephant's) eyes were light blue, surrounded by salmon-colour; his hair fine, soft and white; his complexion pinkish-white; his tusks like long pearls; his ears like silver

## The white elephant

shields; his trunk like a comet's tail; his legs like the feet of the skies; his tread like the sound of thunder; his looks full of meditation; his expression full of tenderness; his voice the voice of a mighty warrior; and his bearing that of an illustrious monarch.'

'That was a terrible affliction, to the people not less than to the king.

'On all occasions of state—court receptions, for example—the white elephant, gorgeously arrayed, is stationed on the right of the inner gate of the palace, and forms an indispensable as well as a conspicuous figure in the picture.

'When the Siamese Ambassadors returned from England, the chief of the Embassy—a man remarkable for his learning and the purity of his character, who was also first cousin to the Supreme King—published a quaint pamphlet, describing England and her people, their manners and customs and dwellings, with a very particular report of the presentation of the Embassy at court. Speaking of the personal appearance of Queen Victoria, he says: 'One cannot but be struck with the aspect of the august Queen of England, or fail to observe that she must be of pure descent from a race of goodly and warlike kings and rulers of the earth, in that her eyes, complexion, and above all her bearing, are those of a beautiful and majestic white elephant.'

from *The English Governess at the Siamese Court* by Anna Leonowens

# Bandoola's birth and the tiger

In November 1897 Po Toke was an elephant-boy of fifteen. Fifteen may not seem a very great age; but the Burmese mature young. He had already picked the girl he wanted to marry, and he had chosen well. Ma Pyoo was beautiful and she was also the daughter of the contractor who owned the herd of elephants with whom he worked. Po Toke was one who aimed high because he had a justifiably high opinion of himself. He already knew more about elephants than any of the oozies of his own age, and more than most of the older men. He was ambitious, but it wasn't just ambition working in a vacuum. He was ambitious about elephants. Sometimes he told himself that he would know far more about elephants than the contractor himself. But that was a fancy he kept to himself. For the last year his thoughts had centred on his charge, Ma Shwe.

His suspicions of February 1896 had been confirmed. Ma Shwe was carrying a calf. Po Toke never knew who the sire was, but he suspected a wild tusker.

Wild elephants consider it the duty of the whole herd to protect an elephant carrying young, but in captivity the 'auntie' system prevails. Instinctively they realise that to protect the young calf against the tiger two elephants are needed, and for a whole year before the birth the expectant mother and her auntie, Mee Tway, had grazed together and got to know one another in preparation for the great and dangerous occasion.

Every oozie is excited when his elephant calves; but Po Toke was especially excited. He was penniless, and he felt in some obscure way that his fortune was bound up with that of Ma Shwe's calf.

And yet there is nothing that an oozie, however thoughtful or ambitious, can do in preparation for the event, apart from keeping his animal in good condition. The choice of site is a matter for the mother and her 'auntie'. No tactful suggestions from outsiders are received.

Ma Shwe and Mee Tway chose well. They selected a spot where the creek made a crook-shaped bend. That meant they were protected on three sides by water, and it was silently running water. The least sound from the river could be heard. There were plentiful supplies of elephant grass, which meant good fodder. And in the centre was a gigantic Nyaung tree. The Nyaung tree is evergreen. Its roots penetrate so deeply that they sap the underground rivers of the jungle, and the Burmans say that under a scorching sun a Nyaung tree will give off a ton of water a day. The tree provided shade, and two natural buttresses protruding from its base made a bay like a natural stall.

When Po Toke left them browsing there at sundown, and walked down the track which the elephants had made in the seven-foot elephant grass, he had to admit that he couldn't have chosen a better place himself. There was fodder, shade, water and silence.

Overnight the mother and the auntie spent a considerable time circling the tree and stamping down the grass until they had flattened an area the size of a circus ring. The maternity ward was complete.

There was little fuss about the birth, though for half an hour there was great tension as Mee Tway went round and round the tree on guard. Then the sun rose and revealed to all the inquisitive eyes of the jungle—squirrels', birds', monkeys'—the tubbiest little male elephant calf ever born.

By the time that Po Toke arrived, the calf was tottering about timidly, as if uncertain where on earth he was. His trunk was just a deformity of a snout which he could scarcely move; and his small piggy eyes were surrounded with wrinkles, and as deep as those of an elephant over three score years and ten. On his little forehead and along his back were masses of long wavy hair in need of brushing. His toe-nails—five on each fore-foot and four on each hind-foot—looked as if they had just been mani-cured. His skin fitted snugly over his baby body, but it was serrated and loose at the folds, like baby clothes. His complexion was the kind of purple you get by mixing blue and pink in a paintbox. His little tail touched his hocks and persistent insects were already teaching him its use.

This is what Po Toke saw when he put his head through the grass. He called to the mother in a loud voice, and when she saw him Ma Shwe rumbled a sort of purr of pride. It was a pride which Po Toke shared; for this was his calf as well as hers. He came over and patted the calf, congratulated the mother and guided the little gaping mouth below the deformity of a trunk to the mother's teats between her forelegs. Mee Tway was grazing about twenty-five yards away. 'Don't stray too far:' shouted Po Toke in a friendly way, and then left the maternity ward, whistling to himself............At noon Po Toke picked up his spear and set off down-creek to visit his charges again. He was only just out of sight of camp when he heard the pattering of feet behind him on the jungle path. It was Ma Pyoo. As an unmarried girl, she wore her hair sadauk fashion in a page-boy bob with two symmetrical points curling behind her ears and forward to frame her cheeks. Her tamain or native skirt was tucked across above her breasts and fastened under her right armpit, leaving her shoulders bare.

'Po Toke,' she said, 'if you really love me as you say you do, promise that you will guard the baby elephant and promise that you will never let anyone ride him except my young brother San Oo, who is in the Monastery School at Yamethin.'

Po Toke promised both these things. 'If I accomplish this,' he thought 'she will surely marry me.'

He waved her good-bye and then hurried on, for this was something to tell his elephants as important as telling his friends of the birth of the calf.

As he approached the maternity ward, he called aloud to warn them of his coming. In answer came great elephantine rumblings to say that all was well with them.

He stayed with them during the afternoon. He kicked a recent dung-dropping from the mother with his bare foot, and as it broke apart, he bent down and looked at it. It was all right. Mother and newly-born were doing well.

Before he left them he gave to Ma Shwe and Mee Tway a ball of molasses each. He made another ball, spat in his hand and rubbed the ball in the saliva. That he gave to the calf to sniff so that it could learn his smell.

As the sun went down, the clearing seemed to be illuminated with a green eerie light. This was the time when some of the jungle-dwellers were thinking of their sleep and others stretching and licking paws and rubbing sleepy eyes awake. Po Toke knew that the coming night would be the most dangerous of all nights for his calf. As he went down to the creek on his way to camp, he saw that Ma Shwe had walked the fifty yards to the river to drink during his absence, and Mee Tway had done likewise at another time. A good mother, a good auntie: they would not leave the calf unguarded. He was happier than he had ever been. He raised his voice and sang a Burmese love-song as he picked his way from boulder to boulder.

The elephants in their clearing heard his voice, so did a young full-grown tiger in a cane-break four hundred yards away across the stream. The tiger had chosen his lair with the same jungle instinct as the elephants had chosen their maternity ward, but with a different purpose. For days he had crossed and recrossed the track behind Ma Shwe. From the day an elephant's second milk falls into her udders, they leave a strong scent on all the leaves and branches that they touch. This scent had been an instinctive challenge to the tiger. He would kill and eat a baby elephant. It was his first attempt, but he knew that his best chance of doing so was within forty-eight hours of the calf's birth. . . .

Before it was dark the tiger left his lair and crossed the creek a long way below the elephants' pitch. He worked stealthily upstream until his sensitive nostrils picked up the scent of the newborn calf being wafted down on the evening breeze. For some distance he boldly followed the open game-track along the bank of the creek. Then he re-entered the jungle, and for a time squatted motionless on his haunches, working himself up for the attack. There was more in this than hunger and a succulent meal; there was prowess. To attack two elephants and kill the calf would be an achievement worthy of the king of the Burmese jungle.

He could not decide in advance whether he would attack the mother or the auntie first. That would depend on how they were standing when he moved in to attack. But he knew that he could not seize the calf until he had stampeded both the adults. He must spring on the back of one and so lacerate her that she fled for safety; then he must unseat himself and stampede the other long enough to give him time to seize the precious calf and carry it off like a cat with a rat in its mouth.

But before he could attack, he knew that he must circle the clearing, because the best line of attack was from upstream. His patience was superb. Twice he moved up to within fifty yards of the clearing, but each time the breeze was coming downstream too fast for him to risk his scent being carried to them when he moved above.

The moon rose higher and higher, but it was not till well after midnight that the breeze dropped. Utter silence fell on the jungle, a silence so deathly that few human beings can endure it without making some sound or movement to reassure themselves. But the elephants made no sound. The two adults stood side by side, as unmoving as statues in the moonlight; and between the forelegs of his mother, with his little head just filling the gap, stood the baby calf, as motionless as they.

Occasionally the ears of the adult animals moved forward as if straining to hear a sound. Then Mee Tway broke the silence—for no reason—she just thumped the end of her trunk on the ground, and it rang hollowly with a metallic sound.

It eased the tension but it started the tiger on his first circuit round the clearing. He was fifty yards out, and he had decided to make his attack from the creek side. Four times he circled without crackling a leaf or a twig—the perfect hunter. He no longer walked with slow, stealthy step. He was now so near that at any moment he might see his quarry in the clearing. His poise was low on the ground. He moved forward with his powerful hind legs tensed under his body, ready instantly to spring. The tip of his tail quivered.

At last he saw the picture he had dreamed of: an elephant's flank clearly silhouetted, and only ten bounds and a leap away. His enormous power was released as he bounded forward and with a seven-foot spring landed on Mee Tway's back. His fore-paws dug deep into the barrel of the elephant's back. The vicious grip of the fore-claws held his weight, while with his hinder claws he lacerated the sides of the wretched elephant. With a murderous snarl he sank his teeth into the elephant's shoulder.

For a second Mee Tway was taken by surprise. Then bellowing with panic fear she was off, making for the nearest jungle, where she could shake this savage terror from her back.

As she reached the edge of the untrodden elephant grass she hesitated for a moment; and in that moment the tiger retracted his claws and slid off, as a child might slide from a bareback pony. Immediately he turned and bounded back to attack Ma Shwe, standing under the Nyaung tree with the buttresses of the tree protecting her flanks. She had the advantage of position. The tiger could only attack head on. He had no opportunity to manoeuvre. She was terrified, but she stood her ground, with the calf huddled between her forelegs.

She took one chance. As the tiger checked before her, she took a pace forward and lashed at him with her trunk. With a lightning swing his right paw struck, the very movement of a cat at a terrier's face. The sharp claws struck home and Ma Shwe shrieked and bellowed with pain; for the trunk is the most sensitive and vital organ of the elephant. But she did not stampede. She replaced her off forward foot to protect the calf, who hadn't moved an inch.

But in that moment the tiger had gained his flank position and sprang up on her withers. His fore-claws dug their hold and his hind-claws tore at her flesh. She rolled and shook herself to fling him off, but still she didn't stampede and still he clung and tore.

Her trunk hung limp. She had no means of touching her calf. The injury had made it quite numb and useless. She felt herself weakening. Was there no relief from this murderous weight?

Then suddenly it seemed as if the Nyaung tree had fallen on her. Something struck her with the force of an avalanche. She sank to her knees with the impact, without damaging the calf. And when she rose again, the murderous weight was gone. Mee Tway had returned, goaded to fury by her wounds, and charged at the tiger clinging to the mother's flank.

The king of the Burmese jungle fell to the ground. He was badly hurt in pride and body. But he managed to slide away back to his jungle lair.

Now the two defiant elephants stood side by side once more, the blood streaming from their wounds, but the calf stood perfect and untouched. They raised their heads and roared and trumpeted a challenge to all the tigers of the Ningyan Forest.

from *Bandoola* by J. H. Williams

# Bandoola and the tamarind tree

The site of Po Toke's camp was a deserted village centuries old. The only signs that the place had ever been inhabited were a huge cultivated tamarind tree, and nearby it a small pagoda so dilapidated that it was now little more than a mound of mud-bricks overgrown with creeper.

To watch the operation of sawing off the tips of Bandoola's tusks, I took up my position on the top of the pagoda mound. Bandoola was securely chained to the tamarind tree without a spark of protest. All visible signs of musth had passed and once again he was as docile as any domesticated animal.

The tamarind tree was excellent for the purpose. Its bole, though short, was of great girth, and its massive branches, radiating out in the form of an umbrella, afforded complete shade. It looked as if it had taken about a century to grow and was good for at least another century.

A rope was fastened to Bandoola's left tusk at the lip. It was crossed over in front of the trunk to the right tusk and back again and then made fast. This was to prevent the small handsaw from cutting the trunk, if Bandoola in a fit of irritation tried to swing his trunk forward. Not that it appeared likely to me, watching from the top of the ruined pagoda, that the elephant would create any disturbance. He made no fuss about the rope being tied round his tusks, and as the first three inches of the tusks, which were to be sawed off, contained no nerve, the operation should cause him no pain.

Po Toke dipped his finger in red betel nut and lime and marked off where he was going to cut each tusk. Then he took up the handsaw. Bandoola watched him, squinting down his tusks. It was rather like a child at the dentist's for the first time, I thought, watching him take the drill. Po Toke caught hold of the tusk with his left hand and began to saw with his right.

For a moment Bandoola was quiet, then suddenly he jerked up his head. Po Toke stepped back, losing grip of tusk and saw at the same moment. Bandoola shook his head and let out bellow after bellow of rage. Po Toke shouted to him to be still, but the elephant took no notice. The other attendants stood back, well out of the way. This wasn't going to be a simple operation. I could feel the air charged with danger.

Bandoola was securely chained to the tree. In the battle of their wills, Po Toke had the advantage, just as he had had the advantage over the calf Bandoola in the pen when he was trained. It was just a matter of time. Po Toke waited for Bandoola to quieten down. He left the saw where it had fallen and spoke to the elephant reassuringly. Bandoola was as silent as a coiled spring.

After a time Po Toke stooped down and picked up the saw. For a moment he held the tusk in his left hand. Then suddenly the spring of Bandoola's anger was uncoiled. He lunged. He strained. He put every ounce of his tremendous body-weight against his chains. But they held. Po Toke, faced with this sudden outburst, stepped back. Into his orders he put his full authority. But Bandoola took no notice. He turned round to face the tamarind tree, seized the tying-chains in his trunk and jerked to snap them, but still they held. Then he raised a forefoot and stamped on the chains already strained to breaking point. The fore-fetters snapped. His forelegs were free.

The oozies fled. Po Toke ran up and joined me on the pagoda. We were helpless. There was nothing to do but watch the furious animal break loose. He wasn't apparently angry with those who had tied him up. His rage was concentrated on the tree and the chains which held him. His mind was made up that something must go.

Having got his forefeet free, he ignored the chains and, raising his tusks high up the tree-trunk to give him leverage, he pushed not only with his whole weight but also with every muscle in his powerful body. A shower of leaves fluttered to the ground; ripe tamarind fruit-pods rained upon the earth and bounced off his body. The whole tree rocked.

The trunk of the tamarind tree came back against Bandoola's trunk and for a moment he rested. Then he heaved against it again. Something snapped, a large root passing underneath him. He rocked the tree rhythmically; there was another snap, a third. His rage became a sort of furious demonstration of power. I watched appalled and yet filled with awe.

Then suddenly there was a rending, and the heaviest branch of the tree snapped and began to fall towards Bandoola. He saw it coming and screamed. He tugged to avoid it. His chains took the extreme strain, but the links did not part. With a volley of explosions as the roots snapped, the whole tree keeled over. Bandoola's screams changed from anger to terror and then they stopped as the tree fell on top of him and buried him from sight.

There is a silence of the forests which follows the crashing of a giant tree, a grave and tragic silence, as if something has suddenly died. Judging from the quiet and the absence of movement, I thought Bandoola was dead too, crushed beneath a tree far more massive even than himself. It was a very peculiar feeling to come down to this battlefield where the corpse of a mighty tree lay obliterating the animal who had killed it.

If Bandoola's chains had broken, he would no doubt have freed himself from the heavy branches which trapped him. But when we examined him, we found that he was lying flat on his side, still chained to the tree by his hind legs.

With incredible speed the elephant men got to work with saws and axes. We had no idea how badly Bandoola was injured. He lay quite motionless during the rescue. The final thing was to smash his chain, and I began to feel that it would never give. But at last with a felling wedge we split a link by driving it into the tree-trunk. Then he slowly rose as if he was recovering from a severe winding. He was as docile as the day he was born. He gave no trouble at all. But no one ever suggested again that his tusks should be tipped.

from *Bandoola* by J. H. Williams

# La Besace

Jupiter dit un jour: Que tout ce qui respire
S'en vienne comparoître aux pieds de ma grandeur;
Si dans son composé quelqu'un trouve à redire,
    Il peut le déclarer sans peur:
    Je mettrai remède à la chose.

Venez, singe; parlez le premier, et pour cause:
Voyez ces animaux, faites comparaison
    De leurs beautés avec les vôtres.
Êtes-vous satisfait?—Moi, dit-il; pourquoi non?
N'ai je pas quatre pieds aussi bien que les autres?
Mon portrait jusqu'ici ne m'a rien reproché;
Mais pour mon frère l'ours, on ne l'a qu'ébauché:
Jamais, s'il me veut croire, il ne se fera peindre.
L'ours venant là-dessus, on crut qu'il s'alloit plaindre,
Tant s'en faut: de sa forme il se loua très-fort;
Glosa sur l'éléphant, dit qu'on pourroit encor
Ajouter à sa queue, ôter à ses oreilles;
Que c'étoit une masse informe et sans beauté.
    L'éléphant étant écouté,
Tout sage qu'il étoit, dit des choses pareilles:
    Il jugea qu'à son appetit
    Dame baleine étoit trop grosse.
Dame fourmi trouva le ciron trop petit;
    Se croyant pour elle un colosse.
Jupin les renvoya s'étant censurés tous;
Du reste, contents d'eux. Mais parmi les plus fous
Notre espèce excella; car tout ce que nous sommes,
Lynx envers nos pareils, et taupes envers nous,
Nous nous pardonnons tout, et rien aux autres hommes:
On se voit d'un autre oeil qu'on ne voit son prochain.
    Le fabricateur souverain
Nous créa besaciers tous de même manière,
Tant ceux du temps passé que du temps d'aujourd'hui:
Il fit pour nos défauts la poche de derrière,
Et celle de devant pour les défauts d'autrui.

from *Fables* by La Fontaine

Illustration by Grandville from *Fables de La Fontaine*

# The overthrow of King Log

Henry said: 'I'm busy every day now. The river is in spate and we are faced with a great jam not three miles from here. I do not know if you would like to come and work with me, or stay at home taking it easy?'

'I'll come. "Work with me" sounds a little ominous, but I'll try.'

I had of course never seen a major teak jam before. The river, a tributary of the Meiping, twisted suddenly here and one log of exceptional size had straddled the stream at this point, held firmly between either bank. Above it more than five hundred logs were held in a solid block. The great pressure tended merely to drive the pin log further and more firmly into the banks. No man or men could hope to dislodge it. Machines such as cranes could not have been brought through the treacherous swamp that fringed the river-bank for fifty yards on either side. It was elephant work.

Henry spoke to his headman, then explained the plan to me. 'Six elephants will wade in with their mahouts and try to ease the pressure of the jam on the pin log. Then Pra Chorn will try to dislodge the pin log. If they fail we get nowhere. If they succeed there is danger, for the released logs will be swept down too fast and we have to get the elephants out undamaged.'

The working elephants were lined up on the bank, Pra Chorn standing apart from the others with Nai Sorn talking to him in the language that good mahouts use when conversing with their beasts. He spoke in Lao, telling him of the task that lay ahead, reminding him of all the feats he had accomplished, saying that this, too, he, and only he, could do. And Pra Chorn seemed to comprehend. Henry went up to him and stood by his side as the elephants that were to hold back the jam lunged one by one into the river, their mahouts riding them, their brown legs tucked in tightly beneath the great grey ears. One by one the brown bodies slid into the water treading gently, slowly, easing their way into mid-stream then across the river until they formed a line. As each beast advanced it had to push a path through the tightly packed logs and only the great strength of the beasts themselves and the cries of encouragement from the mahouts and some beating enabled them to do this.

The moment the line was formed Pra Chorn, without a word from Nai Sorn, plunged into the gap. I noticed that the mahout carried no stick.

'Pra Chorn will not have it,' said Henry. 'He only works if left to himself.'

In the water Pra Chorn seemed larger than ever. The whole of his great back was above water and his head and shoulders were clear to see and to guide him. He approached the pin log from downstream. For a moment he stood there silhouetted against the sky, a primeval frieze of dignity and power, then, in one sudden movement, he lowered his head, twined his tusk under the log and heaved. The log stood fast. It was viciously jammed, but perhaps it was loosened a little for Pra Chorn seemed not the least disturbed. He drew back and waited while the mahouts on the line of elephants above him urged their beasts to hold back the jam. Then, as suddenly as before, Pra Chorn stooped, this time to conquer. The log was free. With a gesture at once proud and con-

57 Japanese brown pottery elephant

58 Chinese porcelain elephant; reign of K'ang Hsi

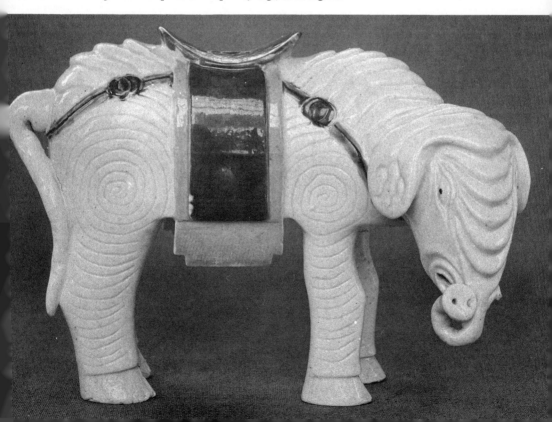

59 Staffordshire elephant by Whieldon, 1750

60 Staffordshire elephant with Rajah and tiger, *c.* 1850

temptuous Pra Chorn took it in his great trunk and flung it behind him as if it were a toy. Then, picking his way with caution, he moved up the bank, the water and mud streaming from him until he was on dry land again. His work was done, but pandemonium broke out in the river. The line of elephants turned to regain the bank and as they did so the avalanche of logs came down swept by the current round the bend. Very quickly the beasts bunched together for protection from that ominous wall of wood. In one tight knot of struggling brown bodies they reached the bank. Pra Chorn regarded them with what appeared to be approval.

The whole operation had taken less than ten minutes, but the suspense had been intense. No one had known if Pra Chorn had met a situation that even his enormous strength could not cope with. Up to the last moment it had seemed possible that the released logs would crush and maim the group of elephants who were now trumpeting on the banks, rolling in dry mud and behaving for all the world like schoolboys released from class.

from *No Other Elephant* by Gerald Sparrow

Reverse of coin said to have been struck by Augustus to commemorate Julius Caesar: coin from Cuperus

# The escape

Nai Sorn placed his hat and cane carefully on a table, grinned, and said:

'We made it, Nai. You remember you saw us off. Well, the Japanese were very close behind us. They were in Chiengmai at dawn. We had just four hours' start. They found out that Nai had escaped. They tortured his head boy by sticking burning cigarettes up his nostrils. He had to tell them the route that we had taken. They were on our track riding fresh Shan ponies. They could commandeer fresh ponies all along the route. No man dare deny them anything. You had but to hesitate to have the water pumped into your belly for them to jump on or for your finger-nails to be slowly extracted. You know what they are like, Nai.' I nodded.

'By the rules they should have caught us, but they never did. Because of Pra Chorn. You know, Nai, that sometimes there are kingly beasts that understand the ways of men, and give their love to one man. Such an elephant was Pra Chorn. He lives still in good retirement in Mandalay. Pra Chorn knew we were being hunted. He knew that if the pursuit caught up with us it was death for Nai and torture and rape for Mem.'

'Wanta, I noticed, was "Mem" again.

'I think I told you that Pra Chorn made his own working hours. He would march from dawn till 10 a.m., no more. But now he marched through the day and half the night—and, Nai, never did an elephant take the giant strides that Pra Chorn took, never did an elephant march so fast.

'Fortunately it was December, Nai, as you remember. Had it been April we could never have escaped. They would have caught up with us the day after leaving Chiengmai, for not even Pra Chorn could have battled against the heat of the spring or early summer. But for us the nights were quite cold and only the noon hours of the day warm. It was cool until eleven, and cool again soon after three. To this alone I can say we owed our good fortune. In those seven shining December days Pra Chorn averaged more than thirty miles a day, sometimes nearly forty. And always he carried his howdah, for the Princess could not walk, and I had to be on the neck of Pra Chorn. Sometimes Nai would walk; at other times, ride, too.

'At first we did not realize how perilously close the Japanese were, but on the fourth day we knew it. There is a point beyond the Three Pagodas where there is a great ravine that holds a river. Not a great river, little more than a torrential stream except in the rains, when it is a turbulent river. We passed across easily, the three of us on Pra Chorn. He was always superb in water, footsure and cunning. We pulled out of the stream and climbed the far side of the ravine, fifteen hundred yards or more. We had almost reached the summit when I heard a shot, then another, then the deadly stutter of a bren gun. Have you ever been exposed to bren-gun fire, Nai! It is a terror. There is no place to conceal one's body. Nai threw himself over his wife, but it was not us they were aiming for. It was the far easier target of Pra Chorn. I could see the bullets eating up the dirt around him when he charged for the summit. The fire followed him, but Pra Chorn swerved and swayed. By some miracle or the intervention of Buddha he was not hit. Had he been, the Japanese knew very well we were at their mercy. Somehow, swerving and darting separately, we reached the top of the ridge, but each of us had a hidden fear. Had Pra Chorn panicked?

'I, Nai, was most concerned of all, for if my elephant had failed us, I would have wept with humiliation and shame. Nai, too, was worried, he told me afterwards, for elephants are panicked by gunfire though they will face all other kinds of battle, perhaps because in the old days the kings rode them to war. I need not have worried, Nai.

'As soon as I crawled over the ridge, safe at last, there he was waiting for us. He had only gone far enough to protect his body from the line of the Japanese fire.

'I recaptured him at once, for he came towards us lifting the Princess first on his great trunk and setting off faster than ever as soon as I was on his neck and Nai was with his wife in the howdah. We had had a grim experience but at least we knew now how far behind us the Japanese were. No more at this time than half a mile, though this included the climb of the gorge which was equivalent to three miles. So we had barely an hour to spare. Pra Chorn knew this too and redoubled his efforts. He was not marching now but surging forward at a great, springing leap that ate up the miles. He had the courage of a lion, Nai, and he gave us courage too. When we fed and watered him now it was as one of us. He was no longer a beast, but a friend who protected us at least as much as we protected him.

'I think, Nai, that owing to the prodigious effort of Pra Chorn, we gained a few hours on the Japanese that day and the following night. I remember that there was a pale lemon moon in its first quarter and I said to my master: "The Lao have a saying that the waxing moon brings good fortune." He smiled then and said that we'd need it.

'I could not help thinking that we kept ahead of the Japanese because we knew the path and they did not and I often wondered whether the country people when the Japanese asked for information told them tales that would set them in the wrong direction. If they did it was a brave but very dangerous game. How dangerous it was we learnt towards the end of that march.

'We had passed near a little village called Kohmit. It was but a hamlet, Nai, but the path to Burma was lost here in a confusion of buffalo tracks and cart-wheel marks. It appears the Japanese asked the way and the villagers, guessing they were pursuing us, gave them false information. We only knew this a little later, for a villager escaped to join our party and he had a terrible tale to tell.

'We had seen a great fire burning in the village after our departure but thought no more of it, for after the harvest as you know the farmers often light bonfires and dance the Ramwong to celebrate.

'But the fire we had seen was no celebration.

'The villager who joined us and begged us to take him with us to Burma to fight against the Japs had lost his mother. She was the old woman who had told the Japanese a pack of lies that delayed them nearly five hours. They were livid with rage, Nai. They stormed back into the village and they poured petrol over the old woman and her nephew and two young girls and tied them to a tree. Then they set them alight. It was a human torch we had seen.

'They got correct information after that, as you can imagine, and now again they were pursuing us.

'Fortune still favoured us. We could easily have been caught even in the last twenty miles, for the Japanese were angry now, beating their ponies to death, then changing them and shooting the discarded ones. We were very near the end when the path split. Nai said: "Here's our chance," and we turned Pra Chorn up the wrong path for two miles, then crossed jungle to the real path. The ground was soft here and the Japanese would see his giant footmarks. To make doubly sure we left a water can as if we had dropped it before we doubled across to the Burma track. I think that trick saved us.

'The Japanese must have taken that decoy turning, for they were not hard on our heels again until the last ten miles. That final stretch over swamp and close jungle was the worst, as I remember it.

'It was then that they almost caught us. I think they feared now that they might lose us after all their efforts, and if they lost us they would lose face with their commander as well as the village people whom they wished to teach a lesson that would be burnt into their memories, the lesson that everyone obeys a soldier of His Imperial Majesty the Emperor of Japan.

'One of their number must have had a pony stronger or fresher than the rest for a little Japanese corporal armed with a bren gun as well as a revolver, came riding after us alone. He spurred his pony towards us at a storming gallop, and I thought: "This is it. He can hold us here at gunpoint until his comrades arrive." On the other hand if we shot him, not as far as we knew yet being at war with Japan, they would say we were murderers and would torture us before we died. We held our fire, but not even the desperate efforts of Pra Chorn could escape this pursuer.

'I was sitting in my usual position kicking the back of Pra Chorn's ears, begging him to go faster, even faster. But we could hear the Jap coming up in a flurry of cries behind us calling us to halt.

'Then Pra Chorn swung round in a split second and without an order from me seized the mounted Japanese in his trunk, shaking him until I thought he would die, but he only dropped his arms and cried out for mercy. Pra Chorn in his charge had sent the man's pony spinning to the ground and now in one furious gesture he trod on the prostrate beast, sending its belly belching out over the green grass.

'The Princess cried out with horror but we were moving again towards the border with the Japanese, his hands bound behind him, our prisoner.

'I say "our prisoner", Nai, but he was not. He was Pra Chorn's prisoner. Pra Chorn in those last hours would not let the little man out of his sight. When we halted at noon as we had to, and our prisoner made as if to go off on his own, Pra Chorn seized him again and shook him terrifyingly. He did not try any tricks after that. It was just as well. I could see the murder in the eye of Pra Chorn. But it was an appalling sight. The elephant had now dominion over the man. The Jap was in abject terror of his captor. It was against nature, Nai, the man being captive of the beast. I had never seen such a thing before nor do I wish to see it again.

'It seemed as if Pra Chorn was determined to keep his prisoner at all costs, for before we reached the border he had terrified the man to such an extent, that he would make not the slightest move without looking apprehensively at Pra Chorn. If Pra Chorn waved his trunk menacingly, the little soldier would stand, frozen with fear, where he was.

'Our last moment of danger came as we approached the frontier post of Melip. It was hardly a village, just two or three huts and a gate barrier with a small Siamese police guard. The Japs had come up again now and were close enough to fire at us while galloping, but either they were not close enough to hit us or the movement of their mounts made their aim too erratic, for no one was hit.

'We had one more desperate hazard. If the Siamese frontier guard delayed us, we were lost, for we had no doubt at all that these determined and vengeful Japanese would secure our surrender.

'Then Pra Chorn did his last deed on that journey, Nai, that has earned him my undying love. He stormed through the Siamese guard and on through the barrier gate as if it were matchwood. We were in British Burma. The Japanese had to rein in their ponies, for they dared not cross the frontier and risk being taken prisoner themselves.

'There was a British officer here and ten men. Nai went up to the officer and said: "We have come to fight against the Japanese."

'The officer looked at the Princess. He looked at the villager who had joined us, he looked at me, and he looked at our trembling Japanese. Finally he looked at Pra Chorn who stood there, proud but exhausted, a King in the sun.

' "Come to fight against the Japs? What, all of you?"

' "Yes," said Nai, "all of us except our prisoner whom we hand over to you."

'Pra Chorn worked in an Army camp, making his own working hours you may be sure, but he was lucky, for he secured a man of dignity and understanding to work with him. The Government gave him a pension at the end and he's resting now, as rest he should, in Mandalay.'

from *No Other Elephant* by Gerald Sparrow

# Nursery elephants

Many observers tell us that no elephant will harm a human child. There are numerous stories, too, of how an elephant will act as a thoroughly responsible baby-sitter. In return children, for the most part, are enthralled by elephants. This relationship, it would have been thought, would have brought far more elephants into the nursery than in fact there are. When one counts up the nursery rhymes on pigs or cats they are legion compared with elephants. In fact, apart from Edward Lear's nonsense alphabet rhymes, there are *no* elephant nursery rhymes.

Lear, one would have thought, would have written largely of the trunk or perhaps the tusks. But no, it was the eye. He does, it is true, mention tusks and trunk yet he was mesmerized by the small size of an elephant's eye compared to the animal's bulk. So far as it is known Lear composed only two elephant rhymes and both were included in nonsense alphabets under the letter E.

One, of which an autographed manuscript exists, was written and illustrated in 1857 for Winifred, William and Barrington Crake. Here it is:

Lear's Alphabet elephant

E was an Elephant,
O! what a size!
With Tusks—and a Trunk—
And with *such* little Eyes!
     E!
O what a great elephant!

The other one puts even more emphasis on the littleness of the elephant's eyes:

E was an elephant,
Stately and wise,
He had tusks and a trunk,
And two queer little eyes.
    e!
O what funny small eyes!

Children's books about animals are not, of course, all fantastical. Preeminent among those which are not are the Jungle Books by Rudyard Kipling. Highly imaginative they are, and even fanciful, perhaps, with their talking wolves, bears, pythons, monkeys and the rest. But they have a solid base of jungle lore which makes them more than pure—or one should perhaps say 'mere'—entertainment. They have no whimsy about them.

High up in the scale of such tales comes *Toomai of the Elephants.* Here we are not presented with the picture of an elephant talking human talk. Kala Nag—or 'Black Snake'—is a servant of man who is devoted to Toomai the son of his mahout and takes him on his back as a mark of friendship to show him the elephants' dance in the midst of the forest. Kala Nag, having enjoyed his holiday with his free companions of the forest, brings Toomai back to his home where he is accepted and proclaimed one of the race of elephant-keepers.

Not all Kipling's elephant tales are designed for children. The splendid extravaganza about Mulvaney's elephant friend Malachi is not for the nursery. The beginning of the story where Mulvaney meets the elephant chasing the gunner officer is inimitable. The gunner officer '. . . fetched wan woild despairin' look on the dog-kyarts and the polite society av Cawnpore, an' thin he dived like a rabbut into a dhrain by the side av the road . . . the elephint was huntin' for the gunner orf'cer. I can see his big fat back yet. . . . He put his head down (by my sowl he nearly stood on ut) to shquint down the dhrain; thin he'd grunt, and run round to the other ind in case the orf'cer was gone out by the back door; an' he'd shtuff his trunk down the flue an' get ut filled wid mud, an' blow ut out, an' grunt, an' swear. My troth, he swore all hiven down upon that orf'cer, an' what a commissariat elephant had to do wid a gunner-orf'cer passed me.'

Malachi then caught sight of Mulvaney and thought he was the gunner-officer and—well, read the story. It is full of meat.

Kipling's other elephant tale—*Moti Guj—Mutineer* is a splendid story of a working elephant and his keeper Deesa who goes on a fortnight's drunk. Moti Guj—which means 'Pearl Elephant'—would obey no one but Deesa. Deesa told Moti Guj that he would be away for ten days and emphasized this by banging Moti Guj ten times on his toenails. He called him 'Light of my Heart', 'Protector of the Drunken', 'Mountain of Might', 'fubsy old pig' and many other names and instructed him to work for another mahout Chihun. This Moti Guj did for exactly ten days. Deesa did not come back on day eleven so Moti Guj struck. Not a stroke of work would he do—well read this story too—it is a lesson in labour relations.

For children, of course, 'The Elephant's Child' far surpasses these two grown-up stories. 'The Elephant's Child' is full of the jingle beloved of children and Kipling was a master of inspired jingle. It would be quite wrong in a book on elephants in art, legend, religion and literature to leave out 'The Elephant's Child'—he is the most famous nursery elephant. Strange, is it not, that the *Just So Stories* animals have no names. 'Old Man Kangaroo', 'The Cat that walked by himself' and so forth. We shall not say much about the 'Elephant's Child' here as he appears in his full glory later on.

Perhaps the only other elephant character in English literature known to all children of today is Heffalump. The trouble is that Heffalump never, in fact, appears. He is a dream beast which Winnie the Pooh and Piglet plan to capture. One suspects somehow that Piglet devised his trap after learning something of the method of catching elephants, from the world of grown-ups. It is so very like the traps described by Pliny and many others. Of course, he is a very stupid Piglet and not at all like that brilliant strategist in the Three Little Pigs who defeated the wolf—Pooh, too, was pretty silly, falling into the pit himself and getting the honey jar stuck on his snout. But Piglet—one suspects that he could never have passed his Eleven Plus and that even if he had gone to a 'Comprehensive School' rather than a Secondary Modern he'd have been put in a very sluggish stream. To imagine that Pooh with the jar on his nose was a Heffalump! It is interesting considering what is known about the attitude of pigs and elephants to each other that Piglet speculated on whether Heffalump was fond of pigs—if so, what sort of pigs—or whether it was fierce with pigs—so perhaps it is not surprising that he fled from Pooh in the trap crying:

'Help, help: . . . a Heffalump; a Horrible Heffalump: Help, help a Herrible Hoffalump: Hoff, hoff a Hellible Horralump: Holl, holl, a Hoffable Hellerump!'

But it is rather sad that the Heffalump only appeared to Piglet in dreams —and oddly enough, E. H. Shepard's drawing of Heffalump makes him look quite like a natural elephant, and if Piglet really dreamed E. H. Shepard's elephant it makes him out sillier than ever to confuse him with Pooh with his snout in the honey jar. No, the story of Heffalump deserves no more than a Beta Plus.

We must, in fact, go to France for childhood's finest elephant, Babar. This tale, with its pictures, is certainly worth an Alpha Plus. Babar is in a class by himself. His only equal is Orlando, Kathleen Hale's Marmalade Cat. One cannot in the very nature of things draw an elephant which can match a cat in sheer beauty, but Jean de Brunhoff has created an elephant's character in the round with a personality as strong as Orlando's. He is the apotheosis of nursery elephants.

Babar's escape from the hunter who killed his mamma, his arrival in town, his friendship with *une vieille Dame* and his entrance into society form a classic of nursery logic and behaviour. Jean de Brunhoff's drawings are utterly convincing. If an elephant went to Paris to buy clothes, these are the clothes he would buy. Asked to tell his forest experiences to his *vieille Dame*'s friends, he takes up the most natural stance in front of the mantelpiece.

Babar has taken his place among the immortals of nurserydom. You will find him conversing on the most familiar terms with This Little Pig who went to market and That Little Pig who stayed at home. In what language?—we hear you ask. One can only say that all this occurred before the Tower of Babel and that all God's creatures understood one another perfectly. You may be quite sure that Babar was present (probably squiring his *vieille Dame*) at the wedding of the Owl and the Pussy Cat and that he had many a talk on philosophic subjects with the pig who gave them the ring. One may be sure that he knew the pigs who overcame Swellfoot the Tyrant in Shelley's drama and that he disapproved profoundly of Napoleon's treatment of Snowball in *Animal Farm*. Indubitably he admired that slick adventurer Puss in Boots, but what did he think of the Elephant's Child? He must, we think, have regarded him with sympathy and gratitude. Even Babar could not have done without his trunk.

One should not bring this tale of nursery—or schoolroom—elephants to a close without at least mentioning Kiouni, the elephant Passepartout found and Phileas Fogg bought (for the fearful sum of £2000) to bridge the gap in the railway between Kholby and Allahabad. Kiouni carried Phileas Fogg and his party, including the lovely Aouda whom Passepartout rescued from a funeral pyre on the way, to catch the train at Allahabad station. But what was then to be done with Kiouni?

Phileas Fogg turned to the Parsee who had guided them on the elephant—

'Parsee,' he said to the guide, 'you have been serviceable and devoted. I have paid for your service but not for your devotion. Would you like to have this elephant? He is yours.'

After all, the elephant had been an integral link, enabling Phileas Fogg to complete his journey 'Around the World in Eighty Days'.

Passepartout not at all frightened

Passepartout's uneasy ride on the back of the elephant

# The Elephant's Child

In the High and Far-Off Times the Elephant, O Best Beloved, had no trunk. He had only a blackish, bulgy nose, as big as a boot, that he could wriggle about from side to side; but he couldn't pick up things with it. But there was one Elephant—a new Elephant—an Elephant's Child— who was full of 'satiable curtiosity, and that means he asked ever so many questions. *And* he lived in Africa, and he filled all Africa with his 'satiable curtiosities. He asked his tall aunt, the Ostrich, why her tail-feathers grew just so, and his tall aunt the Ostrich spanked him with her hard, hard claw. He asked his tall uncle, the Giraffe, what made his skin spotty, and his tall uncle, the Giraffe, spanked him with his hard, hard hoof. And still he was full of 'satiable curtiosity! He asked his broad aunt, the Hippopotamus, why her eyes were red, and his broad aunt, the Hippopotamus, spanked him with her broad, broad hoof; and he asked his hairy uncle, the Baboon, why melons tasted just so, and his hairy uncle, the Baboon, spanked him with his hairy, hairy paw. And *still* he was full of 'satiable curtiosity! He asked questions about everything that he saw, or heard, or felt, or smelt, or touched, and all his uncles and his aunts spanked him. And still he was full of 'satiable curtiosity!

One fine morning in the middle of the Precession of the Equinoxes this 'satiable Elephant's Child asked a new fine question that he had never asked before. He asked, 'What does the Crocodile have for dinner?' Then everybody said, 'Hush!' in a loud and dretful tone, and they spanked him immediately and directly, without stopping, for a long time.

By and by, when that was finished, he came upon Kolokolo Bird sitting in the middle of a wait-a-bit thorn-bush, and he said, 'My father has spanked me, and my mother has spanked me; all my aunts and uncles have spanked me for my 'satiable curtiosity; and *still* I want to know what the Crocodile has for dinner!'

Then Kolokolo Bird said, with a mournful cry, 'Go to the banks of the great grey-green, greasy Limpopo River, all set about with fever-trees, and find out.'

That very next morning, when there was nothing left of the Equinoxes, because the Precession had preceded according to precedent, this 'satiable Elephant's Child took a hundred pounds of bananas (the little short red kind), and a hundred pounds of sugar-cane (the long purple kind), and seventeen melons (the greeny-crackly kind), and said to all his dear families, 'Good-bye. I am going to the great grey-green, greasy Limpopo River, all set about with fever-trees, to find out what the Crocodile has for dinner.' And they all spanked him once more for luck, though he asked them most politely to stop.

Then he went away, a little warm, but not at all astonished, eating melons, and throwing the rind about, because he could not pick it up.

He went from Graham's Town to Kimberley, and from Kimberley to Khama's Country, and from Khama's Country he went east by north, eating melons all the time, till at last he came to the banks of the great grey-green, greasy Limpopo River, all set about with fever-trees, precisely as Kolokolo Bird had said.

Now you must know and understand, O Best Beloved, that till that very week, and day, and hour, and minute, this 'satiable Elephant's Child had never seen a Crocodile, and did not know what one was like. It was all his 'satiable curtiosity.

The first thing that he found was a Bi-Coloured-Python-Rock-Snake curled round a rock.

''Scuse me,' said the Elephant's Child most politely, 'but have you seen such a thing as a Crocodile in these promiscuous parts?'

'*Have* I seen a Crocodile?' said the Bi-Coloured-Python-Rock-Snake, in a voice of dretful scorn. 'What will you ask me next?'

''Scuse me,' said the Elephant's Child, 'but could you kindly tell me what he has for dinner?'

Then the Bi-Coloured-Python-Rock-Snake uncoiled himself very quickly from the rock, and spanked the Elephant's Child with his scalesome, flailsome tail.

'That is odd,' said the Elephant's Child, 'because my father and my mother, and my uncle and my aunt, not to mention my other aunt, the Hippopotamus, and my other uncle, the Baboon, have all spanked me for my 'satiable curtiosity—and I suppose this is the same thing.'

So he said good-bye very politely to the Bi-Coloured-Python-Rock-Snake, and helped to coil him up on the rock again, and went on, a little warm, but not at all astonished, eating melons, and throwing the rind about because he could not pick it up, till he trod on what he thought was a log of wood at the very edge of the great grey-green, greasy Limpopo River, all set about with fever-trees.

But it was really the Crocodile, O Best Beloved, and the Crocodile winked one eye—like this!

''Scuse me,' said the Elephant's Child most politely, 'but do you happen to have seen a Crocodile in these promiscuous parts?'

Then the Crocodile winked the other eye, and lifted half his tail out of the mud; and the Elephant's Child stepped back most politely, because he did not wish to be spanked again.

'Come hither, Little One,' said the Crocodile. 'Why do you ask such things?'

''Scuse me,' said the Elephant's Child most politely, 'but my father has spanked me, my mother has spanked me, not to mention my tall aunt, the Ostrich, and my tall uncle, the Giraffe, who can kick ever so hard, as well as my broad aunt, the Hippopotamus, and my hairy uncle, the Baboon, *and* including the Bi-Coloured-Python-Rock-Snake, with the scalesome, flailsome tail, just up the bank, who spanks harder than any of them; and *so*, if it's quite all the same to you, I don't want to be spanked any more.'

'Come hither, Little One,' said the Crocodile, 'for I am the Crocodile,' and he wept crocodile-tears to show it was quite true.

Then the Elephant's Child grew all breathless, and panted, and kneeled down on the bank and said, 'You are the very person I have been looking for all these long days. Will you please tell me what you have for dinner?'

'Come hither, Little One,' said the Crocodile, 'and I'll whisper.'

Then the Elephant's Child put his head down close to the Crocodile's musky, tusky mouth, and the Crocodile caught him by his little nose, which up to that very week, day, hour, and minute, had been no bigger than a boot, though much more useful.

'I think,' said the Crocodile—and he said it between his teeth, like this—'I think to-day I will begin with Elephant's Child!'

At this, O Best Beloved, the Elephant's Child was much annoyed, and he said, speaking through his nose, like this, 'Led go! You are hurtig be!'

Then the Bi-Coloured-Python-Rock-Snake scuffled down from the bank and said, 'My young friend, if you do not now, immediately and instantly, pull as hard as ever you can, it is my opinion that your acquaintance in the large-pattern leather ulster' (and by this he meant the Crocodile) 'will jerk you into yonder limpid stream before you can say Jack Robinson.' This is the way Bi-Coloured-Python-Rock-Snakes always talk.

Then the Elephant's Child sat back on his little haunches, and pulled, and pulled, and pulled, and his nose began to stretch. And the Crocodile floundered into the water, making it all creamy with great sweeps of his tail, and *he* pulled, and pulled, and pulled.

And the Elephant's Child's nose kept on stretching; and the Elephant's Child spread all his little four legs and pulled, and pulled, and pulled, and his nose kept on stretching; and the Crocodile threshed his tail like an oar, and *he* pulled, and pulled, and pulled, and at each pull the Elephant's Child's nose grew longer and longer—and it hurt him hijjus!

Then the Elephant's Child felt his legs slipping, and he said through his nose, which was now nearly five feet long, 'This is too butch for be!'

Then the Bi-Coloured-Python-Rock-Snake came down from the bank, and knotted himself in a double-clove-hitch round the Elephant's Child's hind-legs, and said, 'Rash and inexperienced traveller, we will now seriously devote ourselves to a little high tension, because if we do not, it is my impression that yonder self-propelling man-of-war with the armour-plated upper deck' (and by this, O Best Beloved, he meant the Crocodile) 'will permanently vitiate your future career.' That is the way all Bi-Coloured-Python-Rock-Snakes always talk.

So he pulled, and the Elephant's Child pulled, and the Crocodile pulled; but the Elephant's Child and the Bi-Coloured-Python-Rock-Snake pulled hardest; and at last the Crocodile let go of the Elephant's Child's nose with a plop that you could hear all up and down the Limpopo.

Then the Elephant's Child sat down most hard and sudden; but first he was careful to say 'Thank you' to the Bi-Coloured-Python-Rock-Snake; and next he was kind to his poor pulled nose, and wrapped it all up in cool banana leaves, and hung it in the great grey-green, greasy Limpopo to cool.

'What are you doing that for?' said the Bi-Coloured-Python-Rock-Snake.

''Scuse me,' said the Elephant's Child, 'but my nose is badly out of shape, and I am waiting for it to shrink.'

'Then you will have to wait a long time,' said the Bi-Coloured-Python-Rock-Snake. 'Some people do not know what is good for them.'

The Elephant's Child sat there for three days waiting for his nose to shrink. But it never grew any shorter, and, besides, it made him squint. For, O Best Beloved, you will see and understand that the Crocodile had pulled it out into a really truly trunk same as all Elephants have to-day.

At the end of the third day a fly came and stung him on the shoulder, and before he knew what he was doing he lifted up his trunk and hit that fly dead with the end of it.

''Vantage number one!' said the Bi-Coloured-Python-Rock-Snake. 'You couldn't have done that with a mere-smear nose. Try and eat a little now.'

Before he thought what he was doing the Elephant's Child put out his trunk and plucked a large bundle of grass, dusted it clean against his fore-legs, and stuffed it into his own mouth.

''Vantage number two!' said the Bi-Coloured-Python-Rock-Snake. 'You couldn't have done that with a mere-smear nose. Don't you think the sun is very hot here?'

'It is,' said the Elephant's Child, and before he thought what he was doing he schlooped up a schloop of mud from the banks of the great grey-green, greasy Limpopo, and slapped it on his head, where it made a cool schloopy-sloshy mud-cap all trickly behind his ears.

''Vantage number three!' said the Bi-Coloured-Python-Rock-Snake. 'You couldn't have done that with a mere-smear nose. Now how do you feel about being spanked again?'

''Scuse me,' said the Elephant's Child, 'but I should not like it at all.'

'How would you like to spank somebody?' said the Bi-Coloured-Python-Rock-Snake.

'I should like it very much indeed,' said the Elephant's Child.

'Well,' said the Bi-Coloured-Python-Rock-Snake, 'you will find that new nose of yours very useful to spank people with.'

'Thank you,' said the Elephant's Child, 'I'll remember that; and now I think I'll go home to all my dear families and try.'

So the Elephant's Child went home across Africa frisking and whisking his trunk. When he wanted fruit to eat he pulled fruit down from a tree, instead of waiting for it to fall as he used to do. When he wanted grass he plucked grass up from the ground, instead of going on his knees as he used to do. When the flies bit him he broke off the branch of a tree and used it as a fly-whisk; and he made himself a new, cool, slushy-squashy mud-cap whenever the sun was hot. When he felt lonely walking through Africa he sang to himself down his trunk, and the noise was louder than several brass bands. He went especially out of his way to find a broad Hippopotamus (she was no relation of his), and he spanked her very hard, to make sure that the Bi-Coloured-Python-Rock-Snake had spoken the truth about his new trunk. The rest of the time he picked up the melon rinds that he had dropped on his way to the Limpopo—for he was a Tidy Pachyderm.

One dark evening he came back to all his dear families, and he coiled up his trunk and said, 'How do you do?' They were very glad to see him, and immediately said, 'Come here and be spanked for your 'satiable curiosity.'

# The Elephant's Child

'Pooh,' said the Elephant's Child. 'I don't think you peoples know anything about spanking; but *I* do, and I'll show you.'

Then he uncurled his trunk and knocked two of his dear brothers head over heels.

'O Bananas!' said they, 'where did you learn that trick, and what have you done to your nose?'

'I got a new one from the Crocodile on the banks of the great grey-green, greasy Limpopo River,' said the Elephant's Child. 'I asked him what he had for dinner, and he gave me this to keep.'

'It looks very ugly,' said his hairy uncle, the Baboon.

'It does,' said the Elephant's Child. 'But it's very useful,' and he picked up his hairy uncle the Baboon, by one hairy leg, and hove him into a hornet's nest.

Then that bad Elephant's Child spanked all his dear families for a long time, till they were very warm and greatly astonished. He pulled out his tall Ostrich aunt's tail-feathers; and he caught his tall uncle, the Giraffe, by the hind-leg, and dragged him through a thorn-bush; and he shouted at his broad aunt, the Hippopotamus, and blew bubbles into her ear when she was sleeping in the water after meals; but he never let any one touch Kolokolo Bird.

At last things grew so exciting that his dear families went off one by one in a hurry to the banks of the great grey-green, greasy Limpopo River, all set about with fever-trees, to borrow new noses from the Crocodile. When they came back nobody spanked anybody any more; and ever since that day, O Best Beloved, all the Elephants you will ever see, besides all those that you won't, have trunks precisely like the trunk of the 'satiable Elephant's Child.

from *Just So Stories* by Rudyard Kipling

61 Tondo from Barhut: the dream of Maya

62 Modern pottery elephant and saddle from Ramsbury, Wilts

# Elephants and inn signs

It is obvious that whoever first described his drunken visions as 'seeing pink elephants'—alas, we do not know who the fellow was—had never heard of the Pink Elephant in the Ajanta cave paintings. Various writers tell us that white elephants are often not really white but pinkish buff in colour. It is true that they are rare and therefore, perhaps, unnatural: human experience does suggest that inebriated persons are apt to see unusual creatures—pink rats, for instance, as well as pink elephants—and even millions upon millions of pink toads, like the chief engineer of the *Patna*, in *Lord Jim*.

Perhaps pink elephants of the imaginary variety were not unknown to the Dartmoor prisoner, who, to the astonishment of the country in general, claimed to be in the habit of slipping away from his working party on the Moor and indulging in a comfortable meal and a pint or two—or three—in that strangely named hostelry, the *Elephant's Nest*.

The authorities on English Inn Signs—Messrs Larwood and Hotten —do not refer to the *Elephant's Nest* and so far as we have been able to discover there is no learned explanation for the name. Those who have studied the Matanga-Lila will recollect that before they became earth-bound, elephants flew through the air at will and even settled in trees. Ethiopian elephants are said to have plucked branches from trees to help them to make obeisance to the sun, moon and stars but there is no reference to their having used the branches to make nests with. An elephant's nest could hardly have escaped notice, it would have been a fairly prominent object and Pliny, Aelian or Solinus would have been sure to mention it—and if there had been the faintest suspicion that such a thing existed Herodotus would have been on to it—or should one say 'into' it—in a flash. And, in parenthesis, who was it that called a certain size of paper 'Double Elephant'? Was it a tipsy artist, used to quaffing doubles, or merely an imaginative paper-maker with grandiose ideas? The speculation is an intriguing one but perhaps it would be unprofit-able to spend too much time upon it.

When the elephant is adopted as an inn sign it is rarely plain or un-accompanied. There is an inn called simply *The Elephant* in Doncaster. Of the Doncaster *Elephant*, so far as is known, no special story is re-corded. Another *Elephant* inn, this time abroad, is however the scene of drama. It was in this *Elephant* that, according to Thomas Mann in his novel *Lotte In Weimar*, Frau Kestner, original of Goethe's Charlotte, stayed when in old age she came to meet Goethe again. The meeting was not a success. And, of course, there was *The Elephant* at which Sebastian was recommended to stay by Captain Antonio in *Twelfth Night*: This is described simply as *The Elephant* 'in the south suburbs' which suggests that it might have been what is now known as *The Ele-phant & Castle*—of which more anon. It is, of course, highly Shake-spearian that Sir Toby and others in the play are indubitably English while Sebastian and Viola were wrecked off Illyria. Now it is an interest-ing thing that in Ljubljana there is a hotel *Slon*—that is the hotel *Ele-phant*—which forty years ago, had a fresco in noble proportions of a sixteenth-century elephant. Ljubljana is not so very far from the Illyrian coast and it is surely not impossible that Shakespeare knew something of an *Elephant Inn* in these parts in his day. It is interesting that Mr

Charles Knight supports the view held by the ancients that the elephant was a sun-worshipper, by observing that the Serbo-Croat word for 'elephant', *Slon*, is so like the word *Slonce*, one form of the word for sun in the same language. Mr A. C. Southern, in a letter to *The Times Literary Supplement* in June 1953, maintains that the *Twelfth Night* '*Elephant*' had nothing to do with the *Elephant and Castle*. In certain 'Vestry' and 'Token' Books providing a census of the districts known as The Clink (1588–1642) and Boroughside (1596–1642) he discovered various relevant entries of which one read, under date July 19, 1598:—

'Item it was ordered that the churchwardens of the Church of St Saviour, Southwark shall calle for an answer of the tenant of the house sometime called the *Redharte* and nowe called the *Oliphant* concerninge the land supposed to be withhelde from the parrishe.'

From other entries the land is described as on Bankside and owned by one Mr Ritche. In later entries, still, under the heading of '*The Elephant*' (alternatively *Elephant Allye*), a group of tenements abutting on Bankside, first in the list of returns of each of the years 1599 to 1605 is a certain John Ford, and in Clink 1601 and Bankside 1602 Ford is described as a 'victualler'.

From that it may be inferred that at the time of the production of *Twelfth Night* there was an inn in the district called *The Elephant* of which John Ford was the landlord. One inn is or was to be found at Sandhill, Newcastle, which takes one back to mediaeval manuscripts and legends—*The Elephant and Fish*. Larwood and Hotten suggest that the fish was in reality the dragon or serpent with which the elephant was in perpetual strife, according to Strabo, Pliny, Aelian and their mediaeval disciples. As the fight required the dragon to squeeze the elephant to death with his tail it is hard to see how it could have been metamorphosed into a fish. The birth of elephants in water according to the bestiaries is referred to in the chapter on elephants in art and legend, and at plate 13 will be seen the representation of the birth. In the illustrations with the elephants are a number of fishes and it seems more probable that the combination of 'Elephant and Fish' merely derives from this fact of the supposed birth in water with fishes to prove it. One may mention, again in parenthesis, that the interest of elephants in fish has been recently proved by Irma, aged 2, an Indian elephant who lives in a zoo at Knaresborough, Yorkshire. With a fisherman friend she regularly goes to sit beside him while he fishes in the River Nidd. Motionless the two companions sit on the bank, their eyes fixed on the float, and wait for a bite. *The Elephant and Friar* is another strange partnership. This sign used to be seen on an inn in Bristol. Larwood and Hotten suggested that it may have come from an earlier sign showing an elephant with his mahout in eastern garments. It has been suggested this sign would better have suited the landlord of an *Elephant and Castle* in Leeds whose name was Priest. As so often with inn signs this landlord adorned his sign with an extremely bad piece of doggerel which read:

'He is a priest who lives within,
Gives advice gratis and administers gin.'

Sign of Cutlers' Company

The *Elephant and Castle* is, of course, the most usual name for 'elephant' inns and the best known is the one which used to stand in London south of the river in Newington Butts and gave its name to the district. The sign now stands in what modern planners call a 'precinct' in the same district.

It has been frequently stated that the name *Elephant and Castle* is a corruption of 'Infanta of Castile'. It is said—whether history or myth is hard to determine—that the Spanish princess who came to wed Henry VIII—Catherine of Aragon—halted here on her journey to London and that Henry met her at this spot. If this were really so and an alehouse were constructed here and named after the Infanta, it is not surprising that Henry's enthusiastic but illiterate subjects got the name wrong. The actual inn the *Elephant and Castle* was however not constructed until 1714. One's inclination is to regard the origin 'Infanta of Castile' as the ingenious invention of some clever wit. In cathedrals and churches many carved elephants and castles appear and it seems more natural that the south-bank *Elephant and Castle* derived from one of these ecclesiastical models.

Another stoutly held theory is that the name is a corruption of 'Eleanor of Castile', daughter of Ferdinand III of Castile and wife of Edward I of England whom she married in 1254. After her death in Northamptonshire in 1290 there was a funeral procession and every place at which the procession stopped was named after her, one spot being *Charing* (or *'chère reine'*) *Cross*. Oddly enough it was in 1254 that Edward's father Henry III received the present of an elephant from Louis IX of France. This elephant (see page 50) arrived in London by water and was housed in the Tower of London. Did he, perhaps, first land on the South Bank of the Thames?

Up to the Second World War and the 'blitz' the 'Elephant', as it was called, was a kind of south bank Piccadilly Circus, full of life, sky signs, a music hall, the biggest cinema in Europe and five pubs roaring into the night. After the blitz people never came back and many think the modern shopping centre built on the site has missed the boat. To reach it people have to go through subways under the traffic. No, the 'Elephant' is not what it was despite the fact that inside there is a shop selling enamelware and pottery called '*The Thoughtful Elephant*'. One can't help thinking that it should have been a trunk shop.

There is a story that about the time the original Newington Butts *Elephant and Castle* was built, an apothecary in Fleet Street who was something of an archaeologist was digging in the neighbourhood of the Fleet in a gravel pit where he discovered the skeleton of an elephant and a flint-headed spear. It was conjectured that the beast had been killed in a fight between the ancient Britons and the Romans. It is, however, hard to see how this elephant could have given its name to the inn. Perhaps it was the elephant declared by Polyaenus (see page 104) to have helped Caesar to defeat Cassivelaunus at the crossing of the Thames.

It is reported that at one time there were at least five *Elephant and Castle* inns in London and there are many others throughout England. In the days when every trader had his sign there was an *Elephant and Castle* at Temple Bar, but this was not an inn. An advertisement from *The Intelligencer* of 14 November 1664 proclaims the efficiency of 'an excellent Bolus for the cure of gout' to be had at '*The Elephant and Castle without Temple-Barre*'. According to *Boyne's Trade Tokens* edited by a Dr Williamson there was a Token with 'The Elephant without' on the obverse, said to represent an Elephant and Castle—and on the reverse 'Tampel Barr, 1650'.

This does not sound a very convivial type of drink but may have been highly useful to frequenters about a hundred years later, in 1756. The *Whitehall Evening Post* for Thursday 13 May to Saturday 15 May of that year has the following interesting advertisement:

*To Be Sold*
At Halletts Warehouse, The Elephant and Castle, Temple Bar having choice of many thousand gallons of best Jamaica Rum of a fine flavour at 7s. 6d. per gallon and by the Puncheon at 7s. 4d. Fine French Brandy at 7s. 9d. per gallon, strong and fine flavour'd. Such or goodness seldom can be obtained, and, Fine Orange Shrub at 6s. per gallon, having a large stock. For ready money, and by applying as above, you may have samples, at 2s. per quart, carriage free to any part of the town.

There are, of course, many heraldic elephants in signs or coats of arms which have nothing to do with inns. Fremlin's Brewery (which has a gilded elephant weathervane at Maidstone), the city of Coventry, Hoveringhams, the Cutlers Company and many other concerns display the elephant. Cutlers used it because of the ivory employed in their trade.

Canute IV of Denmark instituted the Order of the White Elephant in 1190. The insignia consists of an elephant of gold and white enamel and a little Moor of black enamel sits upon the neck.

In modern times the elephant, as a political emblem, represents the American Republican Party. It appeared in a cartoon in *Harper's*

*Weekly* in 1874. The elephant labelled 'Republican Votes' was shown in a jungle in a rage, sweeping aside the covering of a pit-fall prepared to catch it, lettered 'Southern Claims Chaos'. At about the same time the donkey became the symbol of the Democratic Party.

Whether the elephant races organized in Orange County State University, California, have anything to do with American politics is not known, but it seems unlikely, as elephant races were common in India as early as the thirteenth century. In fact, rioting which led to the fall of the Kalingun Dynasty was started by a dispute over such racing between two rival theological colleges.

But this is perhaps too remote from the subject of inn signs to pursue further.

# The man and the elephant

Balahvar said: This transitory life resembles a man pursued by a raging elephant. And it cornered him inside a fearsome abyss. Then he caught sight of some trees on to which he climbed and then saw two mice, one black and one white, which were gnawing away the roots of the trees up which the man had clambered. And he looked down into the chasm and noticed a dragon, which had parted its jaws and was intent on swallowing him. And he looked up above and saw a little honey trickling down the trees, and he began to lick it up. And now he remembered no longer the peril into which he had fallen. But the mice gnawed through the trees, and the man fell down, and the elephant seized him and hurled him over to the dragon.

Now, O king's son, that elephant is the image of death, which pursues the sons of men; and the trees this transitory existence; and the mice are the days and nights; and the honey is the sweetness of the passing world; and the savour of the passing world diverts mankind. So the days and nights are accomplished and death seizes him and the dragon swallows him down into hell; and this is the life of men.

from the *Sermons of the Hermit Balahvar of Ceylon on a mission to Prince Iodasaph*

Elephant worshipping sun and moon

# The elephant's prayer

Dear God,
It is I, the elephant,
Your creature,
Who is talking to you.
I am so embarrassed by my great size,
And think it is not my fault,
If I spoil your jungle a little with my big feet.
Let me be careful and behave wisely,
Always keeping my dignity and poise.
Give me such philosophic thoughts,
That I can rejoice everywhere I go,
In the lovely oddity of things.
Amen.

from *Prayers from the Ark*, by Carmen Bernos de Gasztold, translated by Rumer Godden

Coin struck by Cardinal Zaberella: coin from Cuperus

SOLI DEO

# Captain Rotton's adventure

Two remarkable volumes were published in 1819 by Mr H. R. Young, of 56 Paternoster Row, in London. They are entitled *Oriental Field Sports, being a complete, detailed and accurate description of the Wild Sports of the East.* The manuscript from which the book was produced is by a Captain Thomas Williamson, who served in Bengal for over twenty years and the splendid colour plates are by Samuel Howitt.

Captain Williamson knows every aspect of his subject and he writes with infectious enthusiasm. In his introduction he declares:

'Herein the British Nimrod may view, with no small satisfaction, a new and arduous species of the Chase. The curious observer of Nature will feel equal transport, in contemplating that part of her works, which she has appropriated to other soils. The Artist may reap a rich harvest of information, enabling him, not only to comprehend more fully the scenery of the torrid zone, but to adorn his own compositions with a greater variety of those beauties which the climate and narrow limits of his own country cannot furnish. . . .

'The Public have at times been amused with various anecdotes relating to elephants, of which the generality may be attributed to fiction; because they are either repugnant to the disposition and nature of that noble animal, or, from local circumstances, highly improbable. Such as evince nothing contrary to docility and wondrous discrimination, may be viewed in general, without too severe a scrutiny: for the Elephant may be said to possess the energy of the horse, the sagacity of the dog, and a large portion of the monkey's cunning.'

Frequently throughout his book Captain Williamson refers to the 'beauty' of the chase. 'The Chase is most pleasing,' he says, 'on plains of grass moderately thick,' and 'the Chase in such a situation was often beautiful at the same time that it was safe.'—and, again, 'Never perhaps was a more beautiful scene beheld'—this last when a single tiger was hunted by a vast party on something like seventy elephants!

All Captain Williamson's sportsmen are European. He writes:

'This certainly may appear strange, but is nevertheless perfectly correspondent with facts. The natives of India consider what we call sporting, to be quite a drudgery and derogatory from the consequence and dignity of such as are classed among the superior orders.'

Many if not most of Captain Williamson's stories are of tiger-hunts with elephants.

The following is a typical example:

'A curious circumstance, illustrative of the anomalies of the sport, occurred to a very worthy officer, Captain John Rotton, who died some years since. He was one of a numerous party assembled for tiger-hunting, and was mounted on a very fine male elephant, that, far from being timid, was very remarkable for a courage scarcely to be kept within the bounds of prudence. This singularly fine animal having, after much beating of thick grass, hit upon the tiger's situation, uttered his roar of vengeance, which roused the lurking animal, occasioning him to rise so as to be seen distinctly.

'No sooner did the tiger shew himself, than Captain Rotton, with great readiness, bending his body a little to the left, took aim at him as he

64 Kubla Khan on four elephants

65 Capture of elephants; from *Indiae Orientalis*

66 Capture of elephants in keddah; from *Indiae Orientalis*

67 Elephants in single combat; from *Indiae Orientalis*

68 Elephants in procession; from *Indiae Orientalis*

69 Elephants on 10th-cent. Persian silk shroud

70 Chasing tiger across river; from *Oriental Field Sports*

71 Elephants and rhino; from *Oriental Field Sports*

72 Babar speaks to his friends

73 Elephant and Castle inn sign

74 Charcoal drawing by Rembrandt

stood up, crosswise, almost close to the elephant's head. The elephant no sooner espied his enemy, than he knelt down, as is common on these occasions, with the view to strike the tiger through with his tusks. At the same time the tiger, sensible of the device, as suddenly threw himself on his back; thereby evading the intended mischief, and ready to claw the elephant's face with all four feet; which were thus turned upwards. Now, whether Captain Rotton had not been in the habit of joining in such rapid evolutions, or that the elephant forgot to warn him to hold fast, we know not; but, so it happened, that the delicate situation in which he was placed, while taking his aim, added to the quickness of the elephant's change of height forward, combined to project him, without the least obstruction, from his seat, landing him plump on the tiger's belly! This was a species of warfare to which all parties were apparently strangers. The elephant, however fearless in other respects, was alarmed at the strange round mass, the Captain being remarkably fat, which had shot like a sack over his shoulder; while the tiger, judging it to be very ungentlemanlike usage, lost no time in regaining his legs, trotting off at a round pace, and abandoning the field to the victorious Captain.'

from *Oriental Field Sports* by Captain Thomas Williamson, 1819

# The elephant and the tortoise or, why the worms are blind and why the elephant has small eyes

When Ambo was king of Calabar, the elephant was not only a very big animal, but he had eyes in proportion to his immense bulk. In those days men and animals were friends, and all mixed together quite freely. At regular intervals King Ambo used to give a feast, and the elephant used to eat more than anyone, although the hippopotamus used to do his best; however, not being as big as the elephant, although he was very fat, he was left a long way behind.

As the elephant ate so much at these feasts, the tortoise, who was small but very cunning, made up his mind to put a stop to the elephant eating more than a fair share of the food provided. He therefore placed some dry kernels and shrimps, of which the elephant was very fond, in his bag, and went to the elephant's house to make an afternoon call.

When the tortoise arrived the elephant told him to sit down, so he made himself comfortable, and, having shut one eye, took one palm kernel and a shrimp out of his bag, and commenced to eat them with much relish.

When the elephant saw the tortoise eating, he said, as he was always hungry himself, 'You seem to have some good food there; what are you eating?'

The tortoise replied that the food was 'sweet too much', but was rather painful to him, as he was eating one of his own eyeballs; and he lifted up his head, showing one eye closed.

The elephant then said, 'If the food is so good, take out one of my eyes and give me the same food.'

The tortoise, who was waiting for this, knowing how greedy the elephant was, had brought a sharp knife with him for that very purpose, and said to the elephant, 'I cannot reach your eye, as you are so big.'

The elephant then took the tortoise up in his trunk and lifted him up. As soon as he came near the elephant's eye, with one quick scoop of the sharp knife he had the elephant's right eye out. The elephant trumpeted with pain; but the tortoise gave him some of the dried kernels and shrimps, and they so pleased the elephant's palate that he soon forgot the pain.

Very soon the elephant said, 'That food is so sweet, I must have some more:' but the tortoise told him that before he could have any the other eye must come out. To this the elephant agreed; so the tortoise quickly got his knife to work, and very soon the elephant's left eye was on the ground, thus leaving the elephant quite blind. The tortoise then slid down the elephant's trunk on to the ground and hid himself. The elephant then began to make a great noise, and started pulling trees down and doing much damage, calling out for the tortoise; but, of course, he never answered, and the elephant could not find him.

The next morning, when the elephant heard the people passing, he asked them what the time was, and the bush buck, who was nearest, shouted out, 'The sun is now up, and I am going to market to get some yams and fresh leaves for my food.'

Then the elephant perceived that the tortoise had deceived him, and began to ask all the passers-by to lend him a pair of eyes, as he could not see, but every one refused, as they wanted their eyes themselves. At last the worm grovelled past, and seeing the big elephant, greeted him in his humble way. He was much surprised when the king of the forest returned his salutation, and very much flattered also.

The elephant said, 'Look here, worm, I have mislaid my eyes. Will you lend me yours for a few days? I will return them next market-day.'

The worm was so flattered at being noticed by the elephant that he gladly consented, and took his eyes out—which, as everybody knows, were very small—and gave them to the elephant. When the elephant had put the worm's eyes into his own large eye-sockets, the flesh immediately closed round them so tightly that when the market-day arrived it was impossible for the elephant to get them out again to return to the worm; and although the worm repeatedly made applications to the elephant to return his eyes, the elephant always pretended not to hear, and sometimes used to say in a very loud voice, 'If there are any worms about, they had better get out of my way, as they are so small I cannot see them, and if I tread on them they will be squashed into a nasty mess.'

Ever since then the worms have been blind, and for the same reason elephants have such small eyes, quite out of proportion to the size of their huge bodies.

from *Folk Stories from Southern Nigeria, West Africa* by Elphinstone Dayrell

# The elephants' graveyard

Some people might describe it as fanciful, if not definitely frivolous, to include in this book the story of Sinbad's seventh voyage. They may scoff at the idea of an elephants' graveyard—or a place remote from the haunts of humanity where elephants go when they know their end is near. Perhaps it *is* a fantastic idea, but plenty of Africans and not a few European explorers have supported it.

Major P. H. G. Powell-Cotton is reported by Lawrence G. Green as a firm believer in elephants' graveyards. Major Powell-Cotton was a pioneer hunter in British East Africa. He declared that he had found an indubitable elephants' graveyard in the Turkana country. He described how he found 'the whole countryside scattered with remains, the fitful sun, as it struggled through the clouds, lightening up glistening bones in every direction. . . . My guide called this "the place where elephants come to die", and assured me that it was no fell disease which had decimated a vast herd, but that, when the elephants fell sick, they would deliberately come long distances to lay their bones on this spot. The place was well-known to the Turkana, who regularly visited it to carry off the tusks.'

Mr Green also mentions Major J. F. Cumming, a district Commissioner in the Sudan, who wrote an article about an elephant cemetery for a scientific journal. Major Cumming is said to have killed an elephant in the Upper Nile valley. When he went the next day to collect the tusks, the elephant had disappeared. It was found eventually under eighteen inches of earth and Major Cumming stated that round about he found the tusk marks of the grave diggers.

There was an African slave trader, nicknamed 'Tippoo Tib' (said to be onomatopoeic for 'rifle fire')—his real name was Hamed bin Mohamed bin Tuma bin Rajab—who made a great deal of money out of ivory. He is reported to have caused 100,000 deaths. This ruffian who, on Stanley's strange recommendation, was appointed by Leopold (King of the Belgians) as Governor of the Congo, is supposed to have found a tract of country which is called 'ivory valley', where thousands of elephants had gone to die, but he never disclosed its location to any white man. As late as 1927, however, a nephew of Tippoo Tib called Mohammed Abdulla produced to the Uganda Government about a hundred fine tusks which might have come from such a place.

Mr Green argues that two particular facts support the theory of the elephant graveyard. The first is the fact that Africans have from time to time appeared with huge loads of tusks which have clearly not been cut from newly killed elephants. Secondly, dead elephants (apart from those killed deliberately) are rarely found.

Proof, however, is wanting and it is a fact that various experienced officials in Africa discount the belief. Yet the numerous tales of elephant behaviour and intelligence at least make the story credible. Did Scheherazade's vivid imagination, stimulated by the urgent necessity of interesting the Commander of the Faithful, invent the story of Sinbad's seventh and last voyage, or was there a basis of truth in it?

## The seventh and last voyage of Sinbad the Sailor

On my return from my sixth voyage, I absolutely relinquished all thoughts of ever venturing again on the seas. I was now arrived at an age which required rest; and, besides this, I had sworn never more to expose myself to the perils I had so often experienced. I prepared, therefore, to enjoy my life in quiet and repose.

One day, when I was regaling a number of friends, one of my servants came to tell me that an officer of the caliph wanted to speak to me. I got up from the table and went to him. 'The caliph', said he, 'has ordered me to acquaint you that he wishes to see you.' I followed the officer to the palace, and he presented me to the prince, whom I saluted by prostrating myself at his feet. 'Sinbad', said he, 'I am in want of you: you must do me a service, and go once more to the King of Serendib with my answer and presents; it is but right that I should make him a proper return for the civility he has shown me.'

In a few days I was prepared for my departure; and as soon as I had received the presents of the caliph, together with a letter in his own hand, I set off and took the route of Balsora, from whence I embarked. After a pleasant voyage, I arrived at the island of Serendib. I immediately acquainted the ministers with the commission I was come upon, and begged them to procure me an audience as soon as possible. They did not fail to attend to my wishes, and conducted me to the palace. I saluted the king by prostrating myself according to the usual custom.

The King of Serendib was rejoiced to find that the caliph returned a testimony of his friendship. Soon after this audience I requested another to take my leave, which I had some difficulty to obtain. At length I succeeded, and the king, at my departure, ordered me a very handsome present. I re-embarked immediately, intending to return to Baghdad, but had not the good fortune to arrive as soon as I expected, for God had disposed otherwise.

Three or four days after we had set sail, we were attacked by corsairs, who easily made themselves masters of our vessel, as we were not in a state for defence. Some persons in the ship attempted to make resistance, but it cost them their lives. I and all those who had the prudence not to oppose the intention of the corsairs were made slaves. After they had stripped us, and substituted old clothes for our own, they bent their course towards a large island at a very great distance, where they sold us.

I was purchased by a rich merchant, who conducted me to his house, gave me food to eat, and clothed me as a slave. Some days after, as he was not well informed who I was, he asked me if I knew a trade. I replied that I was not an artisan, but a merchant by profession, and that the corsairs who sold me had taken from me all I possessed. 'But tell me,' said he, 'do you think you could shoot a bow and arrow?' I replied that it had been one of my youthful sports, and that I had not entirely forgotten how to use it. He then gave me a bow and some arrows, and making me mount behind him on an elephant, he took me to a vast forest at the distance of some hours' journey from the city. We went a great way in it, and when he came to a spot where he wished to stop, he made me alight. Then showing me a large tree, 'Get up that tree,' said he, 'and shoot at the elephants that will pass under it, for there is a prodigious quantity in this forest: if one should fall, come and acquaint me of it.' Having said this, he left me with some provisions and returned to the city: I remained in the tree, on the watch, the whole night.

I did not perceive any during the night; but next day, as soon as the sun had arisen, a great number made their appearance. I shot many arrows at them, and at last one fell. The others immediately retired, and left me at liberty to go and inform my master of the success I had met with. To reward me for this good intelligence, he regaled me with an excellent repast, and praised my address. We then returned together to the forest, where we dug a pit to bury the elephant I had killed. It was my master's intention to let it rot in the earth, and then to take possession of its teeth for commerce.

I continued this occupation for two months, and not a day passed in which I did not kill an elephant. I did not always place myself on the same tree; sometimes I ascended one, sometimes another. One morning, when I was waiting for some elephants to pass, I perceived, to my great astonishment, that instead of traversing the forest as usual, they stopped and came towards me with a terrible noise, and in such numbers that the ground was covered with them, and trembled under their footsteps. They approached the tree where I was placed, and surrounded it with their trunks extended, having their eyes all fixed upon me. At this surprising spectacle I remained motionless, and so agitated by fright that my bow and arrows fell from my hands.

My fears were not groundless. After the elephants had viewed me for some time, one of the largest twisted his trunk round the body of the tree, and shook it with so much violence that he tore it up by the roots, and threw it on the ground. I fell with the tree; but the animal took me up with his trunk, and placed me on his shoulders, where I remained more dead than alive. He put himself at the head of his companions, who followed him in a troop, and carried me to a spot where, having set me down, he and the rest retired. Conceive my situation! I thought it a dream. At length, having been seated some time, and seeing no other elephants, I rose, and perceived that I was on a little hill of some breadth, entirely covered with bones and teeth of elephants. This sight filled my mind with a variety of reflections. I admired the instinct of these animals, and did not doubt that this was their cemetery or place of burial, and that they had brought me hither to show it to me, that I might desist from destroying them, as I did it merely for the sake of possessing their teeth. I did not stay long on the hill, but turned my steps towards the city, and having walked a day and a night, at last arrived at my master's. I did not meet any elephants in my way, which plainly evinced that they had entered farther into the forest, to leave me an unobstructed passage from the hill.

As soon as my master saw me, 'Ah, poor Sinbad!' exclaimed he, 'I was in pain to know what could have become of you. I have been to the forest, and found a tree newly torn up by the roots, and a bow and arrows on the ground: after having sought you everywhere in vain, I despaired of ever seeing you again. Pray relate to me what has happened to

Sinbad at elephants' graveyard

you, and by what happy chance you are still alive.' I satisfied his curiosity, and the following day, having accompanied me to the hill, he was with great joy convinced of the truth of my history. We loaded the elephant on which we had come with as many teeth as he could carry, and when we returned he thus addressed me: 'Brother—for I will no longer treat you as a slave, after the discovery you have imparted to me, and which cannot fail to enrich me—may God pour on you all sorts of blessings and prosperity! Before Him I give you your liberty. I had concealed from you what I am now going to relate. The elephants of our forest destroy annually an infinite number of slaves, whom we send in search of ivory. Whatever advice we give them, they are sure, sooner or later, to lose their lives by the wiles of these animals. God has delivered you from their fury, and has conferred this mercy on you alone. It is a sign that he cherishes you, and that He wants you in the world to be of use to mankind. You have procured me a surprising advantage; we have not hitherto been able to get ivory without risking the lives of our slaves, and now our whole city will be enriched by your means. Do not suppose that I think I have sufficiently recompensed you by giving you your liberty; I intend to add to it considerable presents. I might engage the whole city to join and make your fortune; but that is an honour I will enjoy alone.'

To this obliging discourse I answered, 'Master, God preserve you. The liberty you grant me acquits you of all obligation towards me, and the only recompense I desire for the service I have had the good fortune to procure for you, and the inhabitants of your city is permission to return to my country.'

'Well,' resumed he, 'the monsoon will soon bring us sufficient vessels, which come to be laden with ivory; I will then send you away with a sufficiency to pay your expenses home.' I again thanked him for the

# The seventh and last voyage of Sinbad the Sailor

liberty he had given me and for the goodwill he showed me. I remained with him till the season for the monsoon, during which we made frequent excursions to the hill, and filled his magazines with ivory. All the other merchants in the city did the same, for it did not long remain a secret.

The ships at length arrived, and my master having chosen that in which I was to embark, loaded it with ivory, half of which was on my own account. He did not omit an abundance of provisions for my voyage, and he obliged me to accept some rare curiosities of that country besides. After I had thanked him as much as possible for all the obligations he had conferred on me, I embarked. We set sail, and as the adventure which had procured my liberty was very extraordinary, it was always on my mind.

We touched at several islands to procure refreshments. Our vessel having sailed from a port of the Indian Terra Firma, we went there to land; and, fearful of the dangers of the sea to Balsora, I unloaded the ivory which belonged to me, and resolved to continue my journey by land. I sold my share of the cargo for a large sum of money, and purchased a variety of curious things for presents. When I was equipped, I joined a caravan of merchants. I remained a long time on the road, and suffered a great deal; but I bore all with patience when I reflected that I had neither tempests nor corsairs, serpents, nor any other peril that I had before encountered, to fear.

All these fatigues being at last concluded, I arrived happily at Bagdad. I went immediately, and presented myself to the caliph, and gave him an account of my embassy. This prince told me that my long absence had occasioned him some uneasiness, but that he had always hoped that God would not forsake me.

When I had related the adventure of the elephants he appeared much surprised, and would scarcely have believed it had not my sincerity been well known to him. He thought this, as well as the other histories I had detailed to him, so curious, that he ordered one of his secretaries to write it in letters of gold, to be preserved in his treasury. I retired well satisfied with the presents and honours he conferred on me, and have since resigned myself entirely to my family, my relations and friends.

from *The Arabian Nights' Entertainments*

# The place where elephants die

Hidden away from the haunts of men, west of a widespread Lake
Out of the scope of human ken, in tangled thicket and brake,
'Mid arching trees where a foetid breeze ruffles the ragged sky,
Is the sombre place where the vanishing race of the Elephants come
    to die.

Many a mighty Lord of Herd, massive of tusk and limb,
Has crept away at the whispered word that signified death to him—
Driven by doom to the murky gloom where the wheeling vultures fly,
Through buffet and blast he has come at last to the Place where the
    Elephants die.

Pile upon pile of bleaching bone, and a foul, miasmic breath
With now and again a mighty moan to break on the hush of death—
Sluggish streams, and the silver beams of a silent moon on high—
God forfend I should meet *my* end in the Place where the
    Elephants die!

Once, they say, in the olden days a venturesome man set forth,
Threaded a path by devious ways, westward and south and north,
Dallied with Death at every breath while many a moon went by
Till he found the brake by the Silent Lake where the Elephants come
    to die.

Tusk upon tusk lay whitely there, under a twisted tree,
Wealth of the world, bleached stark and bare—and he gazed upon his
    fee
Dreaming the dream of a mighty scheme—and ambition fluttered high
Till he sank, and slept—and the rumour crept through the Place where
    the Elephants die.

But the Elephant Clan were close at heel—for the place was theirs
    to hold,
Sacrosanct to the common weal, out of the mists of old—
And the word went forth from south to north, and the herds came
    thundering by
To kill the Man who had braved the Clan in the Place where they came
    to die.

Only a native tale, you say, laughing in light disdain?
Maybe so—but of what avail to jest when the facts are plain?
Let him who has found on his camping ground or under the open sky
One elephant dead *then* shake his head at 'The Place where the
    Elephants die!'

from *Songs Out Of Exile* by Cullen Gouldsbury

# The elephant

Clumsy feet
And waving trunk
Flapping ears
And rounded tusks
And enormous toes
And all made of leather
It was an elephant
In the hot desert
With round feet
And a straight back
And smoking teeth
And bending legs
And a round head
And waving tails
And a grey coat
And some crumpled skin
Which makes patterns
And quite friendly
With a trunk to lift trees
And small eyes
And brown paper ears
And strong pointed tusks
Made of ivory
And very white
And his ears like waving leaves
And stumpy feet
On the desert ground
And his body
As big as the world
And as heavy as a mountain
And as tall as the tallest tree
And he sways from side to side
When he is walking
In the desert. . . .

by Sarah Jane Eyles (aged 7) of Chichester, Sussex. Winner of first prize in British *Good Housekeeping* Poetry Competition.

# The elephant of the Bastille

In the middle of the eighteenth century, one Charles François Ribart designed a vast elephant to be erected in Paris as a *'Grand Kiosque à la Gloire du Roi'*. The designs were published by Pierre Patte in Paris in 1758 in a volume entitled *'L'Éléphant Triomphal'*. The elephant was to have been of immense size and to have contained a restaurant, pleasure gardens and a hall for music. It is hardly necessary to say that this monstrous creature was never constructed. But it is a most curious fact that Napoleon had the idea of building a great elephant in the Place de la Bastille and a model of this beast was actually erected. It is this animal which is described by Victor Hugo in *Les Misérables*, to which the *gamin* Gavroche took the two children, whom he found hungry and deserted in the streets of Paris, for shelter on the night of the escape of Babet, Brujon, Gueulemer and Thénardier from the prison of La Force.

*Les Misérables* was published in 1862 and Hugo refers to the elephant as having still been standing twenty years before. A picture of this elephant is reproduced on this page, and is described as

> *'Vue de la fontaine de l'éléphant élevé sur la Place de la Bastille. Ce monument qui a 60 pieds de haut, est le travail le plus extraordinaire qu'on ait vu.'*

Project for elephant fountain; print by Julienne, 1820

Victor Hugo gives its height in *Les Misérables* as 40 feet. Another picture, described as *'Projet de fontaine éléphant sur la Place de la Bastille, démolie en 1840'* is reproduced on plate 78. The latter is more splendidly ornate than the former. It is hard to say which of these two monsters was Gavroche's 'house' in the story.

'It was an elephant,' writes Victor Hugo, 'forty feet high, constructed of timber and masonry, bearing on its back a tower which resembled a house, formerly painted green by some dauber, and now painted black by heaven, the wind and time. In this deserted and protected corner of the place, the broad brow of the colossus, his trunk, his tusks, his tower, his enormous crupper, his four feet, like columns produced, at night, under the starry heavens, a surprising and terrible form. It was a sort of symbol of popular force. It was sombre, mysterious and immense. It was some mighty, visible phantom, one knew not what, standing erect beside the invisible spectre of the Bastille.

'Few strangers visited this edifice, no passer-by looked at it. It was falling into ruins; every season, the plaster which detached itself from its sides formed hideous wounds upon it.

'As soon as twilight descended, the old elephant became transfigured; he assumed a tranquil and redoubtable appearance in the formidable serenity of the shadows. Being of the past, he belonged to the night; and obscurity was in keeping with his grandeur.'

The interior of the elephant, which Gavroche had made his home and into which he took the children, was swarming with rats, but Gavroche had constructed a sort of cage of wire, in which he and the children were safe from their depredations. But the children were nervous. The older one could not sleep.

'Sir?' he began again.
'Hey?' said Gavroche.
'What are rats?'
'They are mice.'
This explanation reassured the child a little. He had seen white mice in the course of his life, and he was not afraid of them. Nevertheless, he lifted up his voice once more.
'Sir?'
'Hey?' said Gavroche again.
'Why don't you have a cat?'
'I did have one,' replied Gavroche, 'I brought one here but they ate her.'
This second explanation undid the work of the first, and the little fellow began to tremble again.
The dialogue between him and Gavroche began for the fourth time:—
'Monsieur?'
'Hey?'
'Who was it that was eaten?'
'The cat.'
'And who ate the cat?'
'The rats.'
'The mice?'
'Yes, the rats.'
The child in consternation, dismayed at the thought of mice which ate cats, pursued:—
'Sir, would those mice eat us?'
'Wouldn't they just!' ejaculated Gavroche.
The child's terror had reached its climax. But Gavroche added:—
'Don't be afraid. They can't get in. And besides, I'm here! Here catch hold of my hand. Hold your tongue and shut your peepers!'
At the same time Gavroche grasped the little fellow's hand across

his brother. The child pressed the hand close to him, and felt reassured. Courage and strength have these mysterious ways of communicating themselves. Silence reigned round them once more, the sound of their voices had frightened off the rats; at the expiration of a few minutes, they came raging back, but in vain, the three little fellows were fast asleep and heard nothing more.

The hours of the night fled away. Darkness covered the vast Place de la Bastille. A wintry gale, which mingled with the rain, blew in gusts; the patrol searched all the doorways, alleys, enclosures, and obscure nooks, and in their search for nocturnal vagabonds, they passed in silence before the elephant; the monster erect, motionless, staring open-eyed into the shadows, had the appearance of dreaming happily over his good deed; and sheltered from heaven and from men the three poor sleeping children.

# On shooting an elephant

To shoot big game for pleasure is a pursuit which must require a peculiar temperament. To kill a man-eating tiger because of his raids on a defenceless village has often been a necessity, while to explore the vast lands in Asia, Africa or America without some form of protection against the mighty beasts of forest and jungle would be foolhardy. Among those beasts are, of course, elephants which because of their ivory face death from more than the explorer defending himself. Nevertheless, to direct successfully a rifle bullet into an elephant's brain and see the splendid creature sag to the ground and die, would make many of us feel like murderers and cause us pangs of outraged conscience.

It is indeed impossible to defend the killing of elephants for pleasure and very hard in terms of present day thought to defend it when it has as its object the acquisition of ivory. But from time to time killing cannot be avoided.

George Orwell in an essay recounting such a killing, describes his feelings when, as a police officer in Moulmein, in Burma, he found himself compelled to shoot an elephant. The creature was a working elephant which had escaped while in the state known as 'Must'. It was terrorizing the town smashing up carts and raiding stores. It had stamped on a wretched Indian workman and ripped the skin off his back.

The unwilling Orwell,—or Blair as we should perhaps call him, for 'Orwell' was his pen-name—was called by his native policemen to come and deal with the menace.

He found the elephant in a paddy field a few yards from a road on the edge of the town. He had taken with him from his office a small rifle, more as a gesture evidently than as a weapon capable of killing an elephant. He describes vividly how the elephant stood there quietly plucking up tussocks of grass, beating the earth out of their roots by banging them against its knees, and stuffing them into its mouth.

A great crowd had followed Blair and looked forward with excitement to the coming fun. Against his will Blair sent to a friend for an elephant gun and, inexpertly, shot and killed the elephant. Whereas an experienced elephant hunter would have killed the beast with one shot Blair took a dozen or so. It is this, perhaps, which makes the story particularly harrowing.

Strangely, however, this is not the central theme of the tale, which is, the overwhelming force of public opinion. Blair did not want to kill the elephant. Indeed, when he saw it, he thought its attack of 'Must' was over and that when its mahout arrived it would consent to be led away and would be quite docile. But he knew that government prestige would slip if he did not shoot the beast and that officialdom would lose a lot of its control over the populace.

The crowd was waiting, so to speak, with its tongues hanging out. It wanted the elephant dead. The people wanted the meat. When they saw it was dying and almost before it was dead, they were on it skinning it and cutting it up. Within a few hours it was a skeleton.

Blair tells how the older Europeans were satisfied he had done the right thing. The younger ones thought he had been wrong to kill a valuable elephant just because it had killed a coolie. Blair himself won-

ders how many people realized that he had done it solely to avoid looking a fool.

One does indeed wonder. From one's knowledge of the later Blair
who had become George Orwell, it is hard to believe that he would have
cared the toss of a coin whether he looked a fool or not. He had too pene-
trating a mind for that.

Reverse of lead coin, said to refer to Catiline's project to seize power in Rome, 65BC:
coin from Cuperus

# On not shooting an elephant

Herklaas de la Buschagne was a great elephant hunter. He was an Afrikaner whose story is told magnificently in *The Hunter and the Whale* by Laurens van der Post. De la Buschagne throughout his life sought for Sway-Back, believed by African hunters to be the greatest elephant in Africa and therefore the greatest elephant in the world. He told the story of his meeting with Sway-Back to Captain Thor Larsen, Captain of the whaler *Kurt Hansen* and how, seeing the elephant in the forest, he suddenly saw him as a great fish. From that moment de la Buschagne made up his mind that he must hunt and kill a whale.

For many years Sway-Back had outwitted all the hunters. From time to time de la Buschagne had come on his spoor. On the final occasion the spoor told him that Sway-Back was getting old. The great elephant had returned to the scene of his beginnings as he felt the circle of his life closing.

Sway-Back, he was convinced, was no longer going to avoid him. He was, come what may, going to live out his last days there on his native ground. He, the man, could avoid or meet him as he chose. But Sway-Back himself was no longer going to take part in the chase.

De la Buschagne said that the realization that at last he had his chance of shooting perhaps the most formidable elephant the world had ever known, made the hair at the back of his head rise. But almost as soon as he realised it it was spoilt for him by that instinctive voice which had set him on Sway-Back's spoor forty years before. Would not the Captain too, he asked, in a similar situation, have expected such a voice to echo, 'Now?' Instead, however, the voice astonished him with a 'Not yet' as imperative as had been its original 'Now'.

Well, like Sway-Back, he too was getting old and about to return to the scene of his beginnings. The burning random years had taught him the futility of going against the voice: he was not prepared to argue with it at so late a day.

So he set about pursuing a normal hunter's day as if nothing unusual had happened. . . . Perhaps he should have another look at Sway-Back's spoor and more would come of it? As he asked himself these questions, the day stood at high noon, the sun directly overhead. . . . .

The bush at that hour was silent of course, except for the mopani beetles. They were to the high noon and the sun what crickets after rain were to midnight and the moon. With quicksilver voices they sang a hymn to the sun that flashed like a mirror with light and shimmered like that passion of sickness called fever mounting to a climax in man's own hissing blood. He loved it as did all the birds, animals, insects and plants of Africa and normally would have allowed it to be for him, for them, a cradle-song of afternoon sleep. So strong and old was his association of rest with the beetle music and the hour that he felt like a man walking in a dream of deepest sleep. This should not surprise the Captain if he knew, as de la Buschagne did, that for its aboriginal children noon and not midnight was the hour in Africa when graves opened and ghosts walked. . . . .

People spoke of midnight blue; but he thought often of Africa's noonday black. It was that colour on this fateful day, and the slumber of

Jumbo worship

76 Jumbo starts for America

77 Project for elephant fountain near Bastille

78 Roman circus

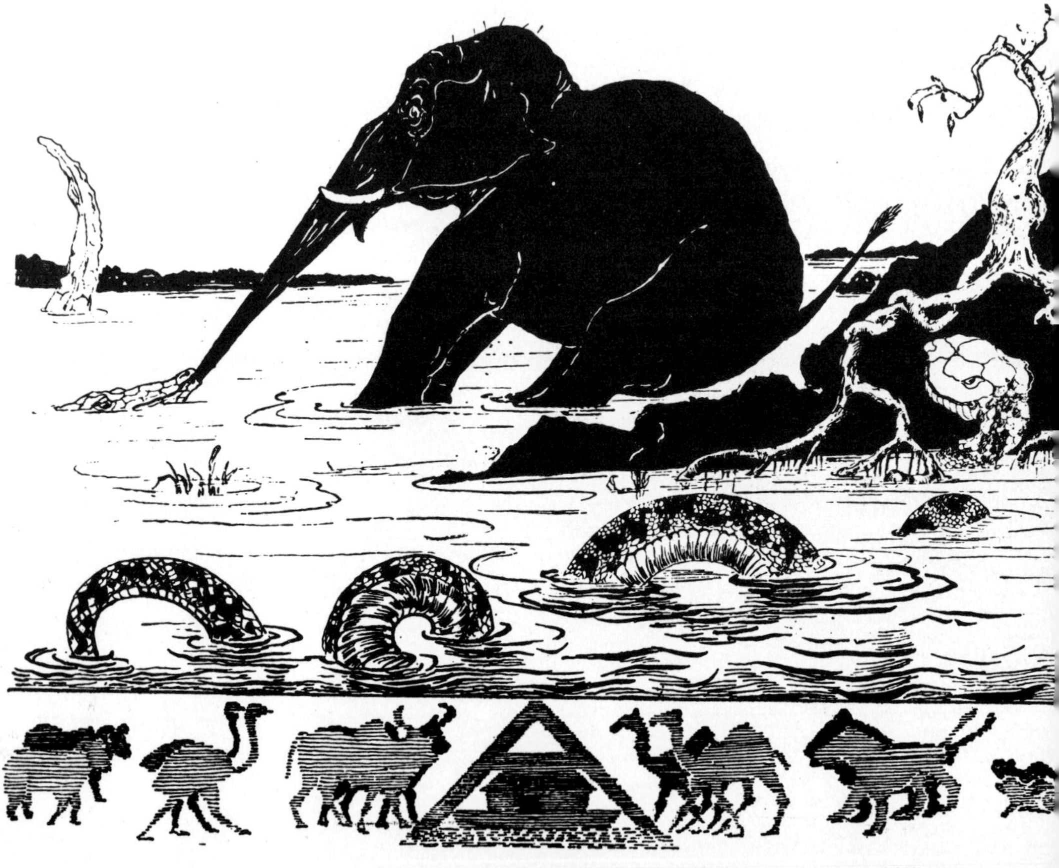

nature around him was more profound than any he had ever experienced. If sleep at night was natural, sleep at so brilliant and seething an hour was supernatural. For instance, he walked by a black mamba coiled on the edge of the narrow track like the spring of a great clock. His foot had come down not a yard from the head of this most vigilant of snakes. Yet so deep was its sleep that not a quiver went through it, and to his relief he had had no cause to awaken this world of noonday slumber with a shot from his gun.

So he continued slowly through a silence composed of that simmering shimmer of silver sound without movement of air or life of any kind. Even the sun above seemed to stand still for a rest on the summit of its compelling sweep and the shadows contracted to a tight blurred blot around the base of trees and shrubs. He called them shadows purely for want of a better word, because so brilliant was the day, so great and intense the reflection of light from the patches of scarlet earth, the leaves of trees scintillating like fish scales in the sea of the sky, and the barley-sugar trunks of mopani trees aglow and translucent as segments of amber, that shade was in reality only a tinted sunlight. Never on the darkest night had he known so eerie a moment as this hour when the great wheel of the sun was poised for its roll down the steep slope of the day into abysmal night.

Despite his training he found himself constantly looking over his shoulder feeling himself to be followed, and not concentrating enough on the ground ahead. Yet it was well he did so, because there came a moment when, turning to look over his right shoulder, something to the east of him caught his eyes. He stopped and with the utmost care turned slowly to face east, his rifle ready.

A bare twenty yards away, he saw the high, broad forehead of an elephant, an enormous pair of ears moving slowly and ceaselessly like fans held in invisible hands in the bush below. Since the animal stood at a slight angle to him he could see also the dark line of a vast back. Prepared as he was by all he had heard over forty years of the proportions of this elephant, even the little that he could see of it surpassed any picture he had been able to imagine. It was Sway-back, of course, and with recognition of the elephant, his rifle was at his shoulder and his finger on the trigger, since knowing the animal's reputation he expected it either to whirl about and make off at high speed, or charge. But the great head, still and immovable as some giant bust from the Valley of the Kings carved by a sculptor of Rameses the Great out of black granite, and the long dark back, remained still and immovable. Only the immense ears rhythmically fanned the melted platinum air. Sway-Back, too, was fast asleep.

Had he moved at all, even just to shift his weight from one foot to another, de la Buschagne was certain he would have shot for, quite apart from his forty years' longing to get this elephant and his tusks, he could not take any risks or chances with an animal of Sway-Back's reputation. But Sway-Back just remained fast asleep.

Nothing it seemed could have proved so conclusively how right de la Buschagne's reading of Sway-Back's spoor and behaviour had been. Sway-Back had made his final pact, his last peace treaty with life. No

# On not shooting an elephant

more evasion, no more travail or travel. Whatever was to come, he was back home where he had begun, to accept all. Sleep, the daily surrender to the will of life, the greatest act of trust possible to its doubting and questing children, was there to demonstrate the completeness of Sway-Back's acceptance. And what a sleep it was! Indeed so much of life was there asleep in the gun-metal being of this, the greatest animal on earth, so deep and so heavy was he with it, that de la Buschagne felt he was looking at the still, immovable centre of a vortex in the steam of existence, drawing all around it from far and wide, down, down, down, like flotsam and jetsam in the maelstrom of a deep sea, to a depth of dreaming never before attained.

He found himself so hypnotised by this colossal example of sleep that even his own eyelids dropped, his gun wavered and his head felt like lead about to drop on his chest. For the first time he experienced what African hunters had often told him, that animals protected themselves by inducing sleep in their hunters; and the greater and more dangerous the animal, the more powerful the temptation to sleep in the hunter. This they had stressed was the moment of extreme peril for the hunter as it invariably preceded the charge of the hunted. The thought brought de la Buschagne wide awake with such a start that his finger nearly pressed the trigger of his gun. But Sway-Back had not moved. He still stood there, the greatest monument to sleep ever erected, and so trusting and so innocent that de la Buschagne might as well have been asked to shoot a sleeping child. Then suddenly he understood. His forty years' quest might be over and his reward was there for the asking; yet he could not take it. The 'Not yet' and the 'Now' were one.

De la Buschagne was evangelically solemn as he said this, looking from me to my Captain and back again like some kind of a nomad who has suddenly found revelation in the realisation that the wasteland of his spirit and the desert around him are one. Hunted and hunter, he said, seemed to have arrived at the same conclusion. In some way that he could not explain, Herklaas de la Buschagne and Sway-Back were one in spirit. For him to kill Sway-Back would have been a kind of suicide. . . . .

How long he had stood there he did not know. Judging by the displacement of the pale shadows of the bush around him it was long. Yet to him it seemed only seconds before he tucked his gun under his left arm and turned. Before he left, on an impulse which we sitting here in comfort fifteen hundred miles away in such different circumstances would probably judge to have been as absurd as it was unnecessary, he took off his hat to Sway-Back. He bowed deeply, hat in hand, to Sway-Back, feeling that he was saying an unique hail and farewell to him for ever. Only then did he swing about to go away as silently as he could in order not to break up the greatest sleep he had ever encountered.

from *The Hunter and the Whale* by Laurens van der Post

# Elephants

The desert stretches far beyond man's ken,
A rolling sea of motionless red sand;
A burning, brassy haze hides all from men
And emptiness spreads silence o'er the land.

No life, no sound. There, countless leagues away,
Replete with food, the lions are asleep
In caves profound. Palms, known of leopards, sway
Where drink giraffes of azure waters deep.

A monstrous sun spins through the sweating air,
Which sees no bird, nor feels the beat of wings;
Some sleepy python, gliding from its lair,
Glistening and scaly, coils itself in rings.

Scorched earth aflame breathes 'neath a cloudless sky
And through the desolate waste where slumber reigns
The elephants, lumbering and wrinkled, hie
Across the desert to their homeland plains.

They march from far horizons, tread the sand
And shroud themselves in whirling clouds of dust;
Straight as a die they come, a massy band,
With mighty feet and bodies brown as rust.

An ancient leader marches in the van,
Gnarled hide, like bark ravaged by time and sapped,
His head a rock, his backbone, like a fan,
Bends to each step, his mind in effort rapt.

Nor fast, nor slow, nor doubting where to go,
He leads his dusty fellows on their way;
They follow, leave a sandy trail to show
The passage of the pilgrims' huge array.

Their ears a-fan, their trunks their tusks between,
Closed eyes, they march. Their swaying bellies smoke,
In sweltering air their sweat like fog is seen
A million humming insects to convoke.

What boots their thirst, what boots the ravening fly,
The sun that sears their hide of wrinkles made?
Plodding, they leave a country parched and dry,
Dreaming of fig-tree forests and their shade.

They see in mind the river in the vale,
Where hippos bellowing plunge and swim at ease,
And where they'd slake their thirst in moonlight pale,
Bend, drink, crush reeds beneath the trees.

Bold and deliberate, they sway along,
A line of darkness o'er the boundless sand;
The desert sings again its soundless song;
Beyond its edge plods on the lumbering band.

after *Les Éléphants* by Leconte de Lisle

# The captive's dream

I will remember what I was, I am sick of rope and chain.
  I will remember my old strength and all my forest affairs.
I will not sell my back to man for a bundle of sugar-cane.
  I will go out to my own kind, and the wood-folk in their lairs.

I will go out until the day, until the morning break,
  Out to the winds' untainted kiss, the waters' clean caress.
I will forget my ankle-ring and snap my picket-stake.
  I will revisit my lost loves, and playmates masterless.

from *Toomai of the Elephants* by Rudyard Kipling

Topsell's elephant

# List of illustrations

The authors and publishers are grateful to all those who have supplied pictures and given permission for them to be reproduced. The following abbreviations have been used in the list below: BM (photos reproduced by courtesy of the Trustees of the British Museum), V&A (Victoria and Albert Museum. Crown Copyright). The authors themselves are responsible for all pictures in which no acknowledgement is made either to source or photographer.

# List of illustrations

N     

# List of illustrations

# Illustrations in the text

# Acknowledgements

As authors, we feel that we have collected together some unusually interesting aspects of the subject. Except for the strange views recorded by ancient and mediaeval writers, the student will not learn much about the natural history of elephants in this book, but he will find what artists, poets, historians and others have found worth while recording about the beast.

In compiling the book, we have made use of many manuscripts, books, pictures, carvings, sculptures and other works of art; but what we have reproduced is a mere fraction of what exists. Perhaps it will stimulate people to probe further into this most engaging subject.

We have been helped in our researches by a great many people; among them we desire particularly to thank Miss Norah Titley, of the department of oriental books and manuscripts of the British Museum; Mrs M. G. Brown, Kirkcudbrightshire County Librarian; the Rev Dr A. J. Arkell, one-time Director of Archaeology in the Sudan; Librarians of the India Office Library; Monsieur Jean Sebire, of the Société Générale, London; Mr Cuthbert Graham, of the Aberdeen *Press and Journal*; Mrs June Carlton of Balmaclellan and Mrs Hilda Macadam of Dalry, for some difficult feats of typing; and last but not least, Mr Bruce Flegg, who not only checked many references for us in the British Museum, but made a number of drawings which have been reproduced in the text.

We have included a short bibliography, but anyone desirous of making an exhaustive study of the subject is referred to the scholarly and comprehensive bibliographies in Richard Carrington's *Elephants* and I. T. Sanderson's *The Dynasty of Abu*.

We should like to record our gratitude to the Deans of Carlisle, Chester, Exeter and Gloucester; and to the Rectors or Vicars of Beverley Minster, Beverley (Saint Mary's); South Burlingham, Holme Hale, South Lopham and Narford, in Norfolk; Denston, in Suffolk; and Tong and Moreton Corbet, in Salop, for allowing us to take photographs for use in this book. We must also express our admiration for the colour photographs taken for us by Mr John Webb.

We should like to apologize to anyone whose express permission we have failed to obtain through misadventure, or inability to trace their address.

For permission to reprint poems and stories, the following acknowledgement is gratefully made to John Heath Stubbs for the extract from *The History of the Flood*; to Rupert Hart-Davis Ltd for the extracts from *Bandoola* and *Elephant Bill* by J. H. Williams; to Jarrolds Publishers (London) Ltd for the extract from *No Other Elephant* by Gerald Sparrow; to Macmillan & Co Ltd, London, and The Viking Press, Inc, New York, for 'The Elephant's Prayer' from *Prayers from the Ark* by Carmen Bernos de Gasztold, tr. by Rumer Godden; to the *Archaeological Journal* for the extracts from *The Elephant in Medieval Legend and Art* by G. C. Druce; to Longmans, Green & Co Ltd for 'The Elephant and the Tortoise' from *Folk Stories from Southern Nigeria, West Africa* by Elphinstone Dayrell.

The Extract from *The Elephant Lore of the Hindus* by Franklin Edgerton is reprinted by permission of Yale University Press, copyright © 1931 by Yale University Press; 'The Elephant' (a chapter heading to *Beast and Man in India*), from *Songs from Books*, 'The Elephant's Child' from *Just So Stories* and 'The Captive's Dream' from *The Jungle Book* by Rudyard Kipling are reprinted by permission of Mrs George Bambridge and Macmillan & Co Ltd, London, and Doubleday & Co Inc, New York; the extracts from *The Hunter and the Whale* by Laurens van der Post are reprinted by permission of William Morrow and Co Inc, New York, © 1967 Laurens van der Post, and The Hogarth Press Ltd, London; 'The Elephant' by Sarah Jane Eyles is reprinted by permission of British *Good Housekeeping*; 'Cupid's Elephant' is reproduced from *The Times* by permission.

# Bibliography

**Abu'l-Fazl 'Allami**: *A'in-i-Akberi*, trs. H. Blochman and H. S. Jarrett

**Aelian**: *Aeliani de natura Animalium*, Book 2, ch. 2, R. Hercher, Paris, 1858

**Aldrovandi, U**: *De Quadripedibus Solidipedibus*, ch. 9, *De Elephanto*, Bologna, 1639

**Anderson, M. D.**: *Animal Carvings in British Churches*, Cambridge University Press, 1938

**Aristotle**: Aristotle's *History of Animals*, trs. Richard Creswell, London, 1862

**Arkell, Dr A. J.**: *Early Khartoum* O.U.P., 1949

**Arkell, Dr A. J.**: *Wanyanga*, O.U.P., 1964

**Arkell, Dr A. J.**: *A History of the Sudan to 1821*, Athlone Press, 1961

**Armandi, P. D.**: *Histoire Militaire des Elephants*, Paris, 1843

**Arrian**: *History of Alexander's Expedition*, trs. Mr Rooke, London, 1729

**Arthus, M. G.**: *Indiae Orientalis*, Frankfurt, 1606

**Bachhofer, Ludwig**: *Early Indian Sculpture*, Zwemmer, 1929

**Ball, Katherine M**: *Decorative Motives of Oriental Art*, John Lane, San Francisco, 1927

**Bond, Francis**: *Wood Carvings in English Churches*, Humphrey Milford, 1910

**Breuil, Abbe H.**: *Four Hundred Centuries of Cave Art*, trs. Mary Boyle, E. Fernand Windels, 1952

**Bridaham, Lester Burbank**: *Gargoyles, Chimeres and the Grotesque in French Gothic Sculpture*, New York, 1930

**Brown, Professor Baldwin**: *The Art of the Cave Dweller*, John Murray, 1928

**Browne, Bishop G. F.**: *Antiquities in the Neighbourhood of Dunecht*, Cambridge University Press, 1921

**Carrington, R**: *Elephants*, Chatto & Windus, London, 1958

**Cox, J. Charles**: *Bench Ends in English Churches*, Humphrey Milford, 1916

**Crawfurd, J.**: *Journey of an Embassy from the Governor-General of India to the Court of Ava, in the year 1827*, London, 1829

**Cuper, G.**: *Gisberti Cuperi: De Elephantis in nummis obviis exercitationes duae*, 1735

**Dayrell, Elphinstone**: *Folk Stories from Southern Nigeria, West Africa*, Longmans, Green & Co, 1910

**De Beer, Sir G. R.**: *Alps and Elephants: Hannibal's March*, G. Bles, London, 1955

**Douglas, Robert**: *Annals of the Royal Burgh of Forres*

**Druce, G. C.**: *The Elephant in Medieval Legend and Art*, Archaeological Journal, ser. 2, vol XXVI: 1919

**Evans, Edward Payson**: *Animal Symbolism in Ecclesiastical Architecture*, Heinemann, 1896

**Funk & Wagnall**: *Standard Dictionary of Folklore, Mythology and Legend*, New York, 1949

**Gibbon, E.**: *The History of the Decline and Fall of the Roman Empire*, London, 1788

**Giteau, Madeleine**: *Les Khmers*, Office de Livre Fribourg S.A., Basle (English version: *Khmer Sculpture and the Angkor Civilization*, Thames & Hudson, 1965)

**Gombrich, E. H.**: *The History of Art*, Phaidon Press, London, 1950

**Hall Burton, Richard**: *Seven League Boots*, G. Bles, 1936

**Holder, C. F.**: *The Ivory King*, London, 1886

**Jennison, G.**: *Animals for Show and Pleasure in Ancient Rome*, Manchester University Press, 1937

**Kipling, J. Lockwood**: *Beast and Man in India*, Macmillan, 1891

**Kipling, Rudyard**: *Just So Stories and other works*, Macmillan, London

**Kircher, A.**: *Athanasii Kircheri China monumentis sacris . . ., illustrata*, Amsterdam, 1667

**Knight, Charles**: *The Elephant in Relation to Man*, Charles Knight & Co, London, 1844

**Kruse, Gosta**: *Trunk Call*, Elek, 1962

**La Decade Philosophique, Litteraire et Politique**: *Du Pouvoir de la Musique sur les Animaux, et du concert donne aux Éléphants*, Paris (1798)

**Lajoux, Jean Dominique**: *Merveilles du Tassili n'Ajjer*: Édition du Chêne, Paris (English version: *The Rock Painters of Tassili*, incl. *The Art of Tassili* by F. Elgar, trs. G. D. Liversage, Thames and Hudson, 1963)

**Larwood, Jacob** and **Hotten, John Camden**: *History of Signboards*, Chatto and Windus, 1866; and *English Inn Signs* (a revised ed. of the same book), Chatto and Windus, 1951

**Lee, Sherman E.**: *A History of Far Eastern Art*, Thames and Hudson, 1966

**Leonowens, A. H. C.**: *The English Governess at the Siamese Court*, London 1870

**Manucci, N.**: *Storia do Mogor*, 1653–1708, trs. W. Irvine, London, 1907

**Maplet, John**: *A Greene Forest*, Cambridge, 1567

**More, Dr**: *Enthusiasmus Triumphatus*, 1656

**Nila-Kantha**: *The Elephant Lore of the Hindus: the Elephant-Sport of Nila-kantha*, trs. Professor Franklin Edgerton, Yale United Press, 1931

**Orwell, George**: *Shooting an Elephant and other essays*, London, 1950

**Phipson, Emma**: *Choir Stalls and their Carvings*, Batsford, 1896

**Pliny, the Elder**: *Natural History*, trs. Bostock & Riley, London, 1855

**Polo, M.**: *The Book of Marco Polo the Venetion*, trs. Sir Henry Yule, London, 1871

**Polybius**: *The General History of Polybius*, trs. Mr Hampton, Oxford, 1823

**Ranking, J.**: *Historical Researches on the Wars and Sports of the Mongols and Romans: in which Elephants and Wild Beasts were employed or slain, etc.*, London, 1826

**Sanderson, I. T.**: *The Dynasty of Abu*, Cassell, 1963

**Scullard, H. H.**: *Numismatic Chronicle*, London, 1948

**Smith, V. A.**: *Akbar the Great Mogul, 1542–1605*, London, 1919

**Sparrow, Gerald**: *No Other Elephant*, Jarrolds, London, 1961

**Topsell, E.**: *The Historie of Foure-Footed Beastes*, London, 1607

**Tyrwhitt-Drake, G.**: *Beasts and Circuses*, Bristol, 1936

**Van der Post, Laurens**: *The Hunter and the Whale*, Hogarth Press, London, 1967

**Wildridge, T. Tindall**: *The Grotesque in Church Art*, William Andrews, 1899

**Williams, J. H.**: *Elephant Bill*, Hart Davis, London, 1950

**Williams, J. H.**: *Bandoola*, Hart Davis, London, 1953

**Williamson, Thomas**: *Oriental Field Sports*, London, 1819

**Works, Ministry of**: *Pictish Sculptured Stones in Scotland*

# Index

Figures in italic refer to plates: illustrations in the text are preceded by *page*

# Index

# Index

# Index

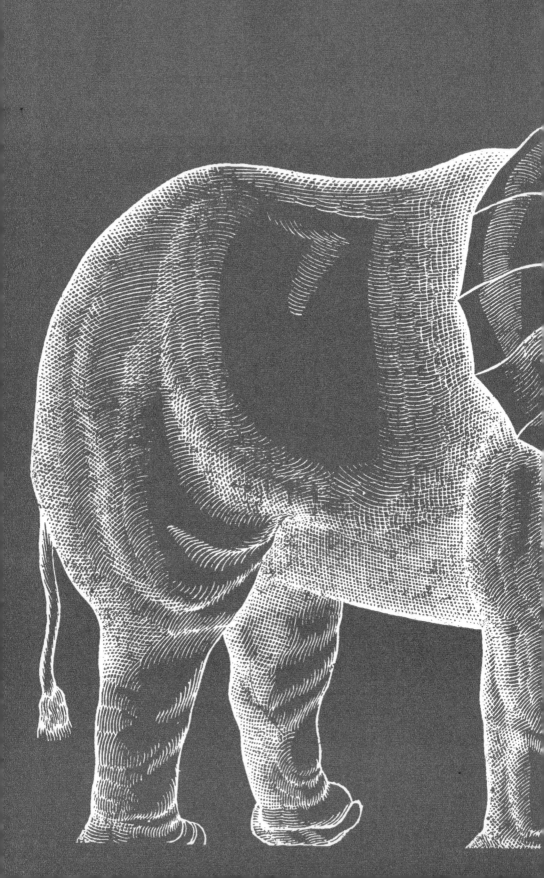